EDUCATING HOMELESS STUDENTS: PROMISING PRACTICES

James H. Stronge
Evelyn Reed-Victor,
Editors

EYE ON EDUCATION
6 Depot Way West, Suite 106
Larchmont, N.Y. 10538

Library of Congress Cataloging-in-Publication Data

Educating homeless students: promising practices / James H.
Stronge and Evelyn Reed-Victor, editors
        p. cm.
    Includes bibliographical references.
    ISBN 1-883001-89-7
    1. Homeless children—Education—United States
    2. Homeless youth—Education—United States I. Stronge,
    James H., 1950- II. Reed-Victor, Evelyn, 1947-

    LC5144.2 .E385 2000
    371.826'942—dc21   99-055009

Production services provided by:
Bookwrights
1211 Courtland Drive
Raleigh, NC 27604

Also Available from Eye On Education

The Directory of Programs for Students at Risk
By Thomas L. Williams

Transforming Schools into Community Learning Centers
By Steve R. Parson

Banishing Anonymity:
Middle And High School Advisement Programs
By John M. Jenkins and Bonnie S. Daniel

What Schools Should Do to Help Kids Stop Smoking
By William L. Fibkins

Making Decisions about Diverse Learners: A Guide for Educators
By Fern Aefsky

Staff Development:
Practices That Promote Leadership in Learning Communities
By Sally J. Zepeda

The Administrator's Guide to School-Community Relations
By George E. Pawlas

Urban School Leadership: Issues and Strategies
By Eugene T. W. Sanders

Data Analysis for Comprehensive Schoolwide Improvement
By Victoria L. Bernhardt

The School Portfolio:
A Comprehensive Framework for School Improvement
By Victoria L. Bernhardt

The Example School Portfolio:
A Companion to The School Portfolio
By Victoria L. Bernhardt, et al.

Research on Educational Innovations 2/e
By Arthur K. Ellis and Jeffrey T. Fouts

PREFACE

In the midst of economic prosperity for most Americans, growing numbers of children and youth are homeless. They live for the moment wherever they can—in campers or motels, doubled up with family or friends, in shelters, or literally on the street. And yet homeless children and youth, moving from place to place, are mostly invisible to the public. The woman with the shopping cart and the panhandler persist as stereotypes for the homeless, in spite of the fact that increasing numbers of *families* are homeless. True images of homelessness include mothers with babies in their arms, children saddened by loss and frightened by danger, youth dismissed as runaways or throwaways, and parents overwhelmed in a maze of service delivery systems. Their individual stories reveal diverse pathways to homelessness —unexpected misfortunes, domestic violence, poor housing and employment options, inadequate preparation for adulthood, substance abuse, mental illness, and no support networks.

Ironically, children and youth who are homeless are often invisible to individuals and agencies with the potential to provide real solutions—schools and universities, service and faith organizations, health and social service agencies, businesses and economic planning groups—the essential resources of every community. How can caring educators and other community members address the complex realities of homelessness for children and youth? Are there constructive approaches being used in school and community programs? This book was created to address these concerns about homelessness through:

1. honest appraisals of the challenges faced by homeless children, youth, and families; and

2. descriptions of promising practices created by individuals and organizations in diverse communities.

While we have focused primarily on the importance of education in nurturing children, youth and families, support is provided by many groups within communities. In fact, many of the hopeful solutions described in this book are built through partnerships—with families, youth, schools, shelters, health and social services, businesses, universities, and volunteers. These "Promising Practices" are highlighted throughout the book, as an encouragement to all educators and community members to see new possibilities for supporting our most vulnerable children, youth, and families.

Several years ago, we visited the Baltimore County Schools at the request of Jill Moss Greenberg and Marie Mayor, two enthusiastic educators and advocates for students in need. We were delighted to meet with school-based teams from every school in the district who were interested in coordinating their supports for homeless students. The efforts of many school and community members were highlighted throughout the day. High school students, Amber Goodman and Lexi Walters, built awareness about the diverse reasons for homelessness, asking audience members to stand as representatives of homeless families, while their varied stories were read. Amber and Lexi had developed a high school project to change their classmates' understanding of homelessness and encourage their donations of personal care items for families. A compassionate bus driver described how he started and ended his bus route at the homeless shelter, to protect the dignity of several children who were embarrassed about living there. Shelter staff, teachers, tutors, and homeless parents described how they worked together to support students' access and success in school.

This book was written to highlight the many creative strategies that are being developed by students, families, educators, and community members in various communities—illustrations of solutions that can grow from understanding the realities of homelessness and the possibilities for working together. We deeply appreciate this opportunity to collaborate with chapter authors, whose ongoing work reflects the partnerships needed for effective support systems. Many authors effectively included the voices and faces of children and youth who are homeless, helping us see and understand their needs more fully. Taken together, these chapters reflect the value of interdisciplinary perspectives, including educational policy and leadership, sociology, psychology, teacher education, special education, social work, law, and social policy. In addition, contributing authors also represent varied organizational experiences of national and state advocacy efforts, state- and community-level services, as well as research and university training programs.

The introductory chapter provides an overview of the educational challenges, federal responses, and promising practices in serving students who are homeless. The remaining chapters have four important foci: students, families, schools, and communities. To focus on the student, chapters include developmental perspectives on the needs of homeless infants, children, and youth, as well as strategies for establishing positive relationships. Chapters 6 and 7 focus on the protective roles of families and other adults in the lives of children, as well as strategies for enhancing those roles. The chapters that focus on schools include strategies for overcoming access barriers, increasing awareness, and planning comprehensive services. In the final section, community strategies are detailed for increasing advocacy, interagency collaboration, and university partnerships. To help readers access additional information, authors have included recommended resources, program descriptions, and contact information.

Just like the children and families we want to support, each school and community has unique features, including resources and priorities, that shape local practices. We hope that this book will provide a meaningful framework for planning and action, based on the realities of homeless children's situations and the needs for school-community partnerships. Every child and youth—including those who are homeless—deserves the benefits of security, care, and education. Together, we can continue our work to fulfill this promise.

Evelyn Reed-Victor
James Stronge

TABLE OF CONTENTS

1

EDUCATING HOMELESS CHILDREN AND YOUTH: AN INTRODUCTION

JAMES H. STRONGE

Homeless students are more like their housed peers than they are different—they have hopes and dreams, and deserve the opportunities that all students deserve. Yet, when children and youth become homeless, realizing those hopes and dreams can become a major challenge. Because of the many adverse conditions associated with homelessness, the students, their parents, and the greater educational community face barriers that must be overcome if students are to be afforded equitable educational opportunities. "Educating Homeless Students: An Introduction"[1] is devoted to exploring the ways and means to open the doors of opportunity for what might well be described as the most at-risk of all identifiable student populations—homeless children and youth.

This introductory chapter is intended to lay the foundation for exploring promising practices in educating homeless children and youth. Specifically, the chapter:

- ♦ provides an overview of problems and concerns related to educating homeless students;
- ♦ details the federal response to homeless education concerns; and,

♦ offers a glimpse of promising practices that may hold the key to designing and implementing successful educational programs for homeless students in schools, shelters, and other community agencies.

WHAT IS THE STATUS OF HOMELESSNESS?

DEFINITION OF HOMELESS

Studies have used a variety of definitions, taking into account not only where the person is residing, but also how long he or she is there. The location element of defining homelessness ranges from literally sleeping on the street to potential homelessness. The length of stay element takes into account point-in-time methodologies (e.g., a one-night count of homeless) and period prevalence counts (e.g., homeless over a given period of time) (National Coalition for the Homeless, 1998a).

For educational purposes, the definition of homeless provided in the Stewart B. McKinney Homeless Assistance Act of 1987 (P.L. 100-77 and amended by P.L. 101-645 and P.L. 103-382), is the prevailing definition. The McKinney Act defines a *homeless* person as one whose nighttime residence is:

♦ a supervised publicly or privately operated shelter designed to provide temporary living accommodations (including welfare hotels, congregate shelters, and transitional housing for the mentally ill);

♦ a public or private place not designed for, or ordinarily used as, a regular sleeping accommodation for human beings (e.g., cars, campgrounds, motels, and other temporary places); and

♦ a doubled-up accommodation (i.e., sharing housing with other families or individuals due to loss of housing or other similar situations).

EXTENT OF HOMELESSNESS

It is difficult to provide an accurate count (or even estimate) of the number of homeless students in America. In explaining the problems associated with determining the extent of homelessness, the National Coalition for the Homeless (1998a) explained that studies are complicated by problems of definitions and methodology. For example, ". . . most studies are limited to counting people who are literally homeless—that is, in shelters or on the streets. While this approach may yield useful information about the number of people who use services such as shelters . . . it can result in underestimates of homelessness" (p. 1).

While we may not know precisely the number of homeless children and youth, we do know that it is a large and apparently growing population (Burt, 1997). Additionally, it is clear that homeless students are not confined to urban areas; in fact, homeless children and their families can be found in large cities, small towns, suburban communities, and rural areas alike.

Figures from the United States Department of Education (USDOE) have shown an increase in the estimated number of homeless students in the last several years (1998). Table 1 provides a summary of the reported numbers of school-age homeless children and youth, as well as school enrollment figures, from data submitted by the states.

As presented in Table 1 (see p. 4), based on reports from the 50 states and U.S. territories, the USDOE estimated there were approximately 272,000 school-age children in the homeless population in 1989. In 1998 (the most recent period for which data are available), an estimate from the Department reported approximately 608,000. In addition to the "not attending school" data reported for 1998, the USDOE also reported data for students *not enrolled* in school. For K–12 students in 1998, 12% were reported as not enrolled. Of these, 10% of K–12 children were not enrolled and 24% of grades 9–12 homeless youth were not enrolled in school during their homelessness; disaggregated data for grades 6–8 were not reported. It is important to note that for 1998, five states and the District of Columbia did not submit reports, which may account for the lower total count in 1998 as compared with 1993. Additionally in 1998, 205,749 pre-school homeless children were reported with approximately 21% enrolled in pre-school programs[2]. These numbers may be an under-estimate because the counts/estimates tend to miss students who do not stay in shelters (Anderson, Janger, & Panton, 1995) as well as adolescent homeless (Powers & Jaklitsch, 1993).

TABLE 1. NUMBERS AND SCHOOL ENROLLMENT OF HOMELESS STUDENTS

Year	Numbers of Homeless Students	Percentage of Students *Not* Attending School
1989	272,773	28
1991	327,416	20
1993	744,266[a]	23
1998	615,336[b]	45[c]

[a]Hurricane Andrew and other natural disasters may account for the particularly high count in 1993

[b]Five states and the District of columbia did not submit reports accounting for the lower total count in 1998

[c]Prior to 1998, data were reported for students *not attending* school; for 1998, data were reported for students *not attending school on a regular basis*. "not attending school on a regular basis" was left to the discretion of the individual states to define.

The National Coalition for the Homeless (1998b) stated that "homeless children are by most accounts the fastest growing segment of the homeless population" (p. 1). Relatedly, a 1997 study conducted by the U.S. Conference of Mayors found that children accounted for 25% and independent youth for an additional 4% of the homeless population in urban areas (Waxman & Trupin, 1997).

WHAT EDUCATIONAL PROBLEMS DO HOMELESS STUDENTS FACE?

Try to imagine the trauma of being homeless. You may be sleeping in a car or living in one temporary shelter after the next. Perhaps you simply do not know *where* you are going to sleep. If you are homeless, it would likely mean moving to strange cities or neighborhoods, not knowing your neighbors, and losing track of friends and family. It would mean becoming rootless, and if you were school age, explaining to classmates why they

can't come over to your house to play. (Stronge &
Hudson, 1999, p. 8)

The above quote epitomizes the often stark realities of
homelessness. In the midst of these realities, making education
a priority in the lives of homeless children and their families is a
formidable task. When the problems that homeless students
bring with them to the schoolhouse door are combined with the
obstacles inherent in the governance and structure of American
public education, the public school seems ill-equipped to deal
with the challenges posed by homeless students. Those challenges can generally be categorized as issues of *access* to school
and *success* in school. A description of the factors that make
school access and success for homeless students such elusive
goals will be explored in the following section.

BARRIERS TO SCHOOL ACCESS

School access barriers for homeless students come in many
forms, including residency, guardianship, school records, immunization, and transportation policies (Anderson, Janger &
Panton, 1995; Helm, 1993; Stronge, 1997; 1999). There have been
numerous court cases involving residency requirements that
have inhibited homeless students from enrolling in school (see,
for example, Rafferty, 1995). Guardianship is another problem
because homelessness sometimes separates families and makes
it difficult, if not impossible, for students to obtain required sig-
natures for school enrollment. This can especially be a problem
for independent homeless youth.

Another barrier to school access is the unavailability of appropriate student records, especially medical records. Most
schools, by state law, mandate proof of immunization as a pre-
condition to enrollment. Helm (1992) stated that records can be
a barrier because parents (a) may not know about the requirements, (b) may not be able to afford immunization or be aware
of public health immunization programs, (c) may have difficulty
contacting the appropriate physician or public health office for
copies of immunization records, and (d) the schools where the
children were previously enrolled may be slow in responding
to requests for document transfer.

BARRIERS TO SCHOOL SUCCESS

Opening the schoolhouse door (i.e., gaining access) is no guarantee of success (Stronge, 1993). Once homeless children are enrolled in school, many problems can inhibit the school's ability to deliver an appropriate educational opportunity, and the students' ability to benefit from it. Potentially inhibiting factors include, among others, problems with educational placement and academic support, inadequate or inappropriate support services, and personal/familial socio-emotional concerns (Stronge, 1999). Educational placement and academic support can be seen in a variety of ways, such as the lack of proper placement in special education and gifted education. Support services, such as transportation, often are inadequate or unavailable. Because homelessness frequently creates personal and family stress, dealing with emotional and social issues can be paramount to making education meaningful for homeless students.

WHAT ARE PROMISING PRACTICES FOR EDUCATING HOMELESS STUDENTS?

Among the promising practices to improved educational opportunities, indeed, to improved lives, for homeless children and youth include building awareness, securing parental involvement and support, providing early childhood education opportunities, addressing special needs of special populations, and coordinating and collaborating in-service delivery. Each of these issues historically has been and, to varying degrees, remains, a barrier to the education of homeless students. However, by focusing on the possibilities rather than the problems, we can find creative and workable solutions, which will enhance the educational opportunities that homeless students receive. Each of these "promising practices" will be discussed in the following section.

BUILDING AWARENESS

One of the problems that continues to plague homeless education efforts is a lack of understanding of the needs of homeless students and their right to an appropriate education. Matters as simple as the school secretary denying parents the opportunity to enroll their child in school because the child "doesn't live in the attendance zone" or as complex as insensitivity and rejection by classmates and teachers (Eddowes & Hranitz, 1989) can effectively block a homeless student's opportunity to receive an education. Studies have recorded a persistent pattern of insensitivity toward homeless students; a problem that stems from lack of awareness (Stronge & Hudson, 1999).

A related problem is that of misperceptions regarding the nature of homelessness. "The homeless" are not one undifferentiated mass; rather "children and their families are homeless for different reasons, ranging from . . . unemployment to escaping domestic violence to parental drug abuse. Children in each of these situations have their special concerns" (McChesney, 1993, p. 377). "There is substantial variability in the type and severity of homeless-related problems experienced within the spectrum of homelessness ranging from individuals who are first-time homeless and are only temporarily in this condition to others who are chronically homeless" (Stronge, 1993, p. 354-55).

Before improved educational opportunities can become a reality, the lack of awareness and its related problems need to be addressed (First & Oakley, 1993). As a start, sensitivity and awareness training for school personnel should be provided (Rafferty, 1995). However, evidence suggests that sensitizing the school staff may not be enough; rather, educating community members and parents of non-homeless students may be necessary. Strategies employed in most states and many school districts to raise awareness include: appointing liaisons at the district and school level; staff development; materials development and distribution; and face-to-face meetings with key constituents (Anderson et al., 1995). Several suggestions for improving awareness are presented in Table 2.

SECURING PARENTAL INVOLVEMENT AND SUPPORT

Parental involvement and support are essential if education is to become and remain a priority for homeless children. Although parents of homeless students often recognize the importance of education for long-term success, they are often

TABLE 2. BUILDING AWARENESS FOR THE NEEDS OF
HOMELESS STUDENTS

Target Audiences	Examples of Awareness Programs and Efforts
Homeless Families	Inform families of rights and responsibilities to education for their children. Build awareness regarding the importance of school continuity. Clarify availability of school-based support services and supplies.
Students	Increase sensitivity of all students to their peers.
Teachers	Increase awareness of the need for emotional and academic support for students.
Special Services Staff	Increase awareness of the need for expedited services and sensitivity in providing services.
Administrators	Build better understanding of homeless student needs and McKinney Act provisions. Emphasize school and community services available for homeless students and families.

too preoccupied with securing basic needs to effectively advocate for their children's educational needs (Yon & Sebastien-Kadie, 1994).

Despite the fact that homeless families typically are lacking in family strength, parents are not lacking in concern and aspirations for their children (Stronge & Hudson, 1999). With encouragement and assistance they can become partners in the educational enterprise. Gonzalez (1992) captured the essence of this sentiment well: "one cannot provide a supportive climate for homeless children without soliciting the help of the parents" (p. 200). In an effort to facilitate the creation of a supportive climate, she offered the suggestions summarized in Table 3.

Enhancing parent-child relationships by emphasizing protective factors of structure, positive interaction, and developmentally appropriate goals can be supported by school liaison personnel (social workers, guidance counselors) and parent education programs (Reed-Victor & Stronge, 1997). Family members also play a vital role that supports the development of their children through modeling behavior, teaching competency, and facing challenges (Reed-Victor & Stronge, 1997). It should be clear that a partnership with parents needs to be forged to assist students in accessing and succeeding in school (Stronge & Hudson, 1999).

TABLE 3. BUILDING PARENTAL INVOLVEMENT AND SUPPORT

Types of Support	Examples of Effective Strategies
School and Community Relations	Foster positive and consistent communication with parents. Build trust between parents and school staff. Provide a "personal touch" in lieu of an air of professionalism.
Parent Efficacy	Demonstrate how parents can assist with school work. Provide suggestions for how parents serve as positive role models for their children.
Parent Training	Provide training that includes parenting skills, preventing or overcoming substance abuse, availability of community services, improving parents' basic skills, and discipline techniques.

PROVIDING EARLY CHILDHOOD EDUCATION OPPORTUNITIES

The research is replete with evidence from programs, such as the Perry Preschool Program, that starting early is paramount for success in learning, particularly for children from impoverished backgrounds (Maughan, 1988). Young homeless children, in particular, have little stability in their lives and lack the comfort, nutritional requirements, and health support necessary for normal development. Additionally, they frequently experience language, cognitive, and behavioral problems (Eddowes, 1993). Issues as practical as a safe place to play can be important: ". . . the absence of easy access to safe outdoor play can be a significant impediment . . ." to parenting and child development (Bartlett, 1997, p. 47).

Despite the overwhelming evidence for the need for early intervention and the call for special attention to early childhood education in the 1994 Amendments to the McKinney Act, early childhood education initiatives continue to lag behind other efforts. For example, Nunez (1994) reported from a New York City study that "nearly 80 percent of school-age children had not attended any school prior to kindergarten" (p. 70). Moreover, the critical need for early childhood education is reflected in the finding that homeless families frequently include two to three children under age 5 (Kling, Dunn, & Oakley, 1996).

The importance of having slots available in high-quality child care programs when they are needed is critical if the problem of nonparticipation is to be alleviated (Eddowes, 1993). Program access is a particularly acute problem due to the fact that demand typically exceeds supply in early childhood programs. Coupled with this supply-demand problem is the fact that homeless children move in and out of a community and, thus, are frequently not in line for a slot in a program. A potential solution to this dilemma is to hold a few slots open in programs like Even Start for homeless children; rather than a slot being filled by a single child for the duration of the program, it could be filled by numerous homeless children as their families move in and out of the community.

Addressing the Special Needs of Special Populations

Homelessness is not unidimensional; each homeless student is an individual with unique needs. However, within the homeless student population, there are discernible subgroups whose similar educational needs especially require effective intervention. Among these subgroups are *independent youth* and *students with disabilities*.

Powers and Jaklitsch (1992) noted that "although homelessness among adolescents is not a new social problem, over the past several decades it has increased in volume, scope, and visibility" (p. 117). Whether they choose to leave home (i.e., runaways) or are forced to leave home (i.e., throwaways), "the consequences of homelessness can be devastating for young people" (Powers & Jaklitsch, 1993, p. 394). A variety of barriers can serve to effectively separate homeless youth from education, including the effects of street life, substance abuse, living conditions, health problems, family background, developmental lags, and emotional and psychological problems (Powers & Jaklitsch, 1993). Anderson et al. (1995) noted the extreme barriers that homeless youth face in merely accessing school:

> Efforts to curb crime or ensure school safety may impede enrollment for homeless teens—for example, curfew laws make them guilty of a crime just because they have no place to go. Schools in some states refuse to admit homeless teens due to liability concerns . . . . In terms of McKinney-funded services, few . . . LEAs . . . provided instructional services to older students. (p. ii)

While there are no simple solutions for getting homeless teens into school and helping them succeed once there, certain strategies can be usefully employed. Vissing, Schroepfer, and Bloise (1994) suggested that independent homeless youth be offered assistance in an effort to accommodate childcare responsibilities, job requirements, the absence of home libraries and places suitable for study, and a host of related problems they encounter. Providing flexibility in school policies and procedures such as admissions criteria, attendance policies, course offerings, and class assignments can be paramount to getting adolescents in school and keeping them there. Additionally, assisting with emotional support, making community resources accessible, and providing special services such as special education and transportation are vital.

Another identifiable homeless sub-population with particularly acute needs includes students with disabilities. "Several factors mitigate against homeless students with disabilities receiving education, let alone *special* education services" (Korinek, Walther-Thomas, & Laycock, 1992, p. 135). Factors such as transiency, difficulty in transferring records, etc., make it difficult to access specialized educational services on a timely basis. Even the stipulations within special education statutes designed to bring services to eligible students can serve as formidable barriers to their education. For example, special education procedural due process rights found in the Individuals with Disabilities Education Act (IDEA, P.L. 101-476) can result in service delivery timelines that are incompatible with homeless lifestyles. "Procedural safeguards designed to protect the due process rights of students with disabilities and to provide maximum involvement of parents set an evaluation pace that makes it difficult to qualify these students for services" (Korinek et al., p. 142). By the time a referral has been made, eligibility has been determined, and a placement can be provided, homeless students may well have moved to a neighboring school district or across the country.

Because factors both within the schools (i.e., organizational characteristics, due process procedures) and within the lifestyle of homeless individuals can contribute to delays or loss of services, special attention to these obstacles must be provided if education is to be provided to needy students. In an effort to address these concerns, Korinek et al. (1992) developed a set of program considerations that can help minimize the problems associated with homeless students and special education. As depicted in Table 4, their suggestions for support might well serve as a practical guide for the delivery of any specialized services to homeless children and independent homeless youth.

TABLE 4. SUGGESTIONS FOR SERVING SPECIAL NEEDS STUDENTS

Types of Support	Examples of Effective Strategies
Educational Placement	School leaders need to actively support the ethical and legal requirements to provide specialized education services. Expedited access to records and services can facilitate school access.
Educational Service Delivery	Individualized programs for basic literacy, gifted education, and a host of other alternatives are vital to success in school. A commitment for a structured, stable, and nonthreatening environment should be provided.
Coordination and Support Services	Collaboration with shelters, social service providers, and parents is vital in order to coordinate efforts. Transitional planning should begin the first day the student arrives because of the likelihood that a move is imminent.
Other Factors	Peer involvement in which a climate of acceptance and support for all students is fostered can enhance school success.

COORDINATING AND COLLABORATING IN SERVICE DELIVERY

A coordinated, collaborative approach to education seems to be especially important when dealing with homeless students. It would be presumptuous to believe that schools alone can solve the problems of the homeless. Although education is fundamental to breaking the grip of poverty (Stronge, 1993), the problems associated with homelessness are multidimensional and rooted in the broader community; so, too, must the solutions to homelessness be multidimensional and based squarely in the broader community.

The McKinney Act requires each state to ensure that coordination among agencies (i.e., state department of education, local school districts, other public and community agencies) serving homeless individuals be emphasized (P.L. 103-382). As Anderson et al. (1995) noted:

> Coordination and collaboration focus on identifying available services and resources and communicating this information to those in need. By promoting coordination and collaboration locally, states have enabled school districts and service providers to stretch their available resources and thus be able to better serve homeless children and youth. (p. 36)

Using Melaville and Blank's (1991) framework, Yon, Mickelson, and Carlton-LaNey (1993) described five variables that have been found to be effective in shaping interagency partnerships (Table 5).

WHERE DO WE GO FROM HERE?

Considerable progress has been made in recent years in converting the concepts of *access* and *success* into reality for homeless students. Tangible evidence can be found across America—in public schools, shelters, and other agencies—of effective programs and efforts to better serve homeless students and their families. Importantly, these programs are beginning to yield dividends.

The collective efforts of the contributing authors of this book offer guidance in furthering our understanding and, hopefully, our capacity to provide successful programs for homeless students. While none of us have the answers to the pervasive problems associated with educating homeless students, we each can make a positive contribution. It is to this end that *Promising Practices for Educating Homeless Students* is devoted.

TABLE 5. DEVELOPING EFFECTIVE COLLABORATIVE
PROGRAMS FOR HOMELESS STUDENTS

Characteristics	Description of Effective Strategies
Climate	Promote a social and political *climate* in which the community, key decision makers, and service providers support one another and make collaboration a top priority.
Process	Develop a *process* of collaboration in which partners accept the goals of others and attempt to resolve difficulties as they arise.
Leadership	The quality of leadership of the *people* who are part of interagency partnerships is critical and their efforts should build on their collective vision, commitment, and competence.
Policies	Because collaborative efforts frequently bring together agencies with differing, if not competing, agendas, it is essential that the agencies establish *policies* that encourage cooperation rather than competition.
Resources	For collaborative ventures to succeed in either coordinating existing services or in creating new services, *resources* must be pooled or reconfigured to meet the needs of the target homeless population.

REFERENCES

Anderson, L. M., Janger, M. I., & Panton, K. L. M. (1995). *An evaluation of state and local efforts to serve the educational needs of homeless children and youth.* Washington, DC: United States Department of Education.

Bartlett, S. (1997). No place to play; Implications for the interaction of parents and children. *Journal of Children and Poverty, 3,* 37-48.

Eddowes, E. A. (1993). Education of younger homeless children in urban settings. *Education and Urban Society, 25,* 381-393.

Eddowes, E. A., & Hranitz, J. R. (1989). Educating children of the homeless. *Childhood Education, 65,* 197-200.

First, P. F., & Oakley, J. L. (1993). Policy, behavior, and research: Changing schooling for homeless children and youth. *Education and Urban Society, 25,* 424-437.

Gonzalez, M. L. (1992). Educational climate for the homeless: Cultivating the family and school relationship. In J. H. Stronge (Ed.), *Educating homeless children and adolescents: Evaluating policy and practice.* Newbury Park, CA: Sage.

Helm, V. M (1992). The legal context: From access to success in education for homeless children and youth. In J. H. Stronge (Ed.), *Educating homeless children and adolescents: Evaluating policy and practice* (pp. 115-132). Newbury Park, CA: Sage.

Helm, V. M. (1993). Legal rights to education of homeless children and youth. *Education and Urban Society, 25,* 323-339.

Kling, N., Dunn, L., & Oakley, J. (1996, Winter). Homeless families in early childhood programs: What to expect and what to do. *Dimensions of Early Childhood, 3-8.*

Korinek, L., Walther-Thomas, C., & Laycock, V.K. (1992). Educating special needs homeless children and youth. In J.H. Stronge (Ed.), *Educating homeless children and adolescents: Evaluating policy and practice.* Newbury Park, CA: Sage.

Maughan, B. (1988). School experiences as risk/protective factors. In M. Rutter (Ed.), *Studies of psycholosocial risk: The power of longitudinal data* (pp. 200-220). Cambridge: Cambridge University Press.

McChesney, K. Y. (1993). Homeless families since 1980: Implications for education. *Education and Urban Society, 25,* 361-380.

Melaville, A. I., & Blank, M. J. (1991). *What it takes: Structuring interagency partnerships to connect children and families with comprehensive services*. Washington, DC: Education and Human Services Consortium.

National Coalition for the Homeless (1998a). *How many people experience homelessness? Fact sheet #2*. Washington, DC: Author.

National Coalition for the Homeless (1998b). *Education of homeless children and youth. Fact sheet #10*. Washington, DC: Author.

Nunez, R. D. (1994). *Hopes, dreams, and promise: The future of homeless children in America*. New York: Homes for the Homeless, Inc.

Powers, J. L., & Jaklitsch, B. (1992). Adolescence and homelessness: The unique challenge for secondary educators. In J. H. Stronge (Ed.), *Educating homeless children and adolescents: Evaluting policy and practice* (pp. 115-132.) Newbury Park, CA. Sage.

Powers, J. L., & Jaklitsch, B. (1993). Reaching the hard to reach: Educating homeless adolescents in urban settings. *Education and Urban Society, 25*, 394-409.

P.L. 100-77, Stewart B. McKinney Homeless Assistance Act of 1987. *Codified at* 42 U.S.C. 11301-11472 (1987, July 22).

P.L. 101-476, Individuals with Disabilities Education Act, 1990. *Codified at* 20 U.S.C. 1400-1476 (1990, October 30).

P.L. 101-645, Stewart B. McKinney Homeless Assistance Amendment Act of 1990. (1990, November 29).

P.L. 103-382, Improving America's Schools Act of 1994. (1994, September 28).

Rafferty, Y. (1995). The legal rights and educational problems of homeless children and youth. *Educational Evaluation and Policy Analysis, 17*, 39-61.

Reed-Victor, E., & Stronge, J. H. (1997). Building resiliency: Constructive directions for homeless education. *Journal of Children and Poverty, 3*, 67-91.

Reed-Victor, E., & Stronge, J. H. (2000 projected publication date). Diverse teaching strategies for diverse learners—Homeless children. In H. Hodges (Ed.), *Educating everybody's children: Diverse teaching strategies for diverse learners (Vol. 2)*. Alexandria, VA: Association for Supervision and Curriculum Development.

Stronge, J. H. (1993). From access to success: Public policy for educating urban homeless students. *Education and Urban Society, 25*, 340-360.

Stronge, J. H. (1997). A long road ahead: A progress report on educating homeless children and youth in America. *Journal of Children and Poverty, 3* (2), 13-34.

Stronge, J. H. (1999). The education of homeless children and youth in the United States: A progress report. In R. Mickelson (Ed.), *Children on the streets of the Americas: Globalization, homelessness, and education in the United States, Brazil, and Cuba.* New York: Routledge.

Stronge, J. H., & Hudson, K. S. (1999). Educating homeless children and youth with dignity and care. *Journal for a Just and Caring Society, 5,* 7-18.

United States Department of Education (1998, December). *Data on homeless children and youth (From ED reports on data submitted by SEAs) Draft Memorandum.* Washington, DC: Author.

Vissing, Y. M., Schroepfer, D., & Bloise, F. (1994). Homeless students, heroic students. *Phi Delta Kappan, 75,* 535-539.

Waxman, L., & Trupin, R. (1997). *A status report on hunger and homelessness in America's cities: 1997.* Washington, DC: U. S. Conference of Mayors.

Yon, M. G., Mickelson, R. A., & Carlton-LaNey, I. (1993). A child's place: Developing interagency collaboration on behalf of homeless children. *Education and Urban Society, 25,* 410-423.

Yon, M., & Sebastien-Kadie, M. (1994). Homeless parents and the education of their children. *The School Community Journal, 4*(2), 67-77.

ADDITIONAL RESOURCES

Journal of Children and Poverty often contains articles relevant to the education of homeless children and youth. The *Journal* is published by the Institute for Children and Poverty, 36 Cooper Square, New York, New York 10003, telephone (212) 529-5252, fax (212) 529-7698.

Journal for a Just and Caring Education. The January 1999, special issue is devoted to issues related to the education of homeless children and youth. For ordering information, contact Corwin Press, Inc. at: 2455 Teller Road, Thousand Oaks, CA 91320, telephone (805) 499-0721, fax (805) 499-0871.

Educating everybody's children: Diverse teaching strategies for diverse learners (Vol. 2). This volume contains a chapter devoted to educating homeless children and youth to be published by: Association for Supervision and Curriculum Development, 1703 N. Beauregard Street, Alexandria, VA 22311, telephone 1-800-933-2723, fax, (703) 299-8631.

ENDNOTES

[1]Appreciation is expressed to Evelyn Reed-Victor, Timothy Davey, Bill Penuel, and Barbara James for their reviews of a draft of this chapter.

[2]Ten states and DC did not report estimates of the number of preschool homeless children in the 1998 report.

[3]An earlier version of this section and the section, "What educational problems do homeless students face?" was published as "A long road ahead: A progress report on educating homeless children and youth in America," in the *Journal of Children and Poverty* (1972) 3 (2), 13-31 by James H. Stronge.

[4]The statute was up for reauthorization by Congress, again, in 1998.

[5]The McKinnery Act will be considered for reauthorization by Congress in 1999 and 2000, too late for inclusion in this text.

2

MEETING THE DEVELOPMENTAL AND EDUCATIONAL NEEDS OF HOMELESS INFANTS AND YOUNG CHILDREN

E. ANNE EDDOWES AND TINA BUTCHER

Children have different opportunities as they confront the world. Most children have parents or other adults to care for them and assist in meeting their needs. One important need is that of a place to live. A majority of children in the United States live in some type of home that gives a measure of permanence in their lives; however, some children are not so fortunate. Against great odds, their parents are trying to provide for the family's needs. Despite the parents' best efforts, it may be impossible for them to provide a home. What happens to a young child when a home is not a possibility? What services supportive of development and education are necessary to assist children in building a bridge from the instability of homeless life to that of a productive adult life? Events that take place in the early childhood years can make a substantial difference in outcomes for homeless children. This chapter will include the following information:

♦ an overview of the developmental needs of all infants and young children;

♦ identification of particular needs of homeless infants and young children;

♦ practices supportive of the education of young homeless children; and

♦ program services important for young homeless children

WHAT ARE THE DEVELOPMENTAL NEEDS OF INFANTS AND YOUNG CHILDREN?

All young children have needs concerning their overall growth and education whether they are homeless or have a permanent place of residence. These needs are related to every area of development: physical; social-emotional; communicative; cognitive and creative. A short overview of selected characteristics of each area of development follows.

PHYSICAL DEVELOPMENT

It is necessary for infants and toddlers to know that their bodily needs will be met. Nutritious food, clean diapers, clothes, and secure surroundings contribute to a child's well-being. As infants become mobile, they need safe space to explore and develop their large muscles. Early gross motor movement, along with sensory experiences, contribute to the development of eye-hand coordination and fine motor skills. As young children grow, they need safe opportunities to practice their skills. In addition, they need medical and dental check-ups and immunizations to assure good health (Eddowes, 1992; Eddowes & Ralph, 1998; Bredekamp & Copple, 1997)

SOCIAL-EMOTIONAL DEVELOPMENT

The early development of social-emotional growth is dependent upon a child's positive interactions with caring adults. Trust is promoted by parents and caregivers who create a predictable environment for infants and continue a stable sense of order throughout childhood. In order to explore their world, toddlers rely on the presence of the parent or caregiver as a secure base. As the young child explores new objects, events, or people, there is a constant checking by looking at or by actually moving closer to the person before the activity is resumed. The stable environment gives young children the security to try new things (Erikson, 1963).

With the assistance of parents and others, young children learn that they can be successful, and this helps build positive self-esteem. They begin to develop autonomy which lays a foundation for self-control. Children who are allowed to express choices and learn self-help skills move toward independence (Kamii, 1982). When children experience positive social interactions, they begin to construct their own understanding of concepts (Bredekamp & Copple, 1997), and learn the rules and social skills related to their culture (Eddowes & Ralph, 1998).

COMMUNICATIVE DEVELOPMENT

This area of development includes listening, speaking, writing, and reading. Infants begin to learn to listen before they can speak. As they begin to make sounds, adults and other children interact with them. These interactions provide infants and young children with practice in listening and speaking. Speech assists children in organizing and integrating many aspects of their behavior (Vygotsky, 1978). Oral language is the foundation for writing. Young children need experiences in manipulating crayons, pencils, and markers on paper so they can practice the fine motor skills necessary to learn to write (Bredekamp & Copple, 1997). In addition, adults should read to very young children often. The children learn that they can gain both information and pleasure from the experience. It provides the basis for their own reading as they move into kindergarten and the early grades (Schickedanz, 1999).

COGNITIVE AND CREATIVE DEVELOPMENT

As they interact with people and materials, young children begin to acquire general knowledge of their world. It is important for infants and young children to explore, experiment, and construct their own knowledge (Piaget, 1970,1973). As infants interact with the environment, they develop concepts of objects, people, and conditions. Young children build a framework to use in solving problems and making decisions. They develop the power of reasoning and judgment (Vygotsky, 1978). As children explore and experiment, their creativity is stimulated. Through various materials and activities (such as art, music, movement, drama, woodworking, and cooking), adults can facilitate cognitive development and creativity to try new ideas (Eddowes & Ralph, 1998).

These areas of development are all important and complement each other as the young child grows and learns. Education and development are closely linked, so that the pace at which development proceeds and abilities evolve is dependent upon the environment and the varied interactions available to each child (Eddowes & Ralph, 1998).

WHAT ARE THE PARTICULAR NEEDS OF YOUNG HOMELESS CHILDREN?

Whether they are in a home setting, childcare program, or school, all infants and young children need safe, secure, and healthy environments which provide some measure of stability. Most homeless children do not have the physical care, space, or stability of environment necessary for their optimum development. Although it may be necessary for them to be more independent than their peers who have homes, they have little chance to practice making wise choices or to learn self-control. Opportunities for positive social interactions may be difficult to achieve. The development of competence necessary in today's world may seem impossible. There may be little opportunity for imagination to thrive. The adults in the lives of young children are usually able to provide environments in which growth, development, and learning will progress; for young homeless children, however, additional help is often necessary. See Table 1 for a summary of the needs of young homeless children.

NEED FOR PHYSICAL CARE

As young homeless children develop, meeting their physical and health needs is very important. Many homeless children do not get the nutritional balance necessary for healthy growth,

TABLE 1. NEEDS OF YOUNG HOMELESS CHILDREN

Overall Need	Specific Need
Physical Care	Nutrition
	Sleep
	Clean Clothing
	Grooming
	Predictable Schedule
Space	Safety
	Privacy
Stability/Security	Trust
	Comfort
	Consistent Interactions
	Continuity
Autonomy/Self-Control	Self-Help Skills
	Choices
	Solving Conflicts
Positive Social Interactions	Self-Worth
	Friends
	Language
Competency/Creativity	Practical Skills
	General Knowledge
	Problem Solving
	Creative Skills

nor adequate sleep and clean clothing. The daily schedule has little predictability and can be very stressful. Medical and dental screenings and check-ups may be nonexistent.

> **Vignette #1:** Megan (6 years) comes into the classroom. Greeting the teacher with a shy smile, she moves directly to her desk. She sits there listening to the other

children talking around her. Then she puts her head down on the desk and falls asleep.

When young children's needs for health and nutrition are not met, they can become listless with little energy and interest for activities in which healthier children engage. They have difficulty in concentrating and attending in classroom settings.

NEED FOR SPACE

Safe Space. Homeless children usually have very little safe space necessary for physical play and motor development. Children who live in temporary shelters are constrained because available space is typically limited. When living in abandoned buildings, tent cities, or other public places, young children may be unable to have room for movement because of unsafe conditions.

Most young children enjoy physical activities; however, they need space and materials to develop both their gross motor and fine motor skills. When young children have little access to space for gross motor movement and the materials necessary to develop fine motor skills, their physical development may not advance in a normal progression.

Personal Space. In addition to physical space, children also have a need for personal space. Although young children learn much from interactions with adults and other children, private space in which to be alone can enhance intrapersonal and emotional growth. It can also help children retreat from excess stimulation, and give them some control over outcomes in their activity (Eddowes, 1993). Most of the time, children with homes have at least a corner of the environment in which they keep personal belongings and can retreat from mainstream activity.

> **Vignette #2:** Celina (3 1/2 years) has just arrived at the childcare center from a homeless shelter. She watches the children playing in different areas of the room. The teacher asks her if she would like to play with others in one of the areas. Celina declines, gets a picture book from the shelf, and climbs up the short ladder to the

reading loft by herself. Later, after she has looked through the book, she joins a group of children playing in the dramatic play area.

In contrast to children who have homes, homeless children may live in crowded shelters or cramped quarters. They have few personal belongings and no place to keep them. Withdrawing even briefly from life situations is difficult. It is important that they have an opportunity at times to withdraw from mainstream activity.

Need for Stability and Security

Little stability is available in the lives of homeless children, who have few of the advantages afforded children living in homes. In a stable environment, infants and toddlers come to expect that they will be fed, have their diapers changed, and be comforted when there is a problem. Consistency, continuity, and predictability contribute to the young child's sense of well-being. In addition, stability of environment gives children the secure base necessary to try new things and develop flexibility in approaching events. A stable environment and consistent interactions between adults and young children assist them in developing trust that there will be predictability in their lives.

> **Vignette #3:** Robert (8 years) has moved three times in the last three months. During that time he has attended two different schools. Each has had a different daily schedule. Now he is attending the third school. The teacher tells the class it is time to line up at the door, but fails to say where they are going. Robert stays in his seat. He does not know where they are going. It is his way of rebelling at the lack of predictability in his life.

Homeless children are unable to have the stability and relative permanence of a home. If there is a shelter of some kind that the family lives in, it is usually very temporary. Because homeless children are denied the security a home can provide, they may have little confidence that the world can be trusted.

Until they believe that an educational setting is a secure, positive, and predictable place, they may not have the confidence necessary to be successful students.

NEED FOR AUTONOMY AND SELF-CONTROL

Young homeless children have a difficult time developing a sense of independence. Striving for autonomy usually begins in the second year of life (Erikson, 1963), and lays the foundation for self-control and future decision-making abilities. When children are allowed to express choices, learn to solve conflicts, and develop self-help skills, they move toward independence (Kamii, 1982).

> **Vignette #4:** Jane (4 years) is playing with several other children in the block area of the childcare center. Both she and another child reach for the same block. Jane yells, "It's mine!" The other child holds onto the block and Jane hits him. The teacher says calmly, "Hitting is not allowed. Is there another way that you can solve the problem?" The other child suggests that there may be another block like the one they both want. Both children look around. Jane says, "There is one. I'll use it." They continue building.

Because young homeless children have few belongings, they may not like to share; however, they can learn these skills with proper guidance. Although they may not be allowed to make many choices due to their family situation, homeless children are usually taught the self-help skills of eating and dressing. The importance of allowing children to make choices may not occur to homeless parents because they have few choices of their own.

NEED FOR POSITIVE SOCIAL INTERACTIONS

Self-Worth. Young homeless children may not have many positive social interactions, because homelessness is very stressful for families. Frequent moving drains energy, and parents may be too worried or tired to have meaningful interactions with their young children. Nevertheless, children can gain much through positive interactions with various adults and children who build their confidence and feelings of self-worth. If young homeless children are to succeed educationally, they need to believe they are valued members of society.

Friends. Friends are an important part of childhood. They provide opportunities for working and relating effectively with other children, fostering healthy social and emotional growth. When children move often, they have difficulty in making friends, or they leave behind any friends that they have made. At school, because they may arrive hungry or unkempt, peers may not be interested in having them for friends.

Language. Social interactions can also provide support for language development, an essential aspect of cognitive development. As young children grow, they need many opportunities for listening, speaking, and exploring books. In addition, they need experiences in drawing in order to organize their thinking, as well as learning control of a pencil.

> **Vignette #5:** Chris (7 years) is sitting in the art area drawing a picture. The teacher asks him to tell her a story about the picture. He does, and she asks him if he thinks that he could write the story on another sheet of paper. He says, "Maybe some of it." The teacher smiles and asks him to try. Later he brings her the paper. He has used invented spelling to write the main points of the story.

Homeless children have little chance to engage in relaxed, appropriate communication experiences. They usually do not have books and drawing/writing materials where they live, nor opportunities to learn to express their ideas.

NEED FOR COMPETENCE AND CREATIVE EXPRESSION

There are many different aspects of competence. Many times it is linked only to linguistic and mathematical ability; however, the emerging view of multiple intelligences also includes the areas of motor, spatial, music, and personal relationships (Gardner, 1983, 1993). Developing cognitive abilities and competence in early childhood is the basis for much of the learning

that will be engaged in throughout life. The challenge is to identify and build on each child's strengths to provide support for
other aspects of development and learning (Hunt, 1961).

Although homeless children need the basic skills of reading, writing, and math, they also need the skills that creative
activities bring. In addition, knowledge of practical skills can
improve their lives. For example, homeless children may have
no idea where food comes from or how it evolves into the meals
that they eat.

> **Vignette #6:** During a large group discussion about food
> in class, Jake (5 years) says that he likes vegetable soup.
> The teacher asks him where the soup comes from. He
> says, "From a can." The teacher and children discuss
> how vegetable soup is made. She tells them that they
> will make vegetable soup tomorrow at school. The next
> day the children all take turns preparing the vegetables
> to cook. After the soup is cooked, they eat it.

While children's cognitive skills can be enhanced through
cooking activities, homeless children usually do not have an
opportunity to assist in those activities with their families. In
addition to the use of cooking and other types of food preparation in class, cognitive and creative skills are enhanced through
sewing and craft activities, carpentry and other activities which
help children learn how things work. Through these kinds of
experiences, homeless children can develop confidence and become more competent in lifelong skills.

WHAT PRACTICES SUPPORT THE DEVELOPMENT AND EDUCATION OF YOUNG HOMELESS CHILDREN?

Because the needs of young homeless children are great, it is
critical that caregivers and teachers recognize these needs and
address them within early childhood settings. In addition to the
lack of a permanent place of residence, these children also experience the effects of poverty, which may include scarcity of food,
clothing, and adequate medical care. They may move from place
to place with such frequency that they are never afforded opportunities to establish a sense of trust with caregivers, create

meaningful friendships, become a part of a classroom community, or receive services which would so greatly benefit them. With this great array of needs, caregivers and teachers for homeless infants and children must be aware of practices that will support their education and development.

Quality early childhood programs seek to address the four components of developmentally appropriate practice as defined by the National Association for the Education of Young Children (NAEYC) (Bredekamp & Copple, 1997). In an earlier publication, Bredekamp noted that:

NAEYC believes that quality is not determined by the length of the program day or by the sponsorship, although these factors can affect quality. NAEYC believes that a major determinant of the quality of an early childhood program is the degree to which the program is developmentally appropriate. (1987, p. 51)

Quality early childhood programs address children from the four perspectives relating to developmentally appropriate practice as outlined in Table 2.

From a developmentally appropriate approach, caregivers and teachers are aware of the typical developmental needs, individual needs, and the social/cultural contexts that affect their students. They also use a variety of sources of knowledge when making decisions. For educators, volunteers, and tutors, significant knowledge of the typical needs of homeless children and practices that address these needs is essential for effectively assisting these children and students. Appropriate practices and informed educators can help to build resilience and allow the child to cope with his or her situation in a healthy manner.

WHAT PRACTICES SUPPORT RESILIENCE IN HOMELESS INFANTS AND YOUNG CHILDREN?

Children who have been identified as possessing resilience, or effective coping skills, demonstrate several characteristics, including age-appropriate sensorimotor and perceptual skills, special interests, sociability, development of autonomy, positive self-concept, and cognitive ability (Reed-Victor & Stronge, 1997). Early childhood programs can support the development of these resilient characteristics while addressing many of the needs that homeless children present.

TABLE 2. FOUR COMPONENTS OF QUALITY EARLY
CHILDHOOD PROGRAMS

Components of Developmentally Appropriate Programs	Practices	Examples
Using knowledge about child development to inform practice.	Practice is appropriate for the age level of the child.	Teachers allow three-year-olds to explore writing using many types of paper and writing instruments rather than by tracing letters on worksheets.
Using knowledge about individual children to inform practice.	Practice is appropriate for the individual needs of the child.	The children use open-ended materials such as blocks or paints regularly to allow for individual expression.
Using knowledge of the social and cultural context to inform practice.	Practice integrates and respects the social and cultural contexts of the child.	When a kindergarten child asks why her friend Billy lives with his grandmother instead of his mom and dad, the teacher uses the opportunity to discuss various family arrangements.
Using multiple sources of knowledge in professional decision making.	Practice examines information from different perspectives.	When an infant frets or cries, caregivers think about the possibility of hunger, wet diaper, food or lactose intolerance, sickness, or need for comfort, and then make an appropriate response.

SUPPORTING PHYSICAL NEEDS

In addressing the physical needs of young homeless children, opportunities for appropriate cleanliness/grooming, ample rest, and adequate nutrition are necessary for typical development to occur. Age-appropriate sensorimotor and perceptual activities also allow children to gain accurate knowledge about the world around them. "Locomotion plays a large role in motor and skill development and includes activities of moving the body through space-walking, running, hopping, jumping, rolling, dancing, climbing and leaping" (Morrison, 1995, pp. 195–196).

As in Vignette #1, homeless children such as Megan may come to school without having their physical needs for cleanliness, rest, nutrition, and physical movement satisfied. Within the classroom or early childhood setting, a caregiver or teacher can provide:

- ◆ bathing, grooming, and clean clothes as the child arrives at the center or school;
- ◆ safe, quiet place and time for the child to rest;
- ◆ cooking experiences that allow the child to explore a variety of healthy foods;
- ◆ opportunities to manipulate small objects such as beads, cubes, and blocks; and
- ◆ activities that allow the child to engage in outdoor activities for motor development.

Temporary living arrangements often provide few opportunities for the homeless child to move about freely, to rest quietly, or to assist in the daily preparation of food. There may be little opportunity for parents to provide for bathing and clean clothes. Such experiences primarily address the physical needs of the child. Maslow (1970) has identified bodily needs as the most basic of needs in the journey toward self-actualization. The satisfaction of these basic needs is essential in freeing the child to pursue social and academic interests.

SUPPORTING CHILDREN'S INTERESTS

Special interests such as hobbies, sports, or other events that promote the self-esteem of the child are vital. Areas within the classroom that encourage these special interests, such as woodworking or cooking, are of special benefit to the homeless child. These special interests are validated when children have areas for their personal belongings and areas that allow them to have personal space.

The descriptions of Celina (Vignette #2) and Jake (Vignette #6) illustrate homeless children's needs for personal space, solitary play and opportunities to explore personal interests. Within the early childhood setting, caregivers, and teachers can provide:

♦ solitary play spaces with books, puzzles, games, or toys that a child can use independently;

♦ areas within the classroom for exploration of cooking, sewing, or woodworking; and

♦ special place at school for items of importance to the child.

Shelters and other temporary living arrangements rarely provide young children with little, if any, space to call their own. This prohibits young children from developing individual interests since personal space is unavailable. Solitary play areas within the classroom allow young children to have a quiet, personal space within which to withdraw when necessary (Eddowes, 1993). "Giving children space and materials of their own can help build a greater sense of acceptance and security, ownership and control" (Klein, Bittel & Molnar, 1993, p. 27). Setting aside adequate space within the classroom can help provide young homeless children with experiences which may otherwise be absent from their lives due to homelessness.

SUPPORTING SOCIAL SKILLS

Developing a sense of humor, communication skills, and the ability to make friends helps children cope in a variety of environments such as childcare, schools, or shelters. Caregivers and teachers promote problem-solving skills by creating opportunities to teach and use cooperation skills, conflict resolution techniques, and decision-making abilities.

Robert's situation in Vignette #3 is indicative of the lack of predictability within the lives of homeless children. Reactions such as Robert's may be perceived as rebelliousness or lack of socialization. It is important for teachers and caregivers to remember to:

♦ maintain a predictable, consistent schedule;

♦ post a classroom schedule in a prominent place within the room;

♦ review the routine and any changes daily;

♦ establish a buddy system to help new students adjust to new routines;

♦ emphasize cooperative learning and active participation to help students work;

♦ together, communicate ideas, and negotiate differences; and

♦ implement a curriculum based on the interests of the students.

"Some children are more dependent upon a predictable environment than others" (Eddowes & Ralph, 1998, p. 67). Because of the lack of structure within the lives of many homeless children, a consistent predictable school setting can lessen fear and anxiety and contribute to the progression of healthy cognitive, social, and emotional development. This predictability and consistency is essential for infants and toddlers in the development of feelings of trust and security. It is also necessary for older children as they move toward a developing sense of independence.

SUPPORTING INDEPENDENCE

Autonomy and self-esteem help children appraise themselves positively, without feeling guilty for the homeless situation they are experiencing. Competence in decision making allows children to feel independent and in control of their situations. This competence fosters a sense of autonomy and allows homeless children to feel some measure of control in their uncertain worlds.

Jane's actions in Vignette #4 demonstrate the need for the development of independence and a positive sense of self-esteem within the young homeless child. By providing an appropriate framework, or scaffold (Berk & Winsler, 1995), within which to respond, the teacher allowed Jane to be successful within her social interactions. Within the early childhood setting, a teacher or caregiver can:

♦ help children problem-solve in situations where sharing must occur;

♦ provide a secure base for infant or toddler exploration;

♦ capitalize on each student's strengths; and

♦ encourage active decision making (such as snack choices or naming the classroom pet).

Kamii (1982, p.78) noted, "Mutual respect is, in fact, essential for the child's development of autonomy." Teachers model respect for children by valuing their ideas and suggestions within decision-making activities in the classroom. Opportunities to make choices enhance a sense of control in the otherwise unpredictable lives of homeless children.

SUPPORTING COGNITIVE SKILLS

Cognitive ability includes concept development within academic areas as well as creative problem solving. Resilient children appear to be flexibile and reflective in their thinking from an early age. This is important in handling difficult situations (Bernard,1992).

Opportunities, such as those provided for Chris in Vignette #5, allow young homeless children to develop cognitive skills within a risk-free environment. Within the classroom, caregivers and teachers can provide:

- ♦ sensory experiences that allow infants and young children to learn about the world;
- ♦ time for children to work on activities and assignments at their own pace;
- ♦ wide variety of appropriate learning and play materials;
- ♦ coaching as children tackle academic tasks and problem-solving activities; and
- ♦ support for homework assignments that may be difficult to complete in a shelter.

Like all children, homeless children need supportive environments in which to take risks and make approximations. These opportunities assist in the development of creativity and problem-solving skills as well as in academic development. Maintaining a relaxed classroom atmosphere, allowing children to work at their own pace, and encouraging students to seek an individualized way of completing projects are several methods of demonstrating acceptance and promoting creativity within the early childhood classroom (Mayesky, 1998).

Teachers of young homeless children have unique opportunities to enhance resilience through the use of developmentally appropriate techniques within the classroom. A thoughtfully planned classroom environment can foster a homeless child's ability to deal with the adverse circumstances that exist in his/her life.

WHAT SERVICES ARE NECESSARY TO MEET THE NEEDS OF YOUNG HOMELESS CHILDREN?

A key strength of early childhood programs that serve young homeless children and their families is the coordination of services. There is a need for coordination between homeless shelters and programs that are available to care for the youngest children while parents are in educational programs, looking for work, or working. Schools should coordinate with shelters and/or childcare centers to provide before- and after-school care that is necessary for young school-age children. Educational services such as transportation, timely and appropriate diagnostic assessments, and access to resource teachers are necessary components of these programs. Community services such as clothing and food banks can assist by communicating closely with school administrators to address needs as they arise. Medical and dental screenings that might detect physical problems, such as vision and hearing losses, are also important services for communities to provide. A summary of services that should be coordinated through homeless shelters, childcare, and school programs is included in Table 3.

EDUCATIONAL SERVICES

Transportation to and from an educational program is the first service that must be provided. Without transportation, the homeless child cannot attend the center or school. Shelters or childcare programs can provide vans to transport young children and public schools can provide bus transportation. When children move, some coordination will be needed to be sure transportation needs are met.

Because many homeless children move frequently from place to place, their school records may be far behind them or lost completely. This may cause children to miss special services for which they are eligible. It may also delay the process of diagnosing difficulties that children may have academically or physically. The coordination of efforts by school personnel can help to speed up this process so that the needs of these young children are met. This is especially essential if the child is eligible to receive services from program such as Title I or if the child has a special need that requires accommodation.

Tutoring services that assist the child in the school or sheltering agency provide individual assistance in the completion of assignments and in the development of new academic skills. Tutors may be teachers, college students, parents, or other adults who wish to volunteer to assist these children. Through a one-on-one tutoring relationship, the child is helped academically, and may also benefit socially and emotionally from the experience.

Homeless children who are sick often have no place to go. Parents are unable to look for a job or may miss work during

TABLE 3. PROGRAM SERVICES FOR YOUNG
HOMELESS CHILDREN

Educational Services	Transportation	Parents and children need transportation to and from the center or school.
	Efficient Record-Keeping	School personnel can assist these children by processing records in a timely manner to assure that a child will receive the services for which s/he is eligible.
	Tutoring	Tutoring programs benefit the young child academically as well as socially and emotionally.
	"Feeling Better" Rooms	"Feeling Better" rooms provide young homeless children a safe and supervised environment when they are too sick to attend their childcare center or school.
Community Services	Food Banks	These agencies can supply families with nutritional food for their children.
	Clothing Banks	These organizations can provide free or inexpensive seasonally appropriate clothing for young children.
	Doctors, Dentists, and Mental Health Specialists	On-site services provided by doctors, dentists, and mental health personnel allow parents to seek care for their children at a central location.

this period of time. Schools or centers that staff a room or an area for children to get well on-site provide the family with a valuable service. The parent can continue to work or look for work and the child can receive necessary attention and care. The establishment of effective services is reliant upon open communication between the family and classroom teachers, administrators, volunteers, and special service personnel.

COMMUNITY SERVICES

The integration of community services, such as food or clothing banks, also provides an important benefit for homeless students. Although the advantages of integrated services are great, many agencies that work with homeless children continue to do so in isolation from others. Schools, such as Benjamin Franklin Day Elementary School in Seattle, Washington, have done much to organize and coordinate services available for homeless families (Quint, 1994).

Classroom teachers can quickly note whether a child comes to the center or school hungry. Such an observation might indicate that the child has not eaten since leaving the school the previous day. Local food banks can help alleviate this problem by providing the family with food. Teachers may also note the need for clothing that is appropriate for the size of the child and for the climate and season. Organizations such as Good Will Industries and the Salvation Army are sources of affordable clothing. Businesses or religious organizations are often willing to provide supplies for infants and toddles, such as disposable diapers and baby formula. Schools or childcare centers may also opt to begin clothes banks of their own to meet these needs.

A partnership with local medical personnel and mental health agencies can be effective in meeting the physical and emotional needs of the young homeless child. The on-site availability of these services increases the family's access to professional medical assistance for their children. Such services can increase the likelihood of timely immunizations for infants and toddlers and of appropriate care for other childhood illnesses. These services contribute to the total well-being of the child within the family.

Young homeless children can benefit greatly from centers or schools that coordinate services which are needed by these children and their families. The identification of needs by the caregiver or teacher and swift communication of these needs to the appropriate agency by center or school personnel can determine whether a child receives the necessary services. These services provide the components of a comprehensive program essential for meeting the needs of young homeless children.

REFERENCES

Bernard, B. (1992). Fostering resiliency in kids: Protective factors in the family, school and community. *Prevention Forum, 12*(3), 1-6.

Berk, L., & Winsler, A. (1995). *Scaffolding children's learning: Vygotsky and early childhood education.* Washington, DC: National Association for the Education of Young Children.

Bredekamp, S. (Ed.) (1987). *Developmentally appropriate practice for programs serving children from birth to age 8* (Rev. ed.). Washington, DC: National Association for the Education of Young Children.

Bredekamp, S., & Copple, C. (Eds.) (1997). *Developmentally appropriate practice in early childhood programs* (Rev. ed.). Washington, DC: National Association for the Education of Young Children.

Eddowes, E. A. (1992). Children and homelessness: Early childhood and elementary education. In J. H. Stronge (Ed.), *Educating homeless children and adolescents: Evaluating policy and practice.* Newbury Park, CA: Sage.

Eddowes, E. A. (1993). Planning retreats for solitary activity in day care. *Day Care and Early Education, 20,* 27-29.

Eddowes, E. A., & Ralph, K. S. (1998). *Interactions for development and learning: Birth through eight years.* Upper Saddle River, NJ: Merrill/Prentice-Hall.

Erikson, E. (1963). *Childhood and society* (2nd ed.). New York: Norton.

Gardner, H. (1983). *Frames of mind: The theory of multiple intelligences.* New York: Basic Books.

Gardner, H. (1993). *Multiple intelligences: The theory in practice.* New York: Basic Books.

Hunt, J. M. (1961). *Intelligence and experience.* New York: Ronald.

Kamii, C. (1982). *Number in preschool and kindergarten: Educational implications of Piaget's theory.* Washington, DC: National Association for the Education of Young Children.

Klein, T., Bittel, C. & Molnar, J. (1993). No place to call home: Supporting the needs of homeless children in the early childhood classroom. *Young Children, 48*(6), 22-31.

Maslow, A. (1970). *Motivation and personality* (2nd ed.). New York: Harper & Row.

Mayesky, M. (1998). *Creative activities for young children.* Cincinnati, OH: Delmar.

Morrison, G. (1995). *Early childhood education today* (7th ed.). Columbus, OH: Merrill.

Neiman, L. (1988). A critical review of resiliency literature and its relevance to homeless children. *Children's Environment Quarterly, 5*(1), 17-25.

Piaget, J. (1970). Piaget's theory. In P. Mussen (Ed.), *Carmichael's manual of child psychology* (3rd ed., vol. 1, pp. 703-732). New York: Wiley.

Piaget, J. (1973). *To understand is to invent.* New York: Grossman. (Original work published in 1948.)

Quint, S. (1994). *Schooling homeless children: A working model for America's public schools.* New York: Teachers College Press.

Reed-Victor, E., & Stronge, J. H. (1997). Building resiliency: Constructive directions for homeless education. *Journal of Children and Poverty, 3*(1), 67-91.

Schickedanz, J. A. (1999). *Much more than the ABC's: The early stages of reading and writing.* Washington, DC: National Association for the Education of Young Children.

Vygotsky, L. S. (1978). *Mind and society: The development of higher psychological processes.* Cambridge, MA: Harvard University Press.

ADDITIONAL RESOURCES: CHILDREN'S BOOKS ABOUT HOMELESSNESS

Bunting, E. (1991). *Fly away home.* New York, NY: Clarion Books. A picture book for children about a father and son who are homeless and stay at the airport. This story portrays a warm family relationship, the hardships of homelessness, and the hopes of the young boy.

Carlson, N.S. (1958). *The family under the bridge.* New York, NY: Scholastic. Living under a bridge, a family struggles to maintain a "normal" life and their integrity as a family.

DiSalvo-Ryan, D. (1991). *Uncle Willie and the soup kitchen.* New York, NY: Morrow. With his grandfather's support, Willie confronts his concerns about homeless people by helping in the local soup kitchen.

Spohn, K. (1994). *Broken umbrellas.* New York, NY: Viking. The daily life of a woman who immigrates to the United States and becomes a "street picker" is depicted in this well-illustrated children's book.

3

MEETING THE EDUCATIONAL NEEDS OF INTERMEDIATE AND MIDDLE SCHOOL HOMELESS STUDENTS

YVONNE VISSING

The middle school years for ages nine through thirteen are perhaps the most stressful for youth, who are no longer children but are not yet adults. It is hard for students to survive the physical and emotional trials and tribulations that typically occur during those years, but the challenges are even greater when one is homeless. The primary institution that can help youth in this age category to acquire skills to address these challenges is the school. Schools are the one resource that has contact with every child in the community. Educational personnel can be trained to identify and assist those children who have special needs and problems, such as housing distress (Vissing, 1996). Thanks to the philosophy of public education, which seeks to enhance all children's growth and development, school personnel are in ideal roles to assist homeless children and their parents. The purpose of this chapter is to explore common developmental, educational, and social challenges experienced by homeless children aged nine through thirteen, and to determine how school personnel can develop programs and practices to assist them.

While numbers of homeless middle school aged children are not well established, existing estimates indicate that the known numbers are the tip of a large and growing iceberg of housing distress (Shane, 1996; Vissing, 1996). The United States Department of Education (1995) indicates that almost a quarter of all homeless students are of middle school age. Over half (57%) of homeless children reported were of elementary school age, while about 20% were of high school age. Their report states that 23% of homeless children and youth were not attending school during the time when they had no housing. The main reasons included a lack of transportation, transiency in living accommodations, lack of school records, and families' preoccupation with finding food, shelter, and employment. With economic distress on the rise, one can anticipate that the housing distress that leads to homelessness will continue to create a significant problem for middle school students—and for the schools.

WHAT DEVELOPMENTAL ISSUES CONFRONT HOMELESS MIDDLE SCHOOL STUDENTS?

While the passage into "adolescence should result in positive outcomes, for increasing numbers of young adolescents, that is not their experience," according to a report by the Carnegie Corporation's study of children aged 9–14. They report that:

> Instead of safety in their neighborhoods, they face chronic physical danger; instead of economic security, they face uncertainty; instead of intellectual stimulation, they face boredom and stagnation; in place of respect, they are neglected; lacking clear and consistent adult expectations for them, many youth feel deeply alienated from mainstream American society. The damage to individual young lives is staggering. American society pays heavily for such outcomes. We pay in the diminished economic productivity of future generations. We pay the increasing bills for crime, welfare and

health care. We pay the immense social cost of living with millions of alienated people. And we pay the moral cost of knowing that we are producing millions of young adolescents who face predictably bleak and unfulfilling lives. (1992, p. 6)

The problems that confront youth aged 9 to 13 are real and significant. Those who are homeless especially need help in order to survive and succeed. Middle school is a pivotal time period when marginal youth can be intercepted and guided toward a path of greater success. When assisting middle school age children, school personnel may require a broader set of skills than do their colleagues in either elementary or high school. This is due both to the demography of who is considered a middle school student, and the developmental needs of this population of children.

While junior high school once consisted only of seventh through ninth grade, today's middle schools incorporate grades five through nine. This means that middle schools can teach children who are as young as nine years old through children who are fourteen or older. A fifth or sixth grader is a very different child than one who is getting ready to enter tenth grade. Yet, all of them could be under a single school roof . This poses significant challenges for middle school personnel. A nine-year-old child likely still lives within a biological family structure, and is too young to negotiate services for him or herself. In this case, the school would need to work with that child's family in order to help the child. But in the scenario of the fourteen-year-old student, this adolescent could be living on his or her own, with other adolescents, or with other people to whom the student has no biological or guardian relationship. A student who is completing ninth grade may desire to be treated as an independent person, and wish to make his or her own decisions about the use of potential services, while a fifth grade child may desire to be taken care of by others.

Psychological and physical developments vary widely throughout middle school. For instance, nine-year-old students may not yet show signs of puberty; fifteen-year-old students could be sexually active. Fifth graders are preoccupied with dif-

ferent educational, peer, and social worlds than are ninth graders. Adult interaction styles need to vary in order to successfully
address the wide range of psychological and developmental
needs of middle school students—especially those who are
homeless.

The result of this demographic and developmental diversity among middle school students is that school personnel who
wish to assist homeless students must be extremely well aware
of the wide range of resources that exist in their communities.
School personnel need to know details about how to help all
types of families who are in economic and housing distress. They
need skills on how to interact with dependent children, and how
to assist adolescents who are surviving on their own. Inevitably,
school personnel must know how to sensitively assist family
units in which there is severe tension.

In any case, whether it is assisting the two-parent family who
is on hard times, the single parent family who is barely making
it, the adolescent who is living with friends or acquaintances, or
the kid who is more or less surviving on his/her own—the school
alone cannot provide all of the needed services. The school is,
however, a convenient point for the homeless student and the
family to enter the community's social service system (Wall,
1998). But the school as point of entry into the social service community is dependant upon two critical factors: (1) the knowledge
base of the school personnel making the referral, and (2), the
range of services accessible within the community.

Sometimes community resources exist that school personnel are not aware of. In this case, it is important for school
personnel to identify specifics about existing services so that students and their families can access them. Other times, the
community may lack key services. If needed services do not exist, the school can provide the impetus for the community's
development of new programs. Working in partnership with the
community, school personnel can help the entire community to
join together in order to help vulnerable students and their families. If the problems of homeless students and their families
continue to exist, students cannot learn, and schools may fail in
their educational mission. Being familiar with community resources ultimately facilitates the creation of educational and

social success. Therefore, key middle school personnel may need to become ferrets of community intervention information.

HOW CAN MIDDLE SCHOOLS ADDRESS EDUCATIONAL ISSUES OF HOMELESS STUDENTS?

Traditional classroom structures and educational models of instruction are often counterproductive in assisting homeless students. If schools are dedicated to the proposition that all students have a right to education, and that different types of students have different learning needs and styles, then school personnel must be equally willing to develop programs for homeless students—just as they have programs for other groups of students, such as those who are talented and gifted, or who require special education. If schools are a representation of a democracy, what is fair for one student must be made fair for all, and schools should proceed with the student of least resource in mind.

Homeless students are not like other students. They have unique challenges and concerns that must be addressed by school personnel in order for academic and social success to be achieved both in and out of, the classroom. Like it or not, schools of today must go beyond their mandate to educate students; they must also address the social, physical, and emotional needs of the homeless students—otherwise, they will fail in their mission to educate all students. If schools are the primary social institution to teach children how to be self-sufficient and productive adults, one has to view the role of the school from a broad perspective. As one New Hampshire principal who worked with homeless students stated:

> We run our schools as if education is the number one priority for all students. The fact is, for many it is not. The fact is, for many kids school shouldn't be their top priority. If they live in homes of chaos and violence, when they don't know what they are going to eat or where they are going to sleep, if they are pregnant or using drugs, or in trouble with their peers—these must be their priorities. For the schools to play ostrich and

ignore the fact that these kids live complicated lives, and have adult problems, this is just plain stupid. Schools must adapt and bend their policies to help the kids, or we are going to lose greater and greater numbers of them. That is the fact. (Vissing, 1996, p. 112)

Middle school students who have housing difficulties today need not be plagued with its residue tomorrow. Identifying which students have special needs, and addressing those needs, can provide students with the resources for success. Schools can best accomplish this when they are willing to establish a flexible and humane environment where students can prosper, instead of enforcing rigid rules merely for administrative purposes, or out of tradition. There are several key areas where schools can develop environments that will benefit the educational process for homeless middle school students.

FLEXIBLE ADMISSION CRITERIA

Middle school children who enter new schools are well aware that they do not know their classmates, their teachers, the location of rooms in the building, or what is expected of them both academically and socially. When homeless middle school students attempt to enter and find themselves "not allowed to attend" right away because they are unable to provide documentation of immunization, age, or records of previous education, it is no surprise that they feel they do not belong there, even before they have attended a single class (Kozol, 1989; Rafferty & Rollins, 1988). School policies, procedures, and practices about admission requirements can be punitive to homeless students who, through no fault of their own, are simply unable to provide the necessary documentation. Schools are encouraged to admit students who want to attend their school on a temporary basis, while the school staff works with the student to obtain the necessary paper work.

Schools are also establishing working relationships with schools in nearby districts since financially strapped students and parents move to where they can find more available, affordable housing. This may mean that the community next door has cheaper housing—but is outside the student's school district. If students want to attend their former school, their educational and social continuity could outweigh the administrative benefits of refusing to admit them because they live outside of district lines.

FLEXIBLE ATTENDANCE POLICIES

Homeless middle school students confront a host of bureaucratic problems that undermine efforts to ensure regular attendance (Rafferty & Rollins, 1989). Attendance rates decline for all students as grade levels increase, since the older the student, the more likely he or she will be employed (Rafferty, 1991). Holding a job and simultaneously going to school is often incompatible. Homeless middle school students seldom have control over the environment in which they stayed the night before. Their parents' situations influence whether or not they can go to school, and many have precarious transportation arrangements. It is common for them to arrive at school late. But when students are penalized for late attendance, it is easier for them to not come at all—because then they can be excused as sick without penalties. Hence, tardy policies frequently create the absenteeism they intend to curb.

Schools are encouraged to use greater flexibility when enforcing penalties for poor attendance and tardiness for the homeless, because as one New Hampshire principal reported:

> Homeless students are not arriving late because they are blowing off school. These kids are busy fighting for survival. So long as they are coming to school—even late, even infrequently—I haven't lost them. I still have a chance to educate them, to help them. They still have faith if they come to school. They haven't given up and dropped out. Should I let a bunch of policies that were written for a different type of student get in the way of doing what is right for this kid? (Vissing, 1996, p. 124)

Attendance policies regarding tardiness and truancy adversely affect both the academic success of the student, and his/

her will to try. Schools have an obligation not to ignore excessive absences or gaps in students' attendance. Instead of having the old-fashioned "truant officer," who was regarded as a punitive strong-arm of education, schools (such as those in Allentown, PA) can create positive "absenteeism specialists" who maintain personal contact with homeless students. The absenteeism specialist visits homeless students and their families and addresses obstacles that inhibit school attendance. The specialist may also deliver food, clothes, alarm clocks, or other needed items to help the family, thus providing items, and building relationships that help students come to school. It may be appropriate to eliminate attendance policies that result in the reduction of grades. They are punitive and serve no good purpose for middle school children whose lives are extraordinarily complicated, and who struggle just to get to school.

FLEXIBLE CLASS ASSIGNMENTS

Homeless students are at a disadvantage to produce the same quality work as students who have home libraries, desks, and other educational resources at their fingertips. Teachers may find homework "unacceptably" messy or torn, unaware that it was written on the dashboard of a car—which also served as the kitchen table for the student who lived in it. Homework assignments are often geared for a more stable, middle class student population, requiring resources that are unavailable to the homeless student. Schools must be sensitive to the fact that many children do not live in situations in which it is possible to do certain types of homework. Teachers need to give assignments for which school resources exist so that all students can accomplish the tasks. Clear instructions on where to go for resources must be provided. If students do not know where to go for help (computers, library resources, etc.), or do not have the time to complete them, they will become discouraged and fail to complete the assignments. This will only exacerbate their problems. Non-punitive alternatives could be made available so that all students have the opportunity to learn and succeed. Homeless students also need plenty of lead time for assignments, since they may be less able than housed students to produce assignments within a limited time frame. Students may have outside jobs with work schedules that interfere with doing homework or studying for a test. They may be asked to watch younger siblings, or have to go with parents from place to place after school hours. Just finding a quiet place to do homework may be impossible. Homeless students may certainly benefit from tutors and extra teacher time to assist them with their homework.

FLEXIBLE AVAILABILITY OF SCHOOL AND COMMUNITY RESOURCES

Homeless students need constructive places where they can go when they are not in school. Schools that open early and close late provide warm, safe places for students. Ideally, being at school provides opportunities for them to get their homework done. Schools are positive environments for students to spend time, since there are caring adult role models, extracurricular activities, and educational resources available. When homeless students have had no place to spend the night, they look forward to coming early to school or staying as late as they can. At school they can find locker rooms where they can shower and cafeterias where they can get something to eat.

Libraries can also be wonderful resources for homeless students, as shown in Baltimore's Helping Hands Homework Assistance Program. There, libraries are matched with shelters to conduct after-school educational support for homeless students. The library programs provide a quiet place for homeless children to study, read, and work on school projects. Participating students also receive several hours of assistance from high school student tutors, who are overseen by an adult mentor.

Community resources near the school, such as churches, agencies, or public buildings, could open early and stay open late to accommodate students who are in need. These non-school buildings could provide services from hot meals to recreation to health or social services to educational tutoring. Creating a more flexible community and educational environment would be immensely helpful to homeless students. But homeless middle school youth also benefit from a sensitive interpersonal touch.

FLEXIBLE TIME TO LISTEN

Studies indicate that homeless middle school children may suffer from low self-esteem and isolation (Bassuk & Rosenberg, 1988; Rafferty & Rollins, 1989). School personnel may be the only ones available to provide students with routine counseling and support. Teachers can help smooth a new student's transition into the classroom, deal with negative confrontations with other students, and make the classroom experience one that results in the student wanting to come back the next day.

Acceptance from classmates and stigmatization is a significant problem for homeless middle school students (Schwartz, 1995). Attentive school personnel can identify when the students need special assistance, and help them to get to the right service. This is important because homelessness is associated with a host of physical, social, emotional, and educational problems. Adolescents prefer to hide their homelessness rather than bring attention to their lack of housing. When they decide to seek help, they will do so only from those whom they trust. Students who do not know where to go for help may seek the assistance of a trusted teacher, secretary, school nurse, or counselor. They may need services from mental health professionals. But managed care in mental health has resulted in limiting the number of times a person can be seen. School social workers and nurses do not have that restriction, and can see the same child daily during the whole year. Sometimes daily assistance is what it takes to help these make-or-break kids.

Kids in crisis need help immediately, and cannot wait weeks, days, or even hours for help. It takes a great deal of courage for them to ask for help, and when they do, help needs to be delivered in a prompt and sensitive manner. Protection of their confidentiality is important for middle school children, who may not come back for help if their confidence is violated.

FLEXIBLE EXTRACURRICULAR ACTIVITIES

Homeless families do not have extra money to pay for their children's recreational activities. As a result, many schools have attempted to create opportunities for homeless students to be involved in programs that otherwise they could not afford. The Children's Center at Martha's Table in Washington, D.C., provides after-school recreation programs for homeless students. The Center's philosophy holds that homeless students require personal attention and emotional support in order to benefit from school instruction. The Center helps students to participate in extracurricular activities so that they can have a more normal childhood experience. In a more elaborate program, the Lady Maryland Foundation assists homeless children to take educational trips in Chesapeake Bay aboard a sailboat. They use parents to serve as chaperons, thereby enhancing the recreational opportunities of the entire household. Schools realize that much learning occurs outside the confines of the classroom, and extracurricular and recreational programs promote both educational and self-esteem development. Linkages between the school, shelter, and community organizations can facilitate the creation of out-of-school educational and recreational options that benefit homeless students.

There are, in sum, a variety of ways to welcome homeless middle school students and to include them in opportunities for educational and social success. Table 1 provides an overview of these strategies.

It is critically important to make sure homeless students get the support they need. However, all too frequently there is a fine line between those who are homeless today, and those who were yesterday, or will be tomorrow (Vissing, 1996). In order to support those students who are homeless, and to avoid future negative stereotyping of homeless people, it is important for housed students to understand more about homelessness.

WHAT CAN MIDDLE SCHOOLS DO TO IMPROVE PEER AWARENESS OF HOMELESSNESS?

Teachers may not necessarily know which of their students are homeless or which are living in distressed housing conditions. Studies indicate that up to 10% of students in school could be experiencing housing distress within the school year (Vissing & Diament, 1996); therefore, it is likely that a student in the classroom, or someone students know at school, will fall into this

TABLE 1. STRATEGIES FOR GREATER INCLUSION OF HOMELESS
MIDDLE SCHOOL STUDENTS

♦ Get students involved as quickly as possible, the older the students, the more at risk they are for dropping out of schol if admission is delayed.

♦ Offer help in completing forms; hesitation may indicate an inability to read. Explain the need for an address, and reassure students you will keep the address confidential—which is a concern for victims of domestic violence.

♦ Give students a locker and make sure they are signed up for free or reduced breakfast and lunch as soon as possible. Homeless students often lack nourishment and a place to put their things.

♦ Provide students and parents with a list of agencies that offer help to those who are new in the area. Have the school counselor meet with the homeless child soon after admission to help secure needed services.

♦ Ensure that children have access to all educational services for which they might be eligible, including Title 1 and bilingual programs.

♦ Make classroom placement based on the class composition, the child's needs, and the teacher's strengths. Teachers should be sensitized to issues that confront students who move frequently, and encouraged to provide extra instruction when needed.

♦ Monitor attendance and provide appropriate follow-up when a student is absent.

♦ Do not establish special lines or use different colored tickets for free and reduced lunch. Be discreet.

♦ Do not grade students down for tardiness or absenteeism. Tardiness or sick days may be unavoidable for homeless students. Flexible grading criteria are helpful.

TABLE 1. STRATEGIES FOR GREATER INCLUSION OF HOMELESS
MIDDLE SCHOOL STUDENTS (CONTINUED)

♦ Give plenty of lead time for assignments. Arrange assignments so students can keep up without having to take things home.

♦ Avoid TV assignments, computer assignments, or other requirements for which all students may not have the same access. Offer tools and supplies needed to complete any required task.

♦ Gym clothes or other clothing may have to be provided. If so, try to find a source to donate them, making private arrangements for giving them to the child.

♦ If cleanliness is an issue, arrange for the student to use the locker room shower on arrival at school and, if necessary, the home economics washer/dryer.

♦ Provide safe opportunities for students to express emotions. Facilitate positive peer relationships.

♦ Determine student strengths and talents, and create opportunities for them to develop. Build hope, trust, and ways to make dreams realities.

category. While most homeless students mask their housing difficulties, they would appreciate it if others were more sensitive to issues of housing distress and homelessness. Peer pressure can be intense during middle school years, and homeless students often suffer emotionally from the words and deeds of unthinking classmates. For instance, Sarah, a 10-year-old girl attending middle school in Minnesota, had lived in a variety of places before she and her family became homeless. She was living in a transitional housing unit when her class began studying homelessness. Sara sat there as her teacher asked, "Who are the homeless?" While her classmates gave stereotypical answers, such as "drunks, bums, bag ladies, and people who don't want to work," Sarah got increasingly upset. Finally, she stood up and

faced her classmates, saying, "If you want to know who is homeless, look at me. I'm homeless," after which she ran out of the
room. This incident became the impetus for the Minnesota Coalition for the Homeless to develop a curriculum guide, and for
Sarah's school to implement it in order to teach students to be
more sensitive. The lesson plan book contains material for immediate application for middle school students, and integrates
classroom activities, field experiences, awareness events, and
serve components into its educational curriculum.

There are other curriculum guides that also provide strategies and information on how to educate middle school students
about homelessness. Several are listed in Additional Resources
at the end of this chapter.

Students find it helpful to read about homeless children and
youth who are their age. In doing so, they can better relate to
homelessness as a real problem experienced by people their age.
But which books should middle school students read? In order
to facilitate age-appropriate reading about homelessness, a list
of recommended books for middle school level students is provided in Table 2.

School libraries would benefit from the inclusion of these
books. They may want to feature the books in a schoolwide
homeless education project. November is typically the month
in which Homelessness Awareness Week occurs. Schools can
contact the National Coalition for the Homeless in Washington,
D.C., for details about this event and how they can participate.

SUMMARY

Middle school children who experience housing distress pose
a challenge for school personnel. School personnel must have a
keen knowledge of community resources for both families and
independent youth in order to meet the needs of this diverse
group of students. School personnel will also need to have an
eclectic understanding of child development, considering the
wide physical, psychological, and social needs of middle school
students.

Schools have the momentary opportunity to cradle vulnerable students in the palm of their hand. The speed and manner
in which they do so may determine the students' success trajec-

TABLE 2. MIDDLE SCHOOL LEVEL BOOKS ON HOMELESSNESS

The Crossing Grades 6-8	Gary Paulsen, Orchard and Dell, 1987
Dew Drop Dead. Grades 5-8	James Howe, Athenaeum and Avon, 1990
Family Pose Grades 5-8	Dean Hughes, Athenaeum, 1989
The Family Under the Bridge Grades 4-7	Natalie Savage Carlson, HarperCollins, 1958.
The Fastest Friend in the West Grades 6-8	Vicki Grove: Putnam, 1990
The Leaves in October Grades 4-6	Karen Ackerman, Athenaeum, 1991
Stay Tuned Grades 6-9	Barbara Corcoran, Athenaeum, 1991
Monkey Island Grades 5-9	Paula Fox, Orchard/ Richard Jackson, 1991
Secret City USA Grades 6-8	Felice Holman, Scribner, 1990
Slake's Limbo Grades 6-8	Felice Holman, Scribner and Aladdin, 1974
Street Family Grades 7-9	Adrienne Jones, HarperCollins, 1987
At the Sound of the Beep Grades 4-7	Marilyn Sachs, Dutton, 1990
Maniac Magee Grades 4-8	Jerry Spinelli, Little Brown, 1990
Patty Dillman of Hot Dog Fame Grades 6-8	Susan Wojciechowski, Orchard and Knopf, 1989

tory. Because communities will vary dramatically in what resources are available to the students, it is important to conduct an assessment of available services, and if service gaps exist. In order to achieve their mandate to successfully educate all students, school personnel are in a unique position to interface with community institutions to build a safety net for at-risk children and families. It is important for school personnel not to forget that homeless middle school students and their families rely upon the school to be the gatekeeper to community resources, and to make students' dreams of success a reality.

REFERENCES

Bassuk, E., & Rosenberg, L. (1988). Why does family homelessness occur? *American Journal of Public Health, 78*, 783-788.

Carnegie Corporation. *A matter of time: risk and opportunity in the out of school hours.* 1992 New York: Carnegie Council on Adolescent Development.

Kozol, J. (1988). *Rachel and her children: Homeless families in America.* New York: Crown.

Rafferty, Y., & Rollins, N. (1989). *Learning in limbo: The educational deprivation of homeless students.* New York: Advocates for Children in New York.

Rafferty, Y. (1991). *And miles to go.* Long Island City, NY: Advocates for Children of New York, Inc.

Schwartz, W. (1995). *School programs and practices for homeless students* (Report No. 105). New York, NY: Clearinghouse on Urban Education. (ERIC Document Reproduction Service No. EDO-UD-95-2)

Shaffer, D. & Canton, C. (1984). *Runaway and homeless youth in New York City: A report to the Ittelson Foundation.* New York: New York Psychiatric Institute and Columbia University of Physicians and Surgeons, Division of Child Psychiatry.

Shane, P.G. (1996). *What about America's homeless children: Hide and Seek.* Newbury Park, CA: Sage.

United States Department of Education. 1995. *Report to Congress: Education for homeless children and youth program.* Washington, DC: Office of Compensatory Education Programs.

Vissing, Y. (1996). *Out of sight, out of mind: Homeless children and families in small town America.* Lexington: University of Kentucky Press.

Wall, J. (1998) Homeless children and their families: Delivery of education and social services through school systems and communities. E. Freeman, C. Franklin, R. Fong, G. Shaffer, & E. Timberlake, *Multisystem skills and intervention in school social work practice.* pp 340-350. Washington DC: NASW Press.

ADDITIONAL RESOURCES: HOMELESSNESS CURRICULUM MATERIALS FOR MIDDLE SCHOOL STUDENTS

On the Street Where You Live, Minnesota Coalition for the Homeless, 122 West Franklin, Suite 5, Minneapolis, MN 55404.

Homelessness Curricula: Five Exemplary Approaches, Pennsylvania Department of Education, Education of Homeless Children and Youth Program, 333 Market Street, 5th Floor, Harrisburg, PA 17126.

Housing and Homelessness: A Teaching Guide, HOUSING NOW!, 425 Second Street NW, Washington, DC 20001.

Teaching About Homelessness, Steven Goldberg, Social Studies Department, City School District of New Rochelle, New Rochelle, NY 10802.

Unsheltered Lives: Teaching About Homelessness in Grades K-12, Vermont Department of Education, Burlington, VT.

4

MEETING THE EDUCATIONAL NEEDS OF HOMELESS YOUTH

WILLIAM R. PENUEL AND TIM L. DAVEY

I'm used to living in a house . . . It was scary at first, but Miss Winnie talked to me a lot and helped me understand why I'm here. She said, "Don't think of it as a shelter. This is a home." But I'm used to having a house I could walk in and out of. I can't even go into the kitchen to get a glass of water. And I'm not used to there being a man's bathroom and a woman's bathroom. I'm also not used to having a Coke machine in my house. (Angel, 14)

WHAT IS THE STATUS OF HOMELESS YOUTH?

STATISTICS

The numbers of adolescents in the United States who are without homes are staggering. Near the end of the 1980s, Janus, McCormack, Burgess, and Hartman (1987) estimated that between half a million and a million young people were homeless in the United States. A more recent study reported that the total number of homeless youth nationwide ranged between 100,000 on any given night to 2 million per year (Cwayna, 1993). The Children's Defense Fund (1992) estimated that 1.5 million youth run away from home each year, and over half of these youth are escaping abusive situations. Of these runaway youth, it is estimated that 6% identify as gay or lesbian (National Network of Runaway and Youth Services, 1991).

DEFINITION

In order to determine their numbers, there have been many attempts made to define what counts as *runaway* or *homeless* in the teenage years (Adams, Gullota, & Clancy, 1985). Typically, runaway youth are defined as those youth who have made a choice to leave their homes, for whatever reason.[1] Homeless youth include young people living with their families in shelters, youth who have been pushed out of their homes (sometimes called *throwaways*), teens doubled up with friends or relatives, and those who are referred to as "street kids," who do not have regular access to a place to call home (McCarthy & Hagan, 1992). While these terms primarily index different states of housing distress (Vissing & Diament, 1997), they can only begin to hint at the lived experiences of these young people.

IN WHAT CONTEXTS DO WE FIND HOMELESS YOUTH AT-RISK?

I got kicked out of my house in July, and at that point there was violence involved. My mother went nuts and came at me with an iron. I ran downstairs and locked the door, she called the police. The police came in and asked me what was going on. My mother started saying that I'm always in Boston with the fags . . . he (the police officer) started cracking all kinds of gay jokes and told me that I should leave . . . (Troix, 17)

While the voices of homeless youth point to the variety of stories young people tell about how they came to live on the streets, in shelters, or with friends, the conditions these young people face are similar regardless of where they live (Whitbeck, Hoyt, & Ackley, 1997). The choices homeless youth make while on the streets are framed by the opportunities afforded by these conditions. Addressing the educational needs of homeless teens means focusing attention on the varieties of risks youth face in their communities, because each context contributes to students' educational success or failure.

COMMUNITY CONTEXTS

It is impossible to describe the broader sociocultural context for homelessness in the United States without considering the dramatic reduction in social services and affordable housing that has resulted from federal and state budget cuts. In the last 25 years, the average benefits for a family of three receiving welfare have declined by nearly half, and in all but one state, maximum benefit levels do not cover the cost of a basic two-bedroom apartment (Children's Defense Fund and National Coalition for the Homeless, 1998).

One result of the reduction in services is that many low-income teens experience housing distress (Vissing & Diament, 1997), in which teens lack a stable physical base where they feel they belong. Teens who run away from home are likely to find life on the street difficult. They may find it hard to find food and shelter, and they may be unable to earn enough money legally to survive (Kufelt & Nimmo, 1987). Many find available hostels and shelters unwelcome and dangerous: they distrust the residents, dislike the rules, and find the workers intrusive (McCarthy & Hagan, 1992).

During the course of their experiences, homeless teens are likely to come into contact with a host of less welcoming community institutions (McCarthy & Hagan, 1992). They may have to live in separate shelters from their parents, for example, because of rules that exclude teenage boys for safety reasons (Foscarinis, 1987). They may have been in foster care and are escaping abuse in their placements (Powers & Jaklitsch, 1992). They may come into contact with social workers and child protection agencies, or as a consequence of involvement in crime be put in jail (McCarthy & Hagan, 1992). If they are able to find services they would like to access, those services may require parental permission, something that might be impossible for the young person to obtain. Finally, young people may be thwarted

in their efforts to provide for themselves by labor laws that pre-
clude their finding work legally.

Community risks:

♦ reduction in welfare benefits

♦ unstable/unavailable housing or shelter

♦ community agencies unwelcoming, intrusive

♦ most social services unavailable without parental consent

♦ youth typically too young for legal employment

FAMILY AND HOME CONTEXTS

Families are in many ways the most problematic of contexts
for homeless adolescents. Nearly half of runaways seeking shelter reported increased conflict between their parents in the
previous three months, 37% reported that their parents were
increasingly absent from the home, and 17% reported parents
going to jail (Rotheram-Borus, Koopman, Haignere, & Davies,
1991). Homeless adolescents are likely to be from physically and
sexually abusive families (Whitbeck & Simons, 1993). Abusive
family backgrounds have a direct effect on further victimization
of adolescents in the streets, by increasing the amount of time
they are at risk, increasing the number of deviant peer associations they have, and exposing them to risky behaviors (Whitbeck,
Hoyt, & Ackley, 1997). Experiences with their parents or guardians teach young people to develop a defensive, self-protective
stance, in which they are unlikely to rely on adults for support
or guidance (Powers & Jaklitsch, 1992).

Risks in the Family

♦ parents absent from home

♦ youth likely to be physically or sexually abused

♦ little or no adult support or guidance

PEER CONTEXTS

As for other adolescents, peers are an important influence on the development of decision-making and problem-solving strategies among homeless youth. Such youth do not appear to have trouble making friends on the street. In a study of youth living on the streets in urban Canada, McCarthy and Hagan (1992) found that only 6% had failed to find one friend since leaving home, and most had formed at least ten friendships.

At the same time, many of these friends may influence homeless teens to engage in risky behavior. These peers are likely to be other youth living on the street who are involved in crime or risky sexual activity, including prostitution. In a study of homeless youth, Whitbeck, Hoyt, & Ackley (1997) found that affiliation with deviant peers was strongly associated with participation in deviant subsistence strategies (e.g., stealing for food), and these strategies in turn were directly associated with the likelihood that the young person would be physically victimized by another.

Risks with peers

♦ increased involvement with risky behaviors

♦ increased involvement in criminal behaviors

♦ increased physical victimization by other peers

SCHOOL CONTEXTS

For many homeless teens, school is not a place associated with opportunity but rather with failure and shame (Powers & Jaklitsch, 1993). Many simply do not attend school, and those who do are often absent (Rafferty & Shin, 1991). When they do attend, their clothing and lack of school supplies often distinguish them from their peers, in ways that stigmatize homeless youth within school culture (Stronge, 1993).

Homeless youth are more likely than not to be experiencing academic difficulties in school as well. They are more likely to be experiencing reading difficulty than other teens (Barwick & Siegel, 1996) and to have repeated a grade (Shaffer & Caton, 1984).

Once homeless, they may be inappropriately placed, or the place-ment process may move too slowly for them to benefit from special services (Stronge, 1993). In many cases, there simply aren't model educational services available for runaway and home-less youth (Powers & Jaklitsch, 1992).

Risks in school

♦ increased number of absences

♦ stigmatized by substandard clothing

♦ lack of necessary school supplies

♦ mobility decreases academic success

WHAT ARE SOME WAYS TO BUILD DEVELOPMENTAL ALLIANCES WITH HOMELESS YOUTH?

Once homeless youth have begun to access services and be-come peripheral participants in youth-serving organizations, they begin to form relationships with adults and peers who have more experience than they with the organization. At this point, programs can provide more structured opportunities for build-ing those relationships so that they become "developmental alliances," wherein young people feel as though they have an ally in a caring adult or peer who will advocate for them and support them in taking positive risks to grow toward more hope-ful futures.

MENTORING

Youth development practitioners, advocates, and research-ers all agree that having one positive relationship with a supportive adult is key to helping young people make healthy decisions about their lives and deal constructively with adver-sity (Dryfoos, 1990). Many young people develop such relationships with adults on their own, but mentoring programs designed to provide young people with structured opportuni-ties to spend time with healthy adults have grown in number across the United States in the past few years. Well-designed mentoring programs have been found to be effective in increasing student attendance in school and in improving students' sense of competence and grades (Tierney & Grossman, 1995). Moreover, such programs may be effective in reducing the risk that young people will become violent or begin to use alcohol, tobacco, or other drugs (Tierney & Grossman, 1995).

Keys to making such mentoring programs work are effective screening procedures, strong training and supervision, and processes for soliciting volunteer, parent, and youth input (Furano, Roaf, Styles, & Branch, 1993). Big Brothers/Big Sisters (BB/BS) of America[2] is a key provider of mentoring services in cities across the United States. BB/BS mentors carefully screen volunteer applicants and solicit parent, youth, and volunteer input as to the kind of match they would like. For the volunteer, there are extensive opportunities for training before and after being matched. Once they have begun seeing their mentee, they may attend in-service training and supervision from BB/BS staff to support the development of their mentoring relationship.

Mentors in BB/BS are focused on developing mutual relationships of respect with youth. They are invited to structure the relationship as a friendship, rather than as a teacher or moral guide (Furano et al., 1993). By developing the relationship through meeting regularly and consistently with one another—whether visiting local parks, seeing a film, or going to a basketball game together—mentor and mentee come to develop a relationship characterized by mutual commitment (Hamilton, 1990).

PEER LEADERSHIP PROGRAMS

In recent years, a variety of programs aimed at using the power of peers to effect change in young people's health behaviors have been developed, sometimes referred to as "peer education" (Baldwin, 1995), "peer helping" (Varenhorst, 1992), and "peer leadership" (Penuel & Freeman, 1997) programs. Such programs typically train and empower young people to teach their peers (same age or younger) about key health concepts and behaviors. They typically rely on experiential and cooperative education methods to engage young people with the material, and they are based on the assumption that young people are more likely to listen to their peers when it comes to difficult topics such as drugs and alcohol, violence, and sexuality. These programs moreover, have been shown to be effective in increasing access to and acceptance of health messages (Baldwin, 1995) and in increasing students' self-esteem (Sawyer et al., 1997). In addition, programs designed to involve young people in such a service capacity have been shown to lead to more positive identity development (Yates & Youniss, 1996).

An example of one such program, developed in Denmark, is called Sjakket[3]. It is financed through the Ministry of Social Affairs and located in Cøpenhagen. Programs like Sjakket are part of larger reforms of the welfare state in Denmark aimed at transforming youth "dependence" on the state into "active participation." To that end, Sjakket focuses on helping street youth become active in helping other street youth with social support and peer counseling. Through the active involvement of peers in helping other youth on the streets, these young people's participation in the broader society begins to shift, and young people begin to reflect critically on their own actions as well as the social organizations around them (Nissen, 1998).

RECIPROCAL TEACHING IN READING

Reciprocal teaching is a way of teaching reading that turns each student into a "teacher" of reading. It has been particularly successful in teaching reading to students with learning disabilities (Palincsar & Brown, 1988) at the elementary level and has been adapted for students experiencing reading difficulty at the high school level (Alfassi, 1998). The approach uses a group problem-solving activity in which students read a passage of text, paragraph by paragraph. During reading, they are taught to practice four comprehension strategies: generating questions about the text, summarizing the text, attempting to clarify word meanings or confusing text, and predicting what might appear in the next paragraph.

During the early stages of reciprocal teaching, the teacher explicitly models the four strategies with students as observers. Each student then takes a turn in leading the group dialogue and practicing the dialogue. The teacher uses what the students do as an informal assessment of the students' mastery of the strategies and adjusts accordingly, providing feedback to students on their reading practice. Critical to the method is the group activity of reading: the entire class shares responsibility for making sense of the text, and part of learning how to read is understood as learning how to negotiate meanings made by different readers of a text. Explicit instruction in reading comprehension and monitoring strategies in the past has been shown to be especially important for new readers and academically delayed readers (Alfassi, 1998).

WHERE DO WE GO FROM HERE?

When I ran the first time I missed the last three days of the school year and thereby failed all of my final exams. This turned most of my C and B averages into F's, causing me to flunk the ninth grade. Starting at a new school in a new town involves a bunch of paperwork, paperwork the schools expect your parents to sign . . . . When I ran the second time, I became a "drop-out." As I'm sure you know, this is not a generally advised practice in our society . . . . In my case, I managed to get into college, in spite of dropping out. I found a back door and started by taking a few courses as a part-time student. After I'd proved myself for a couple years, and built up my abilities to handle a full-time course-load, I applied. They couldn't argue with me as I'd already succeeded. It took me five and half years to get a four-year degree, but I did it. Now I have more employment opportunities, and at my last job earned more than twice as much per hour as I ever did before. (Evan, reflecting at 26.)

Although Evan was able to beat the odds and make a successful transition from the street, not all youth are as fortunate. The following are three educational practices that are effective in reaching homeless youth earlier to prevent some of the dangers of street life and to ensure this kind of success.

Effective Educational Practices

♦ Integrate support services within schools

♦ Develop system-wide standards for learning and assessment tools to monitor student progress

♦ Train individuals to be advocates for homeless youth

INTEGRATING SCHOOL-LINKED SERVICES

Many communities have begun to form partnerships that develop school-linked services for children and their families (Levy & Shepardson, 1992). These "full-service schools" (Dryfoos, 1994), as they are sometimes called, are based on the premise that the current social service delivery system is not adequately well-coordinated to meet the pressing social, educational, and health needs of today's students from low-income families (Morrill, 1992). Schools, for their part, are stable and dominant institutions in many children's lives. School-linked services are designed to build on schools' importance in the community by acting as key participants in planning, governance, and coordination of services on-site or near the school. In order to meet the service needs of students, schools partner with health and social service organizations, parents, and other community groups to develop clear goals and objectives and establish mechanisms for communication, collaboration, and integration of the service delivery system (Center for the Future of Children, 1992).

One program that seeks to create such an integrated service delivery system is California's Healthy Start Initiative[4]. California's Healthy Start Initiative is designed to provide school-based and school-linked services to students and their families that address interrelated health, mental health, social, and academic needs (Wagner & Gomby, 1996). Each Healthy Start site is a partnership of schools, health and human service organizations, community organizations, teachers, and parents. While there is no single service delivery model that all sites adopt, the services must be integrated, which means that school staff and staff from partner organizations must share information and training opportunities. Case management is a key component of the program for each "core client" in Healthy Start, which provides a means for integration of services at the individual level. Services are accessible, being at the school and having hours beyond the normal school day. There is a focus on the family and on culturally appropriate delivery of services.

To be sure, many homeless students may be alienated from the traditional school system and thereby fail to benefit from school-linked services. For those students, alternative community school models hold promise. Such schools are often located in low-income neighborhoods and may, in their curriculum and organization, more closely resemble the kinds of youth organizations where young people feel most at home (Heath & McLaughlin, 1994). Intermediate School 218[5] in the Washington Heights community of New York City is an example of such a school. The Children's Aid Society worked with the New York City Board of Education to plan community schools, which would be open six days per week, from the hours of 7 a.m. to 10 p.m., year-round. The goal of the project was to create a school that would serve as a multi-service center, providing any services needed by neighborhood children, youth, and families. Some of these services include daycare, recreation, drug and teen pregnancy prevention counseling, medical and dental care, mental health, supplemental education weekend, and summer camp services (Carnegie Council on Adolescent Development, 1992). Since IS 218 opened in March 1992, three more schools have opened in Washington Heights, currently reaching nearly 7,000 students and their families.

SYSTEM-WIDE STANDARDS AND ASSESSMENT

School reform efforts in recent years have focused increasingly on the development of clear standards or expectations of student performance and on assessments designed to measure students' progress toward meeting those standards (Rothman, 1997). Standards-based reform efforts assume that setting challenging content and performance standards are a critical means of improving student achievement in different subject areas (McLaughlin & Shepard, 1995). Assessment reform typically follows the development of new standards for student performance, with increasing attention to measuring student performance on more open-ended or "authentic" tasks, in contrast to multiple-choice norm-referenced tests (Posner, 1994).

The National Center on Education and the Economy[6] (1997) has argued that setting high standards and developing assessment tools aligned with those standards that are shared across different educational settings, whether schools or adult literacy centers, can be particularly helpful to nontraditional students, such as high school dropouts. When coupled with a counseling and referral system to help such students consider their educational alternatives, such standards-based reform can have a positive impact for students in both community and school settings, according to the report.

When homeless youth change schools, not only do the people and places change, but so do the academic expectations for students. Rarely are curricula aligned in such a way that students are expected to master the same skills; thus, they may fall behind, not because they lack any skills at all but because they have not had a chance to participate in the building of local school cultures that set expectations, outline curricula, and measure student progress. If districts are able to develop shared frameworks for learning and assessment, then students who change schools often are given a fairer chance at doing well in school.

ADVOCACY AND POLITICAL EMPOWERMENT

Reform aimed at transforming the educational opportunities and outcomes for homeless teens is a process requiring involvement of many people and institutions. Community agencies, school districts, principals and teachers, support personnel, and students must all be engaged in a well-coordinated effort for change. Such efforts and change do not happen without the inclusion of those who are to benefit from the programs—namely homeless youth—in key decisions that affect their social, economic, and educational futures. To that end, the political empowerment of homeless youth—as valued voices within the community—is key. Others within the youth-serving community must become empowered as well to argue on behalf of homeless teens before local, state, and national politicians for solutions to the variety of social problems associated with homelessness.

Effective advocacy, of course, requires knowledgeable advocates. School personnel especially must have an understanding of the needs and unique situations of the homeless teens they serve, and to that end training has proven an effective means of raising awareness within districts (Stronge, 1993). Such training would benefit youth even more if young people, themselves, were involved in delivering such training and if the training reached a partnership of community agencies and schools all engaged in attempting to better serve homeless youth. Ultimately, building relationships with homeless youth not only will support young people's positive educational futures, but also it will transform all those who seek to serve these young people so that they become allies and advocates in the wider world.

REFERENCES

Adams, G., Gullota, T., & Clancy, M. (1985). Homeless adolescents: A descriptive study of similarities and differences between runaways and throwaways. *Adolescence, 20,* 715-724.

Alfassi, M. (1998). Reading for meaning: Efficacy of reciprocal teaching in fostering reading comprehension of high school students in remedial reading classes. *American Educational Research Journal, 35,* 309-322.

Allington, R.L., & McGill-Franzen, A. (1989). School response to reading failure: Chapter 1 and special education students in grades 2, 4, and 8. *Elementary School Journal, 89,* 529-542.

Baldwin, J. (1995). Using peer education approaches in HIV/AIDS programs for youth: A review of the literature. *Peer Facilitator Quarterly, 12,* 34-38.

Carnegie Council on Adolescent Development. (1992). A matter of time: Risk and opportunity in the nonschool hours. *Report of the Task Force on Youth Development and Community Progams.* New York: Carnegie Corporation of New York.

Center for the Future of Children. (1992). Analysis. *The future of children, 2,* 6-18.

Children's Defense Fund. (1992). *The state of the art of America's children.* Washinton, DC: Author.

Children's Defense Fund and National Coalition for the Homeless. (1998). "Welfare to what: Early findings on family hardship and well-being. Washington, DC: National Coalition for the Homeless.

Cwayna, K. (1993). *Knowing where the fountains are: Stories and stark realities of homeless youth.* Minneapolis, MN: Deaconess Press.

Dryfoos, J. (1990). *Adolescents at risk.* New York: Oxford University Press.

Dryfoos, J. (1994). *Full-service schools.* San Francisco: Jossey-Bass.

Foscarinis, M. (1987, February 24). *The crisis in homelessness: Effects on children and families.* Testimony for the Hearing before the Select Committee on Children, Youth, and Families. House of Representatives, 100th Congress, 1st session, Washington, DC.

Furano, K., Roaf, P.A., Styles, M.B., & Branch, A.Y. (1993). *Big Brothers/Big Sisters: A study of program practices.* Philadelphia: Public/Private Ventures.

Hamilton, S.F. (1990). *Apprenticeship for adulthood.* New York: Free Press.

Heath, S.B., & McLaughlin, M. (1994). *Identity and inner city youth: Beyond ethnicity and gender.* New York: Teachers College Press.

Janus, M., McCormack, A., Burgess, A., & Hartman, C. (1987). *Adolescent runaways.* Lexington, MA: Lexington.

Kufelt, K., & Nimmo, M. (1987). Youth on the street: Abuse and neglect in the eighties. *Child Abuse and Neglect, 11,* 531-543.

Levy, K., & Shepardson, W. (1992). Look at current school-linked service efforts. *The future of children, 2,* 44-55.

McCarthy, B., & Hagan, J. (1992). Surviving on the street: The experiences of homeless youth. *Journal of Adolescent Research, 7,* 412-430.

McLaughlin, M.W., & Shepard, L.A. (1995). *Improving education through standards-based reform: A report by the National Academy of Education Panel on Standards-Based Education Reform.* Stanford, CA: National Academy of Education.

Morrill, W.A. (1992). Overview of service delivery to children. *The future of children, 2,* 32-43.

National Center on Education and the Economy (1997). America's education challenge: Helping all students meet high standards. Rochester, NY: Author.

National Coalition on Homelessness. (1998).

National Network of Runaway and Youth Services. (1991). *To whom do they belong? Runaway, homeless and other youth in high-risk situations in the 1990s.* Washington, DC: Author.

Nissen, M. (1998, June). *Mobilizing street kids: The action contexts of independence.* Paper presented at biennial meeting of the International Society for Cultural Research and Activity Theory. Aarhus, Denmark.

Palincsar, A.S., & Brown, A. (1988). Teaching and practicing thinking skills to promote comprehension in the context of group problem solving. *Remedial and Special Education, 9,* 53-59.

Penuel, W.R., & Freeman, T. (1997). Participatory action research in youth programming: A theory in use. *Child and Youth Care Forum, 26,* 175-186.

Posner, M. (1994). "Working together for youth: A guide to collaboration between law enforcement agencies and programs that serve runaway and homeless youth." University of Oklahoma: National Resource Center for Youth Services.

Powers, J.L., & Jaklitsch, B. (1993). Reaching the hard to reach: Educating homeless adolescents in urban settings. *Education and Urban Society, 25,* 394-409.

Rafferty, Y., & Shin, M. (1991). The impact of homelessness on children. *American Psychologist, 46,* 1170-1179.

Robertson, M. (1989). *Homeless youth: Patterns of alcohol use.* Berkely, CA: Alcohol Research Group.

Rotheram-Borus, M.J., Koopman, C., Haignere, C., & Davies, M. (1991). Reducing HIV sexual risk behaviors among runaway adolescents. *JAMA: The Journal of the American Medical Association, 266,* 1237-1241.

Rothman, R. (1997). *Measuring up: Standards, assessment, and school reform.* San Francisco: Jossey-Bass.

Sawyer, R. et al. (1997). How peer education changed peer sexuality, educators' self-esteem, personal development, and sexual behavior. *Journal of American College Health, 45,* 211-217.

Shaffer, D., & Caton, C.L.M. (1984). *Runaway and homeless youth in New York City.* New York: Ittleson Foundation.

Stronge, J.H. (1993). From access to success: Public policy for educating urban homeless students. *Education and Urban Society, 25,* 340-360.

Tierney, J.P, & Grossman, J. (1995). *Making a difference: An impact study of Big Brothers/Big Sisters.* Philadelphia: Public/Private Ventures.

Varenhorst, B. (1992). Developing youth as resources to their peers. *Journal of Emotional and Behavioral Problems, 1,* 10-14.

Vissing, Y.M., & Diament, J. (1997). Housing distress among high school students. *Social Work, 42,* 31-41.

Wagner, M., & Gomby, D. (1996). Evaluating a statewide school-linked services initiative: California's healthy start. In J. M. Marquart & E. Konrad (Eds.), *New directions in program evaluation: Evaluation of human services integration activities.* San Francisco: Jossey-Bass.

Whitbeck, L.B., Hoyt, D.R., & Ackley, K.A. (1997). Abusive family backgrounds and later victimization among runaway and homeless adolescents. *Journal of Research on Adolescence, 7,* 375-392.

Whitbeck, L.B., & Simons, R.L. (1993). A comparison of adaptive strategies and patterns of victimization among homeless adolescents and adults. *Violence and Victims, 8,* 135-152.

Yates, M., & Younniss, J. (1996). Community service and political-moral identity in adolescents. *Journal of Research on Adolescence, 6,* 271-84.

RESOURCES

For more information on the Beat the Street program, you can visit their Web site at http://www.nald.ca./bts.htm or e-mail the program at bts@ican.net. Their address is: 290 Jarvis St, Toronto, ON Canada M5B 2C5, and their telephone is 416-979-3292. Violetta Ilkiw, Program Coordinator at Beat the Street, recommends *Gimme Shelter! A Resource for Literacy and Homelessness Work* as a helpful tool on teaching older teens critical literacy skills. The book is available online at http://www.nald.ca/lithome.htm or by calling St. Christopher House in Toronto at (416) 539-9000.

For more information about California's Healthy Start Initiative contact Healthy Start and After School Program partnerships Office at California Department of Education. (916) 657-3558. Developing information about the After School Learni .g and Safe Neighborhoods Partnerships Program is available at the Healthy Start Web site http://www.cde.ca.gov/syfsbranch/lsp/hshome.htm.

For more information on programs serving homeless teens in Denmark, including Sjakket and another program for homeless teens called "Projekt Gadebørn" ("Homeless Kids Project"), you can e-mail the Danish Ministry of Social Affairs at 01k@sm.dk.

ENDNOTES

[1]In this chapter, youth who are defined as runaway will be included in the term "homeless youth" unless otherwise noted.

[2]To find out more about mentoring programs, please visit Big Brothers/Big Sisters of America's website at http://www.bbbsa.org or call their National Headquarters in Philadelphia at (215)567-7000.

[3]For more information on programs serving homeless teens in Denmark, including Sjakket and another program for homeless teens called "Projekt Gadebørn" ("Homeless Kids Project"), you can email the Danish Ministry of Social Affairs at 01k@sm.dk.

[4]For more information about California's Healthy Start Initiative contact Healthy Start and After School Program partnerships Office at California Department of Education. (916) 657-3558. Web site: http://www.cde.ca.gov/syfsbranch/lsp/hshome.htm.

[5]Information on Intermediate School 218 of New York City can be obtained through the Children's Aid Society, 105 East 22nd Street, New York, New York 10010. Web site: http://www.childrensaidsociety.org/cas/comsch.html

[6]Information on the New Standards Project, a collaboration between the National Center on Education and the Economy and the Learning Research and Development Center, can be found at: http://www.ncee.org/ourprograms/nspage.html.

5

MOVING TO EDUCATIONAL SUCCESS: BUILDING POSITIVE RELATIONSHIPS FOR HOMELESS CHILDREN

LINDA J. ANOOSHIAN

A considerable amount of recent research converges on the conclusion that close personal relationships as well as less intimate social involvements are essential to psychological adjustment and well-being. In a sense, psychologists have simply documented something many people take for granted; specifically, that interpersonal commitments are more than commonplace in human experience, they are essential to life, growth, and happiness. (Jones & Carver, 1991, p. 395)

What happens if, for homeless children, social isolation and rejection become more commonplace than such interpersonal commitments? In school settings, children's failed relationships can be formidable barriers to educational success. This chapter focuses on how social relationships pose both risk and protective factors for the increasing numbers of children facing the terror of homelessness.

RELATIONSHIPS AS A FOCUS FOR EDUCATIONAL PRACTICE

Background and supporting materials for educators—to be reviewed in this chapter—will reinforce that the social isolation of homeless children is often pervasive and this isolation is a barrier to educational success. Without this background, one might question the focus on social and personal relationships for children who are tired, hungry, and/or hopelessly behind in basic academic skills. From a more optimistic perspective, researchers have noted that quality relationships (e.g., through extracurricular activities, substitute caregivers) can provide children with resilience in facing adversity (Rutter, 1990). For example, resilient children—those who seem to thrive through tough times—often report an adult who took a special interest in them. The primary message of this chapter is that educators can and should devote considerable efforts to helping homeless children build positive relationships in school settings. Supporting materials for this recommended educational practice are organized in terms of answers to specific questions.

WHY FOCUS ON RELATIONSHIPS?

As suggested by the opening quote, relationship problems likely contribute to other documented problems of homeless children. In fact, this was confirmed in extensive structured interviews that were part of research conducted in both Boise, Idaho, and Hartford, Connecticut; relationship problems were tied to many of the negative effects associated with homelessness for children. Other researchers have reported developmental delays and numerous emotional, health, and educational problems (e.g., Bassuk & Gallagher, 1990; Bassuk & Rubin, 1987; Dail, 1990). Since social isolation appears to be a contributing factor, one viable approach to addressing these problems is to build positive relationships.

WHY DO HOMELESS CHILDREN EXPERIENCE ISOLATION?

In addressing relationship problems, it is important to recognize that "isolation" is *not* synonymous with *physical* distance or separation from others; the concern is with the scarcity of social attachments and high-quality social interactions experienced by homeless children. For example, consider a homeless child in an emergency shelter who becomes aggressive in response to crowding and lack of privacy. In addition to being deprived of meaningful social interaction, such social crowding creates further perils associated with lack of both privacy and "personal places." As Berck (1992) noted:

> Most families end up disconnected by distance and circumstance from everything familiar—friends, neighbors, schools. It is as if they become lost in the middle of their own city. (p. 30)

When mothers and families become disconnected from meaningful relationships, children necessarily experience isolation as well. During our interviews in Boise and Hartford, mothers often commented that friendships disappeared the day they became homeless (e.g., entered the shelter).

Social isolation and distrust often emerge from past histories of victimization and personal trauma, histories more prevalent for homeless than other poor women. In this context, Dail (1990) points out much of homeless women's distrust is strongly based in reality; these mothers "have learned distrust as a means of survival in their social circumstances. Suspicion and apprehensiveness are what they find they need most" (p. 300). In many cases, school personnel may need to work with parents to gain their trust in allowing children to participate in activities designed to help with relationship building (e.g., after-school programs, mentor programs).

Extreme isolation of homeless mothers is important to understanding the pervasiveness of the social isolation experienced by their children. As noted earlier, social isolation of the mother necessarily means isolation of the family unit and, hence, further isolation of the children. In addition, supportive social networks for mothers are associated with more positive parenting (see Hashima & Amato, 1994). In contrast, both poverty and social isolation are associated with problematic patterns of parenting and child abuse; the combination of poverty and lack of social support yields an "especially dangerous situation for children" (Hashima & Amoto, 1994, p. 400). Also, social isolation of the mother increases vulnerability to depression. We know that depression is frequent among homeless mothers and that maternal depression and poor mother-child relationships are clearly linked (Dail, 1990). By understanding how social isolation—including problematic parent-child relationships—contributes to the perils of homelessness, we gain useful frameworks for educational practice.

ISN'T ISOLATION A FAMILY PROBLEM RATHER THAN A SCHOOL PROBLEM?

Yes and no. Clearly, social isolation often reflects that the stresses of homelessness make positive family interactions difficult. Yet, understanding the family origins of relationship difficulties helps to reinforce that successful educational practices must include strategies for building positive relationships. Numerous authors have pointed to the difficulties in parenting being associated with stresses on the family system and the social chaos of shelters (e.g., Boxill & Beaty, 1990). Children acquire models for social interaction from their interactions with parents (Hetherington & Martin, 1986). Hence, it is not surprising that poor parent-child relationships are often associated with feelings of loneliness for children (Jones & Carver, 1991).

As we have seen, parent-child relationships often reflect the economic stresses associated with poverty. If economic stresses cannot be eliminated, poor relationships interfere with educational success, and "family matters" become "school matters."

EVEN IF PARENT-CHILD RELATIONS ARE STRAINED, DON'T MOST CHILDREN GET THE SUPPORT THEY NEED FROM SIBLINGS?

Several authors have observed that strong sibling relationships sometimes contrast with immature or strained peer interactions. The implication is that positive sibling interactions can protect children or make them more resilient in facing other negative influences in their lives (Bassuk & Gallagher, 1990). Unfortunately, there is good reason to be skeptical. Stresses that negatively influence parent-child interactions (e.g., hunger, transience) are likely to strain sibling relationships as well. In fact, researchers have found that family conflict and poor parent-child relationships are associated with sibling conflict and aggression (Brody, Stoneman, McCoy, & Forehand, 1992). In the research conducted in Boise and Hartford, it appeared that difficulties in sibling relationships contributed to the overall pattern of isolation experienced by homeless children. Children who reported poor parent-child relationships were likely to report problems with sibling relationships as well.

WHAT ABOUT OTHER OPPORTUNITIES FOR SOCIAL INTERACTIONS AND POSITIVE RELATIONSHIPS OUTSIDE BOTH THE FAMILY AND SCHOOL SETTING?

The literature on resilience points to a variety of potential sources of social support and connections outside the family (Rutter, 1990). For example, resilience is sometimes associated with special interests, extracurricular activities, supportive teachers or clergy, or substitute caregivers or role models outside the family (Rutter, 1990). But, as suggested earlier, the very factors that interfere with effective relationships within the family also decrease the likelihood of other sources of social support. For example, Johnson (1992) noted that 95% of homeless elementary school children reported that they missed friends more than anything else. In a similar vein, Tower (1992) argued that the inconsistencies in the lives of homeless children lead to confusion and the inability to trust or commit to any social relationship; the conditions of homelessness lead to distrust of *any* adult. As Hausman and Hammen (1993) concluded, "virtually all the high risk conditions that have been studied for their negative impact on mothers and children come together in the situation of homelessness" (p. 365). A primary goal of this chapter is to demonstrate that the pervasive risk conditions for homeless children often reflect the pervasiveness of their social isolation.

Since classroom and other school activities involve consistent social interactions, aren't educational practices that target increased attendance sufficient? For some, schools can provide a source of healthy social interactions away from the stresses imposed on family life. In this regard, it is well recognized that peer groups and schools are especially important for children undergoing stress (Hetherington & Martin, 1986). Consistent with this perspective, Horowitz, Springer, and Kose (1988) found that homeless children had more positive attitudes about school than poor housed children, perhaps reflecting that schools provided avenues for adapting or escaping from stressful family situations. Schools provide a ray of hope for quality relationships for homeless children.

Unfortunately, homeless children who overcome other barriers to regular school attendance often experience more negative labeling and rejection than social support. Across the country, schools pose problems for homeless children; they are ostracized by their peers, experience negative labeling and stereotyping, feel ashamed, and attempt to hide the fact that they are homeless (Tower, 1992). These observations are particularly sobering in the context of the extensive research literature in child development pointing to clear relations between poor peer relationships and widespread negative outcomes including avoidance of school, poor school performance, school drop-out, and mental health and adjustment difficulties (e.g., Coie & Cillessen, 1993; Jones & Carver, 1991). Developmental psychologists have long recognized that peer rejection has clear negative consequences for children.

WHEN FAMILIES MANAGE TO ACQUIRE HOMES AND ECONOMIC STABILITY, WILL POSITIVE RELATIONSHIPS FOR CHILDREN NATURALLY FOLLOW?

Probably not—educational practice should include building positive relationships for children with histories of homelessness. There are two ways that self-perpetuating cycles of difficult relationships can continue to plague these children. First, proximity to other human beings may have come to evoke anxiety and distrust. Various authors have noted the distrust, insecurity, and sense of danger experienced by homeless individuals, particularly homeless children: "the ability to feel safe and secure eludes many victims of homelessness" (Johnson, 1992, p. 159).

Second, poor self-esteem is likely to emerge from social isolation. Problematic parent-child relationships are associated with poor self-esteem for the child; loneliness and self-esteem are closely connected (e.g., Jones & Carver, 1991). In turn, poor self-esteem can perpetuate the cycle of difficult relationships for children who have been homeless. In addition to negative views about the self, social isolation leads to negative views about others. For example, social rejection leads to negative beliefs about peers that, in turn, contribute to further difficulties with peer relations.

BUILDING POSITIVE RELATIONSHIPS: STRATEGIES FOR SUCCESS

Awareness programs in schools should address the diversity of potential sources of social isolation for homeless children as well as the devastating consequences of that isolation. In addition to awareness programs, strategies for success in building positive relationships should focus on increasing social support, improving social skills, and addressing the insecurity and shame that can keep children in a self-perpetuating cycle of difficult relationships.

BUILDING AWARENESS: HOW CAN SCHOOLS USE THIS INFORMATION ABOUT THE DIVERSE SOURCES OF SOCIAL ISOLATION FOR HOMELESS CHILDREN?

Information about the social isolation of homeless children—including its pervasiveness and consequences—should be an important component of homeless awareness programs in schools. It is important that school personnel (from office staff to principal) understand the potential significance of social exchanges (from short hallway conversations to extended teacher-student interactions) for homeless children. Specific guidelines for teachers should be included in these awareness programs. For example, teachers should know to avoid removing children from positive social situations (e.g., group play) in disciplinary action. Teachers should gain sensitivity when making specific classroom requests. For example, when teachers ask children to bring food, photographs, favorite toys, money, or other objects for specific projects, homeless children may be embarrassed to let others know they don't have these things. That embarrassment contributes to continued social isolation.

BUILDING AWARENESS: WHAT ELSE DO SCHOOL PERSONNEL NEED TO KNOW TO IMPLEMENT SUCCESSFUL STRATEGIES?

The background materials included in this chapter were also designed to help educators when advocating for specific programs and/or school policies for building positive relationships. Unfortunately, some requests for specific social programs (e.g., extracurricular activities, peer support groups) may be met with skepticism. In addressing this skepticism, it will be important to be armed with evidence that social and emotional functioning in childhood is predictive of a variety of outcomes, including poor academic functioning (e.g., Ollendick, Weist, Borden, & Greene, 1992) and school drop-out (Cairns, Cairns, & Neckerman, 1989). Timberlake (1994) has also confirmed close links between psychosocial adjustment and academic functioning for homeless students. Specifically, homeless children with academic problems were significantly worse in psychosocial functioning in classrooms than homeless children who were academically successful. Information included in this chapter should help make the case that positive relationships are not "extra fluff," but rather are essential to the educational success of homeless children. Specific strategies for success should include a three-fold emphasis on:

♦ increasing social support,

♦ building social skills, and

♦ interrupting the self-perpetuating cycle of difficult relationships for homeless children.

SOCIAL SUPPORT: WITH ALL OF THE SOCIAL AND OTHER DIFFICULTIES, IS IT REASONABLE TO THINK THAT SOCIAL SUPPORT WITHIN THE SCHOOLS CAN MAKE A DIFFERENCE FOR HOMELESS CHILDREN?

Despite other difficulties, social support may be more important for homeless than other at-risk children. Graham-Berman et al. (1996) reported that quality of social relationships reliably predicted adjustment difficulties for homeless, but not for low-income children. Further, strategies of providing social support for homeless children have been successful. Consistent with the success of mentor programs—as described in chapter 12—remarkable positive changes have been observed for homeless children in Boise, Idaho, who were assigned adult "school buddies" through the Big Brothers Big Sisters program, even when the match lasted for only a short period (2-4 months; when the child moved to another school). Based on the pervasiveness of their social isolation (as reviewed earlier), we were concerned that many of the children would not have the minimal social skills needed to benefit from the mentor relationship. To the contrary, children relished the attention that came through one-on-one relationships with adults dedicated simply to being good friends. Careful attention to chapter 12 is recommended for educators seeking strategies for addressing the social isolation of homeless children.

Other programs for providing social support to homeless children have also been successful and they make a difference. Rainbow Days offers a two-day professional training for support groups for homeless children (see Additional Resources). In addition to focusing on coping skills and esteem building, the curriculum includes materials designed to help children learn about friendships and relationships. School staff could choose among a number of different options for implementing such support groups. Staff and/or volunteers could be trained to serve as group facilitators; support groups could meet at schools and/ or shelter settings.

City Park School in Dallas achieved impressive levels of academic achievement from homeless students through programs that emphasize psychosocial as much as instructional needs (Gonzalez, 1990). For example, the school follows a systematic procedure for orienting new students to the school as well as provides diverse after-school extracurricular and recreational activities. For inner-city children with many of the same risk factors as homeless children—poverty, community violence, and family distress—formal after-school programs are associated with more positive outcomes than other types of after-school care (mother care, informal adult supervision, self-care) including "better grades and conduct in school as well as better peer relations and emotional adjustment" (Posner & Vandell, 1994, p. 454).

SOCIAL SUPPORT: SINCE THE PRIMARY GOALS OF EDUCATION ARE ACADEMIC, IS IT REALLY NECESSARY TO ADDRESS PEER RELATIONSHIPS IN ADDITION TO POSITIVE RELATIONSHIPS WITH ADULTS (TEACHERS AND STAFF)?

Yes, successful strategies for educational success will require significant efforts in supporting positive peer relationships for homeless children. Classroom expectations are that children should be able to interact in friendly and constructive ways with classmates; a child's failure to do so poses a significant educational risk. In general, the quality of peer relationships within the school is predictive of a wide variety of educational outcome measures, including attendance and drop-out rates (Cairns et al., 1989; Coie & Cillessen, 1993; Ollendick et al., 1992).

Successful strategies for educating homeless children must include interventions that provide homeless children support networks of peers. Some successful school programs involve:

♦ "special friends" for homeless children (Eddowes, 1992);

♦ buddy programs, and other approaches to intervention that emphasize supportive peer relationships within the school context (see Johnson, 1992); and

♦ after-school programs—whether they involve peer support groups (like those described for Rainbow Days), recreational activities, clubs, or other extracurricular activities (see Johnson, 1992).

Halpern (1992) noted that, in addition to quality adult relationships, peer groups in after-school programs can provide children with support and opportunities for "discussing worries and fears, learning to work cooperatively, and learning to trust others" (p. 226).

Although not directed specifically at homeless children, Ramsey (1991) summarized three complementary approaches to promoting positive peer relationships. First, Ramsey summa-

rized a variety of ways in which teachers can organize classrooms to promote positive social environments including:

♦ designing classroom activities with a variety of social
  interactions, including small groups, partners, group
  activities, and independent projects;

♦ maintaining flexibility so that activities with positive
  exchanges can be lengthened, and activities with negative exchanges can be shortened; and

♦ structuring groups and activities so that all members
  can participate equally and develop a sense of com-
  munal effort.

Second, Ramsey provided guidelines for when and how
teachers should intervene in cases of negative or problematic
social relationships in the classroom. Examples include:

♦ designing strategies for helping children meet their
  needs in more productive ways;

♦ involving peers to help them change images and attitudes toward the child(ren) involved in the negative
  social interactions; and

♦ supporting children's efforts to manage or negotiate
  their own conflicts (rather than rushing with an expe-
  dient solution).

Ramsey also summarized diverse activities and materials that
teachers can use to support peer relationships and the development of social skills and peer relationships (e.g., role playing,
cooperative games, social problem-solving exercises).

Educating peers about homelessness is also an important
strategy for providing supportive environments for homeless
children (see Tower, 1992). Otherwise, the stigma associated with
homelessness may remain as a formidable barrier to socially integrating homeless children into classrooms. As noted by James
et al. (1997), "When nonhomeless students become aware of the
adversities and challenges that students without homes contend
with on a daily basis, they sometimes soften their approach to

their peers who are in homeless situations" (p. 97). Similarly, based on interviews in which homeless students emphasized both positive (e.g., friendships) and negative aspects of peer interactions in school (e.g., being teased), Daniels (1995) recommended that school counselors initiate school programs to enhance "awareness and respect for persons with diverse personal backgrounds" (p. 351).

SOCIAL SKILLS: HOW CAN WE TEACH SOCIAL SKILLS TO CHILDREN WITH SO MANY DIFFICULTIES?

Basic social skills provide the foundation for positive relationships that, in turn, maintain esteem and academic performance. Many programs for developing social skills have been developed for at-risk children. By focusing on *conditions* of homelessness, educators can select programs for direct instruction in social skills that have been developed for children experiencing similar relationship problems (Gresham & Evans, 1987; Pedro-Carroll, 1997).

As a first step, educators should investigate what other programs might already be available in their district. For example, specific sections of programs designed for children experiencing the trauma of divorce could be easily adopted for homeless students; the Children of Divorce Intervention Program (CDIP; Pedro-Carroll, 1997) contains sessions on coping with changes and social problem solving that could be quite helpful to homeless children. As another example, Ramsey (1991) recommends the PATHS curriculum (Providing Alternative Thinking Strategies)[1] for children with relationship problems; the program involves a series of classroom activities for improving self-control, emotional understanding, and problem-solving skills.

There are several programs for improving social skills that have proved quite effective for children with relationship problems (independent of housing status). The Social Decision Making and Problem Solving Program[2] (Elias & Clabby, 1989, 1992) is based on clear empirical evidence that specific social skills are reliably associated with the quality of peer relationships and that those social skills "can be enhanced through training and practice" (Bruene-Butler et al., 1997, p. 243). Consistent with these two areas of empirical evidence, Bruene-Butler et al. summarize extensive empirical evidence of program effectiveness. For older children, the Social-Competence Promotion Program for Young Adolescents (SCPP-YA)[3] includes classroom-based instruction focused on self-control, stress management, social problem solving and communication skills, and preventing antisocial and aggressive behavior (Weissberg, Barton, & Shriver, 1997).

INSECURITY AND SHAME: HOW CAN WE BREAK THE CYCLE OF SELF-PERPETUATING ISOLATION AND DISRUPTED RELATIONSHIPS FOR HOMELESS CHILDREN?

As reviewed in earlier sections, children's low self-esteem can lead to a self-perpetuating cycle of isolation and rejection. Of course, strategies that focus on building positive relationships and/or removing stigma should also improve self-esteem. In fact, several strategies already discussed have complementary goals of improving self-esteem and social relationships (see for example, Rainbow Days; Johnson, 1992; Ramsey, 1991). Graham-Berman (1996) reports close ties between social support and perceptions of self-worth for both homeless and low-income children. Beyond working on esteem and positive relationships in the school setting, educators should also be well informed about possible referrals to services in the community (e.g., counseling and/or support groups).

SOME HOMELESS CHILDREN DON'T SEEM TO CARE ABOUT THEIR NEGATIVE CIRCUMSTANCES. OTHERS REJECT THOSE WHO TRY TO SHOW WARMTH AND CARING. YET OTHERS HAVE REAL STRENGTHS AND DON'T SEEM TO NEED HELP. HOW CAN THE SAME STRATEGIES WORK FOR ALL THESE CHILDREN?

Many homeless children adopt coping strategies of becoming aggressive, even hostile; aggressive responses may reflect a way of expressing anger or, for some, a way to control the environment (Tower, 1992). Although some research suggests that homeless children may also react to their circumstances by withdrawing and becoming depressed (Bassuk & Rubin, 1987), interview research with children in Boise and Hartford pointed to aggression as the more common coping strategy. In many at-risk environments, children quickly learn that depression can be dangerous, leaving them vulnerable to attack by others; becoming aggressive is a way of protecting oneself. Maintaining appearances of "not caring" or "being tough" may be learned strategies for protection. When trying to be supportive of homeless children:

♦ be patient;

♦ don't be surprised if your initial efforts are met with lack of caring or actual rebuff;

♦ look for ways in which children can control their classroom environment without being aggressive; and

♦ be persistent in maintaining positive social interaction and support (avoid the erroneous conclusion that children really don't want your support).

Davis (1996) notes that desperation, loss of hope, and poor esteem often lead to an apparent "I don't care" attitude among homeless adults. Like adults, children may also cope with stressful events by minimizing negative events. While their words may express apathy, it would be a mistake for teachers or other school personnel to conclude that homeless children don't care. In fact, Mickelson and Yon (1994-1995) reported that, despite strong stereotypes and expectations to the contrary, homeless children are very motivated to perform well in school. Timberlake (1994) also reported that, surprisingly, teachers depicted about one-third of homeless students as "attending regularly, earning all passing grades, being well-adjusted, and demonstrating psychosocial strengths in the classroom" (p. 273). Obviously, it is important to recognize individual differences among homeless children in both their academic motivation and in their use of coping strategies that might erroneously convey a lack of motivation. Regardless of whether or not homeless students are currently experiencing academic and/or psychosocial problems, continued attention to positive relationships will be important to their future educational success.

IF CHILDREN ARE TIRED AND HUNGRY, WHAT'S THE POINT OF TRYING TO HELP WITH SOCIAL RELATIONSHIPS?

Of course, sleep deprivation and/or hunger exacerbate problems with social relationships. Clearly, it makes little sense to focus on building positive relationships without also initiating broader school programs (e.g., getting children signed up for free or reduced meal programs, including nutritional snacks as part of after-school program, working with shelters and food kitchens to help ensure that children do not come to school hungry and tired). The interview research in Boise and Hartford also pointed to direct links between the frequency of skipping meals and the pervasiveness of shame or disapproval reported by homeless children. Not only were children hungry, but their hunger appeared to reinforce the shame associated with being poor. Other research findings indicated that, the more shame that children reported, the lower their self-esteem and the greater the likelihood of disrupted relationships (e.g., bullying and/or victimization).

BROADER PERSPECTIVES: THE TOTAL SCHOOL PICTURE AND POLICY IMPLICATIONS

The preceding section emphasized how strategies for building positive relationships must be integrated with broader school programs. In earlier sections, schoolwide awareness programs were recommended. There is limited value to integrating homeless students in their classrooms if they experience disgust from office staff when coming to school tardy wearing dirty clothes. With awareness programs, schools recognize that negative attitudes are major contributors to the isolation and rejection experienced by homeless children. Further, in emphasizing broader perspectives, Moroz and Segal (1990) concluded that "Schools can and should play an important role in connecting homeless children and families to a coordinated network of community services designed to help them" (p. 139). For example, educators could work with shelter staff in promoting social support for families and children who have been marginalized and isolated.

In taking a still broader perspective, it is clear that, despite our best efforts in building positive relationships for children, the very state of homelessness will necessarily continue contributing to isolation and strained relationships. Can support groups ever compensate for the inability to invite a friend over to play after school or the strain in relating to a mother preoccupied with thoughts of where to spend the next night? Some sources of isolation and loneliness are inevitable consequences of lacking a permanent home. As long as the number of families living in poverty exceeds the number of low-income (affordable) housing units, we will have homeless families. Wright and Lam (1987) concluded that:

> . . . in a hypothetical world where there are no alcoholics, no drug addicts, no mentally ill, no deinstitutionalization movement, indeed, no personal or social pathologies at all, there would still be a formidable homelessness problem, simply because at this stage in American history, there is not enough low-income housing to accommodate the poverty population. (p. 53)

Hence, from a broader policy perspective, only major policy changes can reduce the numbers of children experiencing the trauma of homelessness. In the meantime, intervention approaches must recognize that healthy development depends on positive relationships.

REFERENCES

Bassuk, E. L., & Gallagher, E. M. (1990). The impact of homelessness on children. *Child and Youth Services, 14,* 19-33.

Bassuk, E., & Rubin, L. (1987). Homeless children: A neglected population. *American Journal of Orthopsychiatry, 57,* 279-286.

Berck, J. (1992). No places to be: Voices of homeless children. *Public Welfare, Spring,* 28-33.

Boxill, N. A., & Beaty, A. L. (1990). Mother/child interaction among homeless women and their children in a public night shelter in Atlanta, Georgia. *Child and Youth Services, 14,* 49-64.

Brody, G. H., Stoneman, Z., McCoy, J. K., & Forehand, R. (1992). Contemporaneous and longitudinal associations of sibling conflict with family relationship assessments and family discussions about sibling problems. *Child Development, 63,* 391-400.

Bruene-Butler, L., Hampson, J., Elias, M. J., Clabby, J. F., & Schuyler, T. (1997). The Improving Social Awareness-Social Problem Solving Project. In G. W. Albee & T. P. Gullotta (Eds.), (pp. 239-267). Thousand Oaks, CA: Sage.

Cairns, R. B., Cairns, B. D., & Neckerman, H. J. (1989). Early school dropout: Configurations and determinants. *Child Development, 60,* 1437-1452.

Coie, J. D., & Cillessen, A. H. N. (1993). Peer rejection: Origins and effects on children's development. *Current Directions in Psychological Science, 2,* 89-92.

Dail, P. (1990). The psychosocial context of homeless mothers with young children: Program and policy implications. *Child Welfare, 69,* 291-308.

Daniels, J. (1995). Homeless students: Recommendations to school counselors based on semistructured interviews. *The School Counselor, 42,* 346-352.

Davis, R. E. (1996). Tapping into the culture of homelessness. *Journal of Professional Nursing, 12,* 176-183.

Eddowes, E.A. (1992). Children and homelessness: Early childhood and elementary education. In J.H. Stronge (Ed), *Educating homeless children and adolescents: Evaluating policy and practice.* Newbury Park, CA: Sage.

Elias, M. J., & Clabby, J. F. (1989). *Social decision-making skills: A curriculum guide for the elementary grades.* Rockville, MD: Aspen Publishers.

Elias, M. J., & Clabby, J. F. (1992). *Building social problem-solving skills: Guidelines from a school-based program.* San Francisco: Jossey-Bass.

Gonzalez, M. L. (1990, June). School + home = A program for educating homeless students. *Phi Delta Kappan,* pp. 785-787.

Graham-Bermann, S. A., Coupet. (1996). Interpersonal relationships and adjustment of children in homeless and economically distressed families. *Journal of Clinical Child Psychology, 25,* 250-261.

Gresham, F. M., & Evans, S. E. (1987). Conceptualization and treatment of social withdrawal in the schools. *Special Services in the Schools, 3,* 37-51.

Halpern, R. (1992). The role of after-school programs in the lives of inner-city children: A study of the "Urban Youth Network." *Child Welfare, 71*, 215-230.

Hashima, P. Y., & Amato, P. R. (1994). Poverty, social support, and parental behavior. *Child Development, 65*, 394-403.

Hausman, B., & Hammen, C. (1993). Parenting in homeless families: The double crisis. Special section: Homeless women: Economic and social issues. *American Journal of Orthopsychiatry, 63*, 358-369.

Hetherington, E. M., & Martin, B. (1986). Family factions and psychopathology in children. In H. Quay & J. Werry (Eds.), *Psychopathological disorders of childhood (3rd ed.)* (pp. 332-390). New York: Wiley.

Horowitz, S. V., Springer, C. M., & Kose, G. (1988). Stress in hotel children: The effects of homelessness on attitudes toward school. *Children's Environments Quarterly, 5*, 34-36.

James, B. W., Lopez, P., Murdock, B., Rouse, J., & Walker, N. (1997). *Pieces of the puzzle: Creating successes for students in homeless situations.* Austin, TX: STAR Center.

Johnson, J. F. (1992). Educational support services for homeless children and youth. In J. H. Stronge (Ed.), *Educating homeless children and adolescents: Evaluating policy and practice* (pp. 153-176). New York: Sage.

Jones, W. H., & Carver, M. D. (1991). Adjustment and coping implications of loneliness. In C. R. Snyder & D. R. Forsyth (Eds.), *Handbook of social and clinical psychology: A health perspective* (pp. 395-415). New York: Pergamon Press.

Mickelson, R., & Yon, M. (1994-1995). The motivation of homeless children. *International Journal of Social Education, 9*, 28-45.

Moroz, K. J., & Segal, E. A. (1990). Homeless children: Intervention strategies for school social workers. *Social Work in Education*, pp. 134-143.

Ollendick, T. H., Weist, M. D., Borden, M. G., & Greene, R. W. (1992). Sociometric status and academic, behavioral, and psychological adjustment: A five-year longitudinal study. *Journal of Consulting and Clinical Psychology, 60*, 80-87.

Pedro-Carroll, J. (1997). The Children of Divorce Intervention Program: Fostering resilient outcomes for school-aged children. In G. W. Albee & T. P. Gullotta (Eds.), (pp. 213-238). Thousand Oaks, CA: Sage.

Posner, J. K., & Vandell, D. L. (1994). Low-income children's after-school care: Are there beneficial effects of after-school programs? *Child Development, 65*, 440-456.

Ramsey, P. G. (1991). *Making friends in school: Promoting peer relationships in early childhood.* New York: Teachers College Press.

Rutter, M. (1990). Psychosocial resilience and protective mechanisms. In J. Rolf, A. Masten, D. Cicchetti, K. Nuechterlein, & S. Weintraub (Eds.), *Risk and protective factors in the development of psychopathology* (pp. 181-215). Cambridge, England: Cambridge University Press.

Timberlake, E. M. (1994, August). Children with no place to call home: Survival in the cars and on the streets. *Child and Adolescent Social Work Journal, 11*(4), 259-278.

Tower, C. C. (1992). The psychosocial context: Supporting education for homeless children and youth. In J. H. Stronge (Ed.), *Educating homeless children and adolescents: Evaluating policy and practice* (pp. 42-61). New York: Sage.

Weissberg, R. P., Barton, H. A., & Shriver, T. P. (1997). The Social-Competence Promotion Program for Young Adolescents. In G. W. Albee & T. P. Gullotta (Eds.), (pp. 268-290). Thousand Oaks, CA: Sage.

Wright, J., & Lam, J. (1987). The low-income housing supply and the problem of homelessness. *Social Policy*, pp. 48-53.

ADDITIONAL RESOURCES

For information on Family Connection Support Group Facilitator Training, contact Rainbow Days, Inc., 8300 Douglas, #701, Dallas, TX 75225, (800) 899-7828.

For useful information on school programs for building social skills and social competence, see Bruene-Butler et al. (1997) and Weissberg et al. (1997) in the reference section.

For information and resources for awareness programs, contact the STAR Center at the Charles A. Dana Center, The University of Texas, 2901 North IH-35, Suite 3.200, Austin, TX 78722-2348, (512) 475-9702. Ask for the manual entitled *Pieces of the puzzle: Creating successes for students in homeless situations* ($50 with accompanying video).

The web site for the National Coalition for the Homeless (http://www2.ari.net/home/nch/wwwhome.html) is also an excellent source of materials for awareness programs.

ENDNOTES

[1]The PATHS Curriculum was designed for educators and counselors for use with elementary-school aged children. It can be obtained from Developmental Research and Programs, 130 Nickerson Street, Seattle, WA 98109 (1-800-736-2630; FAX 206-286-1462; ask for Sally Christie). Further information can be obtained from Mark Greenberg, Ph.D., Psychology, University of Washington, Seattle, WA 98195 (206-685-3927; FAX 206-685-3944; e-mail mgp@u.washington.edu).

[2]*Social Decision Making Skills: A Curriculum Guide for the Elementary Grades* (see Elias & Clabby, 1989) contains coordinated lesson materials and follow-through activities for the elementary grades. Additional information as well as an excellent review can be found in Bruene-Butler et al. (1997).

[3]SCPP-YA is a 45-session program with classroom-based instruction and environmental supports. Additional information can be found in Weissberg et al. (1997).

6

RESILIENCE AND HOMELESS STUDENTS: SUPPORTIVE ADULT ROLES

EVELYN REED-VICTOR

Attention Salem!
One nice family - Dad, Mom, Jared,
Casey and me are homeless.
That's why we live here.

We don't have enough money for a house yet.
Mom and Dad worry about this.
Me and Jared do too.
But not Casey. He's a baby.
Will someone help us?
P.S. We are nice. - Ryan, age 7[1]

INTRODUCTION

Most seven-year-olds in the United States take their housing for granted and have little idea about their parents' financial worries. But Ryan and his peers who are homeless experience uncertainties that are usually reserved for adults. Ryan asks for help and assures his anonymous readers that his family is nice. Children and youth who are anxious about their basic security need the warmth and reassurance of adults, particularly their family caregivers. And this becomes a great challenge for parents who are themselves struggling with the complexities of homelessness and its root causes.

Educators and community members who work with homeless children are concerned about supporting the vital role of families as protectors and providers for their children's basic physical and emotional needs. In numerous studies of children and youth who are resilient, caring adults provided the nurture, guidance, and advocacy that helped children bounce back from stressful and traumatic circumstances. In this chapter, adults' roles in fostering children's resilience will be reviewed in the context of homelessness and its diverse stressors. Family and staff concerns about homelessness will be summarized. In addition, promising practices will be detailed which: (1) build the role of family caregivers; (2) provide respite for children and family caregivers; and (3) create other avenues for securing adult support.

WHAT IS RESILIENCE?

In spite of high-risk situations, some children and adolescents appear to be resilient or adaptable (Felsman, 1989; Garmezy & Masten, 1991). The basic question about resilience is: "Why do some people collapse under pressure while others seem unscathed by traumatic circumstances such as severe illness, death of loved ones, and extreme poverty, or even by major catastrophes such as natural disasters and war?" (National Institute of Mental Health, 1995, p. 26). Developmental studies have identified protective processes within child, family, school, and community systems, which support the competence of children and youth who are challenged by various risk factors. Table 1 illustrates some of the factors that have been studied to address fundamental questions about resilience; these risk and protective factors are relevant in considering the stressors of homelessness for developing children and youth.

Resilience is a complex process because it involves patterns of stress, children's individual differences, environments that

TABLE 1. RISK, PROTECTION, AND OUTCOMES IN SELECTED
STUDIES[a]

Risk Factors	Protective Factors	Outcomes
Neighborhoods with high crime rates & limited economic resources	Family warmth High parental expectations & close monitoring	High academic achievement
High poverty neighborhoods	Caring school community	Student engagement Sense of belonging High academic achievement
Prematurity, low birth weight Low maternal education Poverty	Responsive & accepting caregiver Stimulating & organized care Safer & less crowded housing	Good health Cognitive & social/adaptive developmental gains in early childhood
Divorce	Child temperament Custodial parent's emotional stability	Positive adjustment
Perinatal stress Chronic poverty Disorganized family Low parental education	Child characteristics Warm caregiving Mentoring Growth opportunities Values-oriented organizations	Graduation Employment Life satisfaction Family stability in adulthood

[a] Baldwin et al., 1990; Battistich et al., 1995; Bradley et al., 1994; Heatherington et al., 1990; Werner & Smith, 1992

provide structure and opportunities, as well as ". . . the avail-ability of personal bonds and intimate relationships" (Rutter, 1979, p. 408). Through this developmental process, resilient children and youth develop problem-solving skills, sociability, responsibility, goal orientation, special interests, and positive self-appraisal. These characteristics help children and youth cope with major stressors, including health problems, poverty and limited resources, family instability, and trauma. Over time, resilient children and youth become "caring, competent, and confident adults" (Werner & Smith, 1992, p. 2).

HOW CAN ADULTS FOSTER RESILIENCE IN CHILDREN AND YOUTH?

Adults can be a central force in nurturing children's competence, through caring interactions, reliable guidance, great expectations, and active advocacy (Werner & Smith, 1992; Zimmerman & Arunkumar, 1994). Those who are a reliable source of nurture and caring build children's trust. They also model behavior, create access to knowledge, advocate for enlarged opportunities, teach competence, and encourage growth in facing challenges (Masten, 1994).

Through these roles, parents, other relatives, school staff, and community members can buffer the effects of stress and reduce children's unnecessary exposure to risk. The links from family relationships and school experiences are important for children's development of competence.

"In the early years, relationships with adults . . . form the infrastructure of development that supports all of what a child is asked to do in school—relate to other people, be persistent and focused, stay motivated to perform, be compliant-assertive, communicate, and explore the world . . . this . . . is transferred to the classroom—in relationships with teachers and in the challenges of classroom adjustment" (Pianta, 1999, p. 17).

HOW DOES HOMELESSNESS AFFECT FAMILIES' PROTECTIVE ROLES?

As detailed in chapters 1 through 4, homeless children and their families face complex and varied difficulties. The experience of homelessness includes a wide range of risks to healthy development including:

♦ health stressors (poor nutrition and health care, perinatal drug exposure);

♦ family circumstances (separation, poor education, unstable mental health);

♦ environmental stressors (high poverty, low resources); and

♦ trauma (accidents, violence). (Masten et al., 1993)

Increasing numbers of young mothers with children are homeless and face extreme poverty (Stronge, 1997); however, the characteristics of homeless families may vary significantly, in terms of size, composition, parents' ages, reason for homelessness, and other significant factors. For example, a parent who has moved her children to a shelter to flee a dangerous domestic situation may have both similar *and* different concerns than a family seeking shelter due to chronic financial distress. Likewise, very young "homeless mothers' overall youth and relative inexperience in managing the day-to-day obligations of money, family, and home complicate their route to self-sufficiency even further than does their lack of work experience" (Nunez, 1997, p. 95).

While their circumstances, needs, and resources may vary, homeless families face significant and complex stressors which complicate the day-to-day challenges of caregiving for their children. The impact of these stressors on children and youth also varies with their circumstances, as well as the characteristics of the children and youth themselves. For youth who have run away to escape family conflicts, their lack of protection or connectedness is profound and may lead to other destructive relationships.

FAMILY CONCERNS

In reviews of families' concerns about their homelessness, the following major concerns and underlying issues are frequently noted (see Table 2). Coping with these issues adds considerable emotional turmoil and insecurity to family rela-

TABLE 2. COMMON CONCERNS OF HOMELESS PARENTS[a]

Concern	Underlying Issue
Basic needs (food, shelter, clothing)	No extended family support
	Not aware of support programs and services
	Poor employment and housing prospects
	Lack of available shelter space
Family separation	Shelters may accept only males or only females
	Fear that children will be placed in foster care if parents can't provide for basic needs
Physical and emotional stress	No privacy in shelters
	No support in caregiving or problem solving
	Threats to safety (lack of shelter or protection from abuse)
Education of children	Transportation and enrollment problems
	Low self-confidence, lack of advocacy
	Unfamiliar with available supports

[a] Bassuk & Weinreb, 1994; Lewitt & Baker, 1996; Yon & Sebastien-Kadie, 1994

tionships. "Some children regress and manifest various behaviors that are attempts to cope with the stress of homelessness" (Bassuk & Weinreb, 1994, p. 39). Older children and youth usually find the disruption from familiar places and relationships distressing; they may also assume a parental role within the family if the adult is overwhelmed and providing little structure or support.

STAFF CONCERNS

Staff in school and community programs also express an array of concerns about children and youth who are homeless. In a survey of six programs in Virginia, staff members (teachers, counselors, social workers, tutors, and family development specialists) described concerns about their students (Reed-Victor & Stronge, 1997). These homeless education programs provided a wide range of services in different settings, including: shelter-based tutoring, school-based educational and social services, community preschools, domestic violence counseling, and comprehensive family services. Staff priorities for increasing support to specific homeless children and youth reflected significant student needs for adult encouragement, protection, structure, modeling, and advocacy. These same concerns have been voiced repeatedly in other locales by staff members, volunteers, and advocates for homeless children, youth, and their families. Although every homeless family's situation is unique, the needs of children and youth for an appropriate balance of adult support, structure, and advocacy are widespread.

HOW CAN THE FAMILY'S ROLE BE SUPPORTED?

Family-centered principles are particularly important in helping families address the realities of homelessness as well as the developmental needs of children and youth. Hanson and Carta (1996) identified the following approaches to supporting families with multiple risks:

1. emphasize family strengths;
2. use informal support systems;
3. focus on family-identified needs;
4. advocate for comprehensive services;
5. reduce bureaucratic barriers.

One of the first steps in this process is dialogue with families about their concerns, priorities, and resources. Initial plans based on the family's perspective help service providers focus their efforts and communicate their respect for the family's protective role. Secondly, a service coordinator can be identified based on the service needs and priorities of the family. Whether the coordinator is based in the shelter, school, or community, this staff member can help the parent identify resources and advocate for support services (including shelter and food, health care, school enrollment, employment, etc.). Although the service coordinator may initially take the lead in this process, the goal should be to support the parent's skills in identifying, accessing, and advocating for resources to meet the family's needs. Given the comprehensiveness and availability of necessary services, as well as existing bureaucratic complexities, families may need considerable and sustained support to establish a secure base.

Staff and volunteers working with homeless families can also acknowledge the efforts of parents to provide for and protect their children. The parent who has removed her children from an abusive situation or moved to a new location with the expectation of greater employment opportunities has acted in a protective way. Likewise, it is important for staff members to recognize the underlying commitment of parents to their children's education, which may be expressed as anger or frustration with the red tape of school enrollment. In this case, acknowledgment of concerns as well as modeling advocacy skills support parents' active roles. For parents who are overwhelmed, simple strategies can be used to encourage their participation in caregiving. For example, the parent's role as provider can be respected by active selection of children's clothes and school supplies from a supply closet. Teachers can also encourage parents' positive relationships with their children by emphasizing students' accomplishments and identifying other avenues for enrichment and expansion of their abilities (for example, through extracurricular activities). Many young mothers also benefit from the modeling and mentoring of experienced parents, whether they are shelter volunteers or staff members in formal parenting education programs. When family relationships are strained by the stress of homelessness, opportunities to observe, practice, and receive feedback about caregiving are valuable.

Caring and respectful interactions may be the most important way to encourage parents' participation in educational opportunities for themselves and their children. Quint's (1994) case study of B.F. Day Elementary School documents a dynamic school program for homeless children. A grandparent described the effectiveness of the school's welcoming atmosphere:

> The very first time I walked through the doors of this school, I knew something was different—I mean different. People actually smiled at you and asked if they could be of assistance . . . I felt so relieved at the end of the first day at the school because I thought, "Finally, someone is there to help me get help." (Quint, 1994, p. 85)

HOW CAN OTHER ADULTS ACTIVELY SUPPORT HOMELESS CHILDREN AND YOUTH?

While homeless parents or adult guardians tackle the complex issues of securing resources for basic needs, other adults in schools and communities can encourage children's development through meaningful relationships based on support, structure, and advocacy. Their relationships may develop in the context of the classroom, school enrichment activities, shelter-based tutoring, childcare, job coaching, community mentoring, recreation programs, or religious organizations. The availability and quality of these relationships among adults and children is fundamental to promoting long-term competence (Pianta & Walsh, 1996; Wang & Gordon, 1994).

SCHOOL-BASED ROLES

Numerous members of the school community play significant roles in welcoming homeless students into the school community (Reed-Victor & Pelco, 1999).

From the outset, office staff and bus drivers are important in welcoming students and families during enrollment and transition into school. In these roles, they are essential as communicators of the school's commitment to including homeless students and as initiators of vital services. School psychologists and counselors can provide support to students, families, and staff through consultation, expedited evaluations, counseling, and coordination among team members. Likewise, the specialized knowledge and community resources available through school nurses and social workers can address significant family, housing, employment, and health concerns that accompany homelessness. Leadership from principals and other administrators is also critical in developing school-based plans for the allocation, coordination, and evaluation of resources to fully meet the needs of children and adolescents who are homeless.

Within most school communities, other families and community volunteers contribute valuable time, expertise, and materials through mentoring programs and emergency supplies to meet specific physical, social-emotional, and educational concerns. Overall, the effectiveness of their efforts is enhanced by their awareness of the realities of homeless students' situations, their compassionate responses, and their coordination of comprehensive supports.

While these staff and volunteers play important roles, teachers may have the most frequent and intensive contact with students who are homeless. The quality of classroom interactions can enhance students' sense of worth, their trust in adults, and their interaction with peers. Teachers model competent behavior and coach student competence through guidance and constructive feedback. Such coaching entails advising students about avoiding pitfalls and bolstering students' confidence in meeting challenges (Masten, 1994). Teachers who carefully scaffold students' learning provide a balance of support, challenge, and autonomy within teaching-learning exchanges. These learning experiences promote students' problem solving, resourcefulness, confidence, and sociability—important factors in coping with stress.

COMMUNITY-BASED ROLES

Likewise, adults in many community programs can have similar roles in the lives of homeless children and youth. Community programs provide increased opportunities for high-quality relationships with adults who are mentors, religious leaders, coaches, counselors, and tutors (Werner & Smith, 1994). Community organizations also serve a protective role through increased resources (physical, social, emotional, recreational), as well as structure through organizational values and activities. The enhancement of family economic stability, through community work, educational and housing opportunities, plays a significant role in promoting child resilience (McLoyd, 1998). In addition, adequate and accessible community services (police and fire protection, medical facilities, family support services) protect the safety, health, and caregiving functions of families as well as children and adolescents' emotional well-being (Taylor, 1997). Through tutoring and other cooperative school projects, community libraries, youth organizations, and civic groups support students' school achievement, community involvement, and self-development (Freiberg, 1994; McLaughlin, Irby & Langman, 1994).

CONCLUSION

As school and community groups plan and implement programs to support families who are homeless, several approaches are recommended: (1) increase the use of existing programs that focus on enhancing competence; and (2) include resilience-oriented principles in existing or new programs. In Table 3, several programs are highlighted to illustrate promising practices that enhance the competence of homeless children, adolescents, and their caregivers.

Throughout this book, many other promising practices are identified that support the competence of children, youth, and families who are homeless. There is clearly not one "solution" to the complex and difficult experiences of homelessness, nor is there a single intervention that promotes resilience. Nevertheless, there are caring adults within families, schools, and communities who can:

♦ respond sensitively to the considerable needs that accompany homelessness;

♦ model problem solving and constructive interactions;

♦ nurture interests, talents, and self-development; and

♦ advocate for integrated, comprehensive supports.

TABLE 3. PROMISING SCHOOL AND COMMUNITY PROGRAMS

Programs	Program Components	Protective Features
Knock on Every Door & Kidstart Georgetown University Washington, DC	Contacts in transient housing & shelters Developmental screening & assessment Family-centered service coordination	Reduced barriers to services Early & preventive services for homeless infants & preschoolers Greater access to services
B.F. Day Elementary School Seattle, Washington	School reform based on needs of homeless students Curricular focus on problem solving & support Integrated service goals (academic, health, housing) Partnerships among staff, families, & community	Supportive classroom & mentoring relationships Comprehensive services Strong staff & family roles in program governance Structure based on shared values Increased expertise & resources (university, business, agency)
Brownsville Cultural Academy Brownsville, Texas	Summer program for homeless & non-homeless youth Integrated academic, cultural & recreational emphasis High interest activities (sailing, computer, horseback riding) Native American focus (drumming, mural creations)	Meaningful, structured activities Integrated learning and extended interests Engaging & challenging activities with mentors & peers Cultural identity affirmed

These adults—whether family members, teachers, counselors, nurses, coaches, youth advocates, community mentors, or volunteer tutors—are important protective forces in supporting the resilience of homeless children and youth.

REFERENCES

Baldwin, A. L., Baldwin, C., & Cole, R. E. (1990). Stress-resistant families and stress-resistant children. In J. Rolf, A.S. Masten, D. Cicchetti, K.H. Nuechterlein, & S. Weintraub (Eds.), *Risk and protective factors in the development of psychopathology* (pp. 257-280). New York: Cambridge University Press.

Bassuk, E.L. & Weinreb, L. (1994). The plight of homeless children. In J. Blacher (Ed.), *When there's no place like home*. Baltimore: Paul H. Brookes.

Battistich, V., Solomon, D., Kim, D., Watson, M., & Schaps, E. (1995). Schools as communities, poverty levels of student populations, and students' attitudes, motives, and performance: A multilevel analysis. *American Educational Research Journal, 32*, 627-658.

Bradley, R. H., Whiteside, L., Mundfrom, D. J., Casey, P. H., Kelleher, K. J., & Pope, S. K. (1994). Early indications of resilience and their relation to experiences in the home environments of low birth weight, premature children living in poverty. *Child Development, 65*, 346-360.

Felsman, J. K. (1989). Risk and resiliency in childhood: The lives of street children. In T. F. Dugan & R. Coles (Eds.), *The child in our times: Studies in the development of resiliency* (pp. 56-80). New York: Brunner/Mazel.

Freiberg, H. J. (1994). Understanding resilience: Implications for inner-city schools and their near and far communities. In M. C. Wang & E. Gordon (Eds.), *Educational resilience in inner-city America: Challenges and prospects* (pp. 151-165). Hillsdale, NJ: Erlbaum.

Garmezy, N., & Masten, A. (1991). The protective role of competence indicators in children at risk. In E. M. Cummings, A. L. Greene, & K. H. Karraker (Eds.), *Life-span developmental psychology: Perspectives on stress and coping* (pp. 151-174). Hillsdale, NJ: Erlbaum.

Hanson, M. J., & Carta, J. J. (1996). Addressing the challenges of families with multiple risks. *Exceptional Children, 62*, 201-212.

Heatherington, E. M., Stanley-Hogan, M., & Anderson, E. R. (1989). Marital transitions: A child's perspective. *American Psychologist, 44*, 303-312.

Lewitt, E.M. & Baker, L.S. (1996). Homeless families and children. *Future of Children, 6* (2), 146-158.

Masten, A. S. (1994). Resilience in individual development: Successful adaptation despite risk and adversity. In M. C. Wang & E. Gordon (Eds.), *Educational resilience in inner-city America: Challenges and prospects* (pp. 3-25). Hillsdale, NJ: Erlbaum.

Masten, A. S., Miliotis, D., Graham-Bermann, S. A., Ramirez, M., & Neeman, J. (1993). Children in homeless families: Risks to mental health and development. *Journal of Consulting and Clinical Psychology, 61*(2), 335-343.

McLaughlin, M. W., Irby, M. A., & Langman, J. (1994). *Urban sanctuaries: Neighborhood organizations in the lives and futures of inner-city youth.* San Francisco: Jossey-Bass.

McLoyd, V. C. (1998). Socioeconomic disadvantaged and child development. *American Psychologist, 53*(2), 185-204.

National Institute of Mental Health. (1995). *Behavioral science research for mental health: A national investment* (DHHS Publication No. 95-3682). Washington, DC: U.S. Government Printing Office.

Nunez, R. D. (1997). Why jobs and training alone won't end welfare for homeless families. *Journal of Children in Poverty, 3*(1), 93 -101.

Pianta, R. (1999). *Enhancing relationships between children and teachers.* Washington, DC: APA.

Pianta, R. & Walsh, D.J. (1996). *High-risk children in schools: Constructing sustaining relationships.* New York: Routledge.

Quint, S. (1994). *Schooling homeless children: A working model for America's public schools.* New York: Teachers College Press.

Reed-Victor, E. & Pelco, L. E. (1999). Helping homeless students build resilience: What the school community can do. *Journal for a Just and Caring Education, 5* (1), 51-71.

Reed-Victor, E., & Stronge, J. H. (1997). *The resilience paradigm: A model for building integrated supports across school, home and community borders for homeless education programs.* Paper presented at the University Council of Educational Administration Conference, Orlando, FL.

Rutter, M. (1979). Temperament: Conceptual issues and clinical implications. *American Journal of Orthopsychiatry, 57*, 316-331.

Stronge, J. H. (1977). A long road ahead: A progress report on educating homeless children and youth in America. *Journal of Children and Poverty, 3*(2), 13-31.

Taylor, R. D. (1997). The effects of economic and social stressors on parenting and adolescent development in African-American families. In R. D. Taylor & M. C. Wang (Eds.), *Social and emotional adjustment and family relations in ethnic minority families.* Mahwah, NJ: Erlbaum.

Wang, M. C. & Gordon, E. (1994) *Educational resilience in inner-city America: Challenges and prospects.* Hillsdale, NJ: Erlbaum.

Werner, E. E., & Smith, R. S. (1992). *Overcoming the odds: High risk children from birth to adulthood.* Ithaca, NY: Cornell University Press.

Yon, M., & Sebastien-Kadie, M. (1994). Homeless parents and the education of their children. *The School Community Journal, 4*(2), 67-77.

Zimmerman, M., & Arunkumar, R. (1994). Resiliency research: Implications for schools and policy. *Social Policy Report of the Society for Research in Child Development, 8*(4).

ADDITIONAL RESOURCES

Geller, S. R. (1998). *Al's Pals: Kids Making Healthy Choices.* Richmond, VA: Virginia Commonwealth University. This resilience-based curriculum for young children (complete with puppets, music, and photographs) has been effective in developing children's social skills and other traits related to resilience. *Here, Now and Down the Road . . . Tips for Loving Parents* is a companion parent education series to help parents support their children's resilience. Materials are available only with accompanying training for teachers and parent educators. Contact: Susan Geller, Wingspan, P.O. Box 29070, Richmond, VA 23242; (804)754-0100.

Masten, A. S. (1994). Resilience in individual development: Successful adaptation despite risk and adversity. In M. C. Wang & E. Gordon (Eds.), *Educational resilience in inner-city America: Challenges and prospects* (pp. 3-25). Hillsdale, NJ: Lawrence Erlbaum. (365 Broadway, Hillsdale, New Jersey 07642). In this chapter, Dr. Masten provides a helpful summary of resilience research, with an emphasis on the role of adults in fostering competence.

Quint, S. (1994). *Schooling homeless children: A working model for America's public schools.* New York: Teachers College Press. This book describes the responsive programs developed at B.F. Day Elementary School to support homeless children and their families in a Seattle neighborhood.

Taylor, T. D., & Brown, M.C. (1996). *Young children and their families who are homeless.* Washington, DC: Georgetown University Child Development Center. (Center for Child Health and Mental Health Policy, 3307 M Street, NW, Suite 401, Washington, DC 20007-3935. 202-687-8807.) This publication describes the Knock on Every Door program and provides case studies of two families.

ENDNOTES

[1]Salem Kaiser Public Schools, 1996

7

SUPPORTING FAMILY LEARNING: BUILDING A COMMUNITY OF LEARNERS

RALPH DA COSTA NUNEZ AND KATE COLLIGNON

Most children are born with the greatest teachers they will ever know: their parents. Yet homeless children, in addition to facing logistical and emotional obstacles to education, frequently find themselves lacking a parent's critical educational support. Parents who are in shelters or moving between doubled-up housing situations are overwhelmed by the conditions of deep poverty and homelessness, and are distracted from their children's education. Equally detrimental to their ability to provide support is homeless parents' own limited education, alienating them from school involvement and impeding them from achieving residential stability.

So long as parents remain unable to support their children's education, specialized programs for homeless children can make only a limited difference. The surest way to support homeless children's education is to support their parents. To ensure that education does not stop once children walk out of the classroom door, schools and homeless service providers have developed "communities of learning." These communities provide:

◆ education for homeless children;

◆ family support services; and

◆ education for homeless parents.

This chapter offers a guide for developing the adult education and family support components of communities of learning,
and for linking these with children's education. As should be
clear from the examples presented here, there is no "correct"
model of communities of learning. Instead, implementation of
this concept of integrated education and support services for
homeless families can and should vary dramatically depending, on local resources and needs. By broadening their vision
beyond education for children, educators and service providers
alike can learn from this guide to break cycles of poverty and
homelessness and ensure a future of success for the thousands
of children and families who are homeless today.

PARENT INVOLVEMENT IN CHILDREN'S EDUCATION: ROLES AND CHALLENGES FOR HOMELESS FAMILIES

WHAT ROLES DO PARENTS PLAY IN THEIR CHILDREN'S EDUCATION?

School is where children go to learn. Every teacher knows,
however, that the success or failure of his/her greatest lesson is
dependent on how that lesson is supported at home, within the
family. Parents play three roles in their children's education:
nurturers, teachers and advocates (Kellaghan, Sloane, Alvarez,
& Bloom, 1993; Maeroff, 1992; Rutherford, Anderson, & Billig,
1997). Fulfillment of all three of these roles ensures that children
focus on, excel in, and have access to school.

Parents as Nurturers. Children cannot concentrate and perform well in school unless they feel well themselves. To feel well,
children need to eat enough nutritious food, get enough sleep,
and maintain good health through regular visits to the doctor.
Their physical well-being also extends to their emotional need

to feel safe, secure, and confident. Children depend on their parents to provide for these physical and emotional needs.

In addition to providing this day-to-day nourishment, parents are responsible for nourishing their children's dreams and the values that help them achieve those dreams. The value of education and school achievement is critical among these; without it, children have little incentive to pursue success in the classroom or to complete the education that enables them to become independent adults. Parents nurture their children's value of education by fulfilling their roles as teachers and advocates.

Parents as Teachers. It has often been said that parents are their children's first teachers. Even before they speak their first word, children look to their parents for clues to learning. As they grow, this learning assistance takes two forms. Parents first assist learning through day-to-day activities, such as engaging children in stimulating conversation, answering children's questions about the world, and reading with them at bedtime. The second form of learning assistance that parents provide involves formal reinforcement of school lessons at home by asking about and discussing what children are studying in school, providing homework help, and even simply making sure homework gets completed.

Parents as Advocates. In addition to nurturing and teaching their children, parents advocate for their children's education by making sure they have access to school and that in-school education is meeting the individual needs of their sons and daughters. Parents' role in ensuring school access encompasses first enrolling their children, and then making sure they get to class every day. Parental advocacy for educational quality begins with efforts to meet their children's teachers to discuss student strengths and problems, as well as how those strengths and problems are addressed within the classroom and at home. Finally, parents advocate more directly for quality in school by volunteering within their children's classrooms, and becoming involved in school decision making through participation in the PTA.

WHAT PREVENTS HOMELESS PARENTS FROM ASSUMING THEIR EDUCATIONAL ROLES?

A variety of factors prevent homeless parents from fully assuming their roles as nurturers, teachers, and advocates for their children's education. These factors both contribute to homelessness and result from its conditions.

Distractions of Homelessness. Homeless parents are discouraged by the same fundamental concerns that distract their children from learning—concerns that are heightened by a parent's additional responsibility for the welfare of her children. Parents in poverty constantly worry about whether their families will have enough to eat or a place to sleep each night. This lack of basic needs satisfaction is compounded by an abundance of other ongoing problems, which frequently lie at the origins of families' homelessness. Sixty-three percent of parents in shelters have a history of family violence as adults, and between 9 and 30 percent report domestic violence as the immediate cause of their current episode of homelessness (Chicago Department of Human Services, 1995; Institute for Children and Poverty [ICP], 1998a). An estimated 38 percent of homeless parents have ongoing drug and alcohol abuse problems, and as many as 71 percent have a history of substance abuse (Mayor's Homeless Budget Advisory Task Force, 1994; Nunez, 1996). All of these issues ultimately force homeless parents into a constant crisis mode—always thinking in terms of their family's short-range needs and fears, rather than the steps necessary to achieve long-term goals. Often, this occurs at the expense of less immediately pressing responsibilities, such as getting children to school every morning or making sure that they do their homework.

Limited Educational Preparation. Even if food and housing crises, domestic violence, and substance abuse did not distract homeless parents, most are ill-prepared by their own education to take on their children's. Between one-third and two-thirds of homeless parents never completed high school (ICP, 1998b; Nunez, 1996). Many also lack basic literacy skills, whether or not they have their diploma (Drury & Koloski, 1995; ICP, 1998a; Nunez, 1996). This limited preparation presents three significant obstacles for parents attempting to take on their roles as their children's educational nurturers, teachers, and advocates:

1. *Low skill levels.* Parents who lack basic literacy and math skills have difficulty reading to their children, assisting their children in their schoolwork, or otherwise supporting school lessons.

2. *Educational alienation.* Parents who lack confidence in their own education, or associate their own educational experiences with a sense of failure or dissatisfaction with school, are frequently hesitant to get involved in their children's education. Even if they do have the basic skills they need, parents can be so self-conscious about their own education that they avoid reading with their children and are too intimidated to meet with their children's teachers.

3. *Family instability.* In today's job market, parents who lack a high school diploma or basic literacy skills cannot find work that pays enough to provide for their family's basic needs and to regain stability. Until their families achieve this stability, homeless children will continue to face educational challenges.

BUILDING A COMMUNITY OF LEARNING: HELPING HOMELESS PARENTS TO HELP THEIR CHILDREN SUCCEED

To overcome the obstacles to homeless children's success, educators and service providers must pave the way to parent education, stability and involvement. Model programs have responded by combining the educational expertise of schools with the experience and services of shelters and community-based organizations to develop communities of learning.

Communities of learning link education for parents and support services for the whole family into education programs for children. This coordination facilitates the ultimate goal of communities of learning: to immerse families in an educational environment with the support they need to make education a whole-family activity. Communities of learning provide an environment packed with supportive educators and peers who are working their way through the same challenges that homeless participants face. Here children can pursue their education while witnessing their parents embracing learning as well and families can focus on the future together.

WHAT DOES "FAMILY SUPPORT" INCLUDE?

Homeless parents cannot be expected to make education for themselves or their children a priority so long as they must continue to worry about whether they will have enough food for the day or when an abuser will resurface. To pave the way to the stability necessary to enable a family to focus on education, communities of learning attend to not only the educational needs of parents and children, but also the other issues that affect their lives, including basic and special needs.

Providing for Basic Needs. Homeless shelters and community-based services have traditionally provided for these basic needs. Both the American Family Inn and the Center for the Homeless provide food services on site, as well as access to emergency clothing supplies, while families reside in apartment-style accommodations until they find permanent housing. While schools are less accustomed to providing for these needs, food boxes, clothing, and housing referrals can become a regular part of day-to-day school activities through appeals to and partnerships with local agencies. SKHP's Homebase Project, for example, established a link to Salem's Emergency Housing Network at the Capitol Inn in order to assist families looking for more stable housing situations.

Health Care. The majority of schools already maintain nurse services on site (Dryfoos, 1994). This medical attention, however, is available only for schoolchildren. Cooperative agreements with local hospitals and medical groups, and especially medical training programs, offer medical services—including general health, immunizations, dental, and prenatal care—to children and parents participating in school, shelter, or community-based communities of learning.

Meeting Mental Health Needs. In some instances, collaboration with community organizations makes it possible to provide specialized services on site at communities of learning. At the American Family Inns, substance abuse treatment is provided at the shelters through an agreement with Camelot and Phoenix House, two local treatment programs. Where on-site specialized services are not possible, basic counseling can give parents and children the opportunity to discuss personal concerns, and receive referrals to quality caregivers. Turning Point provides this basic counseling, as well as mental health assessments, for residents of the Center for the Homeless. Adults in need of treatment for mental illness or substance abuse are then referred to the nearby Madison Center, through yet another cooperative agreement. Finally, issues of domestic violence and substance abuse can be addressed more generally among participants in communities of learning, whether or not these problems have yet been identified, by integrating discussion into the regular educational curriculum.

WHAT DOES "PARENT EDUCATION" INCLUDE?

Limited education among homeless parents constrains critical involvement in their children's education, as well as their options for leaving poverty and homelessness behind. Wherever possible, communities of learning offer parents a continuum of educational programs to meet multiple needs. This continuum incorporates:

♦ literacy;

♦ adult basic education;

♦ General Equivalency Diploma (GED) preparation;

♦ referrals to higher education;

♦ job training and placement; and

♦ life skills training.

In providing any or all of the components of the educational continuum, it is important to remember that homelessness and poverty affect a parent's ability to participate in adult education and the curricular content required for their retention within a program. To achieve success, adult educational curricula for homeless parents must be:

♦ relevant to a parent's day-to-day life;

♦ provided in a non-traditional one-on-one or workshop format (anything to avoid negative associations with previous classroom-based educational experiences);

♦ basic enough to help those with even the lowest literacy skills;

♦ flexible to accommodate unpredictable participation rates resulting from frequent moves and erratic schedules; and

♦ offered in conjunction with transportation and childcare to overcome logistical barriers to participation.

Linking Education with Day-to-Day Life. Before any education program can assist homeless parents, it must first capture their interest and make them feel comfortable enough to get involved. One method is by providing an entry into education via doors less visibly marked "school." Many homeless parents, whether or not they have a need or feel a need for continuing education, want assistance to strengthen the basic skills they will use to care for their families in permanent housing. These "life skills" include:

♦ parenting;

♦ health and nutrition;

♦ stress and time management;

♦ budgeting;

♦ housing and apartment maintenance;

♦ accessing community resources; and

♦ coping with domestic violence and substance abuse.

Independent workshops on life skills familiarize parents with education staff and help parents to gain confidence in their ability to succeed within an educational environment.

Provision of separate life skills workshops draws parents into the educational process. The incorporation and reinforcement of these concepts within other education programs also maintain parent interest by keeping sometimes esoteric academic lessons relevant to daily lives, and further strengthen the skills on which families most depend. The literacy programs at the Center for the Homeless and the American Family Inns, for example, strengthen skills by reading materials that parents come across every day, such as the ingredients on the back of a cereal box, or the details of a lease. The job-training program at the American Family Inns incorporates life skills by emphasizing not just job skills development, but also more basic job readiness issues such as reading the want ads, preparing resumes, and writing thank-you letters.

Making Parents Comfortable. The success of any education program for parents who are homeless is contingent upon its provision in a non-traditional atmosphere, as well as acknowledgment that many parents will bring to the program very low literacy levels. Replication of the school environment is not an objective of any education program targeting adults who once made the decision to leave school. Instead of lectures, interactive group activities or workshop formats involve parents more directly in the ideas and skills presented, and avoid negative associations with previous school experiences. Handouts geared toward a sixth grade literacy level also make it possible for parents of all educational backgrounds to feel successful in their participation, rather than exacerbating the feelings of frustration and failure frequent among adults who have difficulty reading. Education programs that must require minimum literacy levels for graduation, such as GED and job skills training programs, create ladders to participation by linking parents with literacy classes.

Breaking Down Barriers to Participation. Once parents are attending and excited about education programs, the logistical obstacles to participation that arise from their lives as homeless parents threaten to prevent ongoing involvement. The search for housing and employment demands attention from homeless parents during the day, and the needs of their children occupy their energies in the evenings. Even if they have the time to participate, homeless parents lack extra money to spend on transportation to programs located at any distance from their temporary residences. In addition, frequent moves between doubled-up housing situations and shelters, as well as final moves from shelters to permanent housing, pose obstacles to ongoing participation, threatening to eliminate the sense of completion and achievement these programs ideally impart to their students.

Flexibility in program length and duration, as well as the availability of childcare, shuttle services, or public transit vouchers, make it possible for homeless parents to manage the demands of their lives and simultaneously build for their families' futures. The need for brief program cycles frequently calls for modification of pre-existing curriculum in order to work with homeless parents. As part of SKHP's services for parents, for example, staff trained by the Red Cross to teach disaster preparedness, HIV prevention, first aide, and babysitting classes come to the Capitol Inn and shelters around the area to provide skills training for parents and youth. To accommodate the rapid mobility of the homeless parents, the training program—first developed to work with the general population—has been condensed from its original daily class structure provided over four weeks to a few full-day Saturday classes. Accessibility to programs for which the curriculum cannot be shortened—such as the work skills and internship component of the job readiness and training program at the American Family Inns—is facilitated by their provision in brief time periods, supplemented by childcare.

HOW CAN FAMILY SUPPORT AND ADULT EDUCATION BE LINKED WITH CHILDREN'S EDUCATION?

Availability of family support, adult and children's education for homeless families does not in itself create a community of learning. These programs do not form a community, nor achieve their highest benefit individually, unless the three components are intertwined. It is this integration that most facilitates whole—family involvement, and helps homeless families come to view education as a joint parent/child venture. The following three suggestions—two general and one quite specific—help bring out the "community" in communities of learning.

Co-location. Location of child and adult education programs and family support services at one site offers dramatic advantages for recruitment, retention and community-building. Co-location of the three components, particularly in schools or shelters:

♦ increases the visibility of additional components for families already participating in one (such as children's education at school or family supports at shelters);

♦ heightens staff recognition, overcoming fears of becoming involved with yet another unfamiliar program; and

♦ reduces transit needs between multiple locations.

All of these benefits together increase opportunities for recruitment and retention. Co-location of these programs also builds community among participants, who see each other in hallways and discuss experiences with different education and service programs, providing yet another recruitment incentive in the form of peer pressure and information. Perhaps most importantly, the hallway visibility of parent and child educators helps parents and children recognize their joint educational project, and develop a united educational goal.

Staff Communication. Internal and interagency communication between staff providing education and support services to homeless children and parents can overcome many of the hurdles to establishing effective communities of learning. Scheduling conflicts need not prevent families from accessing the programs they need if staff check with each other before finalizing times and dates. Even more important, communication between educators and service providers, child and adult program providers prevents critical information about family needs from falling through programmatic cracks. Educators working with children who discover a history of domestic violence, for example, can help parents and children access appropriate services. Issues of client confidentiality necessarily limit the specific information that can be shared among staff members. However, even at its most general, staff communication can improve family access to necessary programs, as well as the appropriateness of education and support programs offered within communities of learning.

Family Literacy. Perhaps one of the most effective links between the multiple components of communities of learning can derive from implementation of a family literacy program (Brizius & Foster, 1993). Family literacy programs are comprised of three elements: adult literacy training, basic skill building workshops, and parent/child activity time. Each of these pieces, except for the parent/child time, would already be included in a community of learning following the guidelines presented above. It is this parent/child time, however, that brings literacy to the entire family. Parent/child time in family literacy programs provides homeless parents and children with a safe place to read, play or participate in organized educational activities together. In this non-threatening environment, with guidance from supervising staff, parents working on their own literacy skills become more comfortable sitting down with their children to read. Most importantly, children have the full attention of their parents—a rare event in the chaotic life of a homeless family—and witness their parents' involvement in educational activities. Indeed, many family literacy programs invite children to participate in parent/child time even without their parents, with an eye toward increasing overall recruitment; children who see their friends reading and playing with their parents pester their own parents to participate. Once they attend, parents are then drawn into the more formal educational aspects of family literacy, and referred to support services as necessary.

HOW CAN I ESTABLISH A COMMUNITY OF LEARNING? ADDRESSING THE BASICS

A community of learning is a *concept* as opposed to a specific *program*. Indeed, its three components can be integrated in any number of ways. Before beginning to build a community of learning, organizations must first answer the following interrelated questions for themselves.

WHO WILL PROVIDE AND COORDINATE SERVICES?

Who will be responsible for providing each of the education and support services, and who will take responsibility for coordinating them? Schools, shelters, and community-based non-profits have all successfully served as lead agencies within communities of learning, although full collaborative decision making has been identified by many researchers as the ideal toward which communities of learning should aspire (Center for the Future of Children, 1992; Dryfoos, 1994). Indeed, a collaborative approach makes the greatest use of community expertise and resources. In fact, it is critical that every community of learning, no matter what its scope or design may be, collaborate with the public school system to some degree in order to prevent homeless children from being isolated from the educational mainstream.

WHERE WILL THE COMMUNITY OF LEARNING BE LOCATED?

Education and family support services can be centralized in a single site, linked through referrals, or both (see Table 1). Each variation offers advantages and disadvantages, all related to the specific sites selected. Referral systems enable families to gain access to the community of learning from multiple entryways. However, it is easy for the collaboration within such networks to remain limited to referrals, as opposed to developing into any identifiable community. Families also may be hesitant to take advantage of multiple referrals due to the logistical obstacles to traveling between locations and the intimidation associated with becoming familiar with a new agency.

Centralized services offer significant advantages for recruitment and referral, as mentioned above. Location at homeless shelters eliminates transportation issues for residents, and facilitates community development as residents and staff members get to know each other outside of the specific program in which they are involved. Centralized services within schools also offer

TABLE 1. THE ADVANTAGES OF DIFFERENT LOCATIONS FOR
COMMUNITIES OF LEARNING

Location	Advantages
Centralized in homeless shelter	Facilitates development of "community" among staff and residents
	Promotes coordination between programs and components of community of learning
	Overcomes transportation barriers
	Aids recruitment between programs
Centralized in school	Promotes coordination between programs and components of community of learning
	Overcomes transportation barriers
	Aids recruitment of families not yet in shelter
	Prevents isolation of homeless families
	Makes use of space available in schools after regular school hours
Scattered site (across multiple agencies), linked through referral	Provides multiple gateways to entry into community of learning

advantages for recruitment and success. Schools are the most
visible institution in every community, and one to which every
family is already connected. What is more, school facilities often remain unused after school hours, providing ready space
for provision of adult education programs. Perhaps most im-

portantly, schools work with all children, whether or not they are identified as homeless, facilitating a non-stigmatic, preventive focus within communities of learning for homeless families, instead of responding once crises already have led to homelessness.

Space and funding limitations in general, however, frequently make centralized services impossible, particularly in the early development stages of communities of learning. As a result, the most common form of education and service provision is partial centralization, supplemented with off-site referrals to specialized services.

WHO COULD PARTICIPATE?

Communities of learning for homeless families need not restrict participants to families in shelters. While a narrow program focus offers advantages in location, scheduling, and coordination, it also can limit the ultimate impact of a program. Families moving between doubled-up housing situations but not yet in a shelter have the same needs as officially homeless families, but have even less access to education and support services. What is more, there are many families who may still be in stable housing but are grappling with their own educational, domestic violence, and substance abuse problems—problems that may ultimately result in homelessness without access to preventive services. School-based communities of learning that open their doors to all families in need reach out to these often overlooked segments of the homeless and near-homeless; remove the stigma of the label "homeless" from participants; and increase opportunities for broad-based community support and funding.

LAYING THE GROUNDWORK: COLLABORATION, COLLABORATION, COLLABORATION

The key to developing successful communities of learning of any kind lies in collaboration between schools, shelters, and community-based agencies. In almost every local community, *somebody* is already providing the education and support services that, when integrated, form communities of learning. Attempts to duplicate such services waste valuable resources in both expertise and funding. Collaboration enables local communities to maximize their resources to best serve homeless families.

Collaboration is a gradual process, dependent on the resources and interests of the collaborating agencies. In general, however, there are four basic steps to follow:

1. Identify existing resources and expertise within the community.

2. Develop an information-sharing relationship between schools and these organizations.

3. Update administrators of schools, shelters, and other service-providing agencies on progress and developments within programs to ensure that they are complementary, not conflicting.

4. Collaborate toward coordinated services.

The ultimate goal of this collaboration is seamless integration of children's education, adult education, and support services, making full use of school, shelter, and local expert resources to establish effective communities of learning. Such close coordination between the multiple components of communities of learning increases the likelihood that once a single family member becomes involved in a single aspect, the entire family can be drawn into all three: children's education, adult education, and support services. Thus, educators and service providers alike can ensure that homeless children receive the educational assistance they need whether or not they have turned to the shelters, and that their families receive the assistance they need to move beyond the problems that threatened children's education in the first place.

AN OPPORTUNITY FOR TODAY AND THE FUTURE

Homeless children need special educational attention both in school and in shelters. This attention can have the most thorough and far-reaching impact if it includes the whole family. Through collaboration with area-wide school, shelter, and community-based resources, communities of learning attend to the whole family by integrating parent education and family support services with education for children.

The vision of comprehensive communities of learning in their entirety can be a daunting one, in part because of its flexible nature. The steps along the way to that vision, however, should be familiar to educators and service providers alike. Outreach to parents, basic casework and service referrals, and communication between schools and service providers are efforts made daily by hundreds, if not thousands, of programs across the country. These efforts are the gateway to communities of learning, and the starting line from which many of the examples presented here began. Individual educators and service providers who persist in placing one foot in front of the other, no matter how slowly, can help change the life of a child.

The blueprint for communities of learning is the collaborative product of multiple programs from across the country. These programs have turned the challenge of educating homeless children into an opportunity to make a difference for an entire family. Service providers and educators must seize this opportunity today by building from these blueprints. This is an opportunity for the future of homeless children.

REFERENCES

Center for the Future of Children. (1992). School-linked services. *The Future of Children 1*, (2). Los Altos, CA: Author, The David and Lucille Packard Foundation.

Chicago Department of Human Services. (1995). *Chicago consolidated plan*. Chicago: Author.

Children's Aid Society. (1993). *Building a community school: A revolutionary design in public education*. New York, NY: Author.

Drury, D., and Koloski, J. (1995). *Learning to hope: A study of the Adult Education for the Homeless Program*. Washington, DC: U.S. Department of Education.

Dryfoos, J. (1994). *Full-service schools: A revolution in health and social services for children, youth, and families*. San Francisco: Jossey-Bass.

Institute for Children and Poverty. (1998a). *The cycle of family homelessness: A social policy reader*. New York: Author.

Institute for Children and Poverty (1998b). *Ten cities, 1997-1998: A snapshot of family homelessness across America*. New York: Author.

Kellaghan, T., Sloane, K., Alvarez, B., & Bloom, B. (1993). *The home envi-ronment and school learning: Promoting parental involvement in the education of children.* The Jossey-Bass Education Series. San Fran-cisco: Jossey-Bass.

Mayor's Homeless Budget Advisory Task Force (1994). *Continuum of care: San Francisco: A five year strategic plan.* San Francisco: Author.

Nunez, R. (1996). *The new poverty: Homeless families in America.* New York: Insight Books, Plenum Publishing.

Nunez, R., & Collignon, K. (1999). Communities of learning: A bridge from poverty and homelessness to education and stability. *Journal of Just and Caring Education, 5,* 72-87.

Rutherford, B., Anderson, B., & Billig, S. (1997). *Parent and community involvement in education. Studies of Education Reform.* Washington, DC: U.S. Department of Education, Office of Educational Research and Improvement.

ADDITIONAL RESOURCES

"School-Linked Services," *The Future of Children,* 2(1). This Spring 1992 issue includes a comprehensive discussion of school-linked ser-vices—including history, evaluation, and practical considerations for implementation-which has survived the test of time. For ordering in-formation, contact the Center for the Future of Children, The David and Lucille Packard Foundation, 300 Second Street, Suite 102, Los Al-tos, CA 94022.

Keeping Schools Open as Community Learning Centers: Extending Learn-ing in a Safe, Drug-Free Environment Before and After School (1997) is complete with planning and budgeting worksheets. This resource is available on-line at http://www.ed.gov/pubs/LearnCenters or from the U.S. Department of Education, 600 Independence Avenue, SW, Washington, DC 20202, telephone 1-800-USA-LEARN.

Strengthening Homeless Families: An Annotated Resource Guide and a Coalition-Building Guide (1996) offer guidelines and additional resources for developing comprehensive support services for homeless families. To order, contact the National Clearinghouse on Child Abuse and Ne-glect, 330 C Street, SW, Washington, DC 20447, telephone (800) 394-3366 or (703) 385-7565.

The New Poverty: Homeless Families in America (1996) by Ralph da Costa Nunez provides a detailed account of full-service, educationally focused shelters for homeless families. Published by Insight Books, Plenum Publishing, 233 Spring Street, New York, NY 10013-1578, telephone (800) 221-9369.

ENDNOTES

[1] The programs discussed in this chapter can be contacted directly for further information. Homes for the Homeless, 36 Cooper Square, 6th Floor, New York, NY 10003, (212) 529-5252. Homeless Children and Families Program, Salem-Keizer Public Schools, P.O. Box 12024, Salem, OR 97309-0024, (504) 399-3353. The Center for the Homeless, 813 S. Michigan Street, South Bend, IN 46601, (219) 282-8700.

8

REMOVING EDUCATIONAL BARRIERS FOR HOMELESS STUDENTS: LEGAL REQUIREMENTS AND RECOMMENDED PRACTICES

MARIA FOSCARINIS AND SARAH MCCARTHY

INTRODUCTION

The impact of homelessness on children can be devastating. Researchers have demonstrated the negative effects on children and youth that include developmental delays, heightened risks to health and safety, hunger and poor nutrition, and psychological and emotional turmoil.[1] Educational achievement is also compromised. Homeless children and youth are more likely to perform below average work, be absent, repeat a grade, drop out, require special education, and score lower on standardized tests.[2] Continuity in school or preschool and the provision of supportive services can make a critical difference by providing stability, a sense of community, and opportunities for academic, social, and emotional growth.

Federal law protects the right of all homeless children and youth to attend public school and preschool and to receive school services; it also requires state and local educational agencies to remove barriers that may deny or delay these children's access to school or services. While compliance with the law's requirements has improved in recent years, homeless children still face barriers.

This chapter reviews those barriers, examines the responsibilities of state and local education agencies under federal law, assesses current compliance with the law, and includes a discussion of the recent growth of separate schools for homeless children. Additionally, the chapter outlines recommended practices.

REMOVING BARRIERS TO ACCESS

Homeless children face significant barriers in gaining access to public schools. Because of their homelessness their enrollment in school may be denied or delayed. As a result, homeless children are at increased risk for academic underachievement, poor attendance, gaps in enrollment, course failure, being held back a grade or dropping out, the loss of special education placements, access to compensatory services, and participation in gifted and talented programs.

Barriers that can prevent homeless children from enrolling, attending, or succeeding in school include:

♦ *Residency requirements.* States and localities typically require parents to prove permanent residence within a school district's geographic boundaries in order to enroll their children in school there. Homeless children living in shelters or other temporary residences may be denied enrollment based on such requirements. Similarly, homeless children may be denied continued enrollment in schools they attended before becoming homeless if they move to a shelter or other such facility outside their original districts.

♦ *Lack of Records*. Delays in the school-to-school transfer of records (such as transcripts, course schedules, individual education plans) or other documentation (such as immunization records and birth certificates) from a previously attended school can prevent homeless children's prompt enrollment in a new school. For homeless children who seek to enroll in school for the first time, the lack of records such as a birth certificate or proof of immunizations can lead to enrollment delays or denials. Homeless children are more likely to change schools as their families move from place to place seeking shelter (often due to time limits imposed by shelters), and their families are likely to have problems with maintaining personal documents such as immunization records or birth certificates.

♦ *Lack of transportation*. Lack of transportation may prevent homeless children from continuing in the school they attended before becoming homeless; it may also prevent school attendance by homeless children living at a temporary address that is outside existing school bus routes.

♦ *Guardianship requirements*. Homeless children may be placed temporarily by their parents with friends or relatives while the parents address the family's lack of housing and other crises. If the intent of the placement is temporary, it is unlikely that the caretaker will seek a court order of legal guardianship. In addition, homeless youth may be living on their own or with friends or relatives who are not their legal guardians. In these situations, requirements that children be enrolled in school by their parents or legal guardians may bar youth living on their own and children living with temporary caretakers from enrolling in school, thus preventing or delaying their attendance.

♦ *School programs*.Homeless children and youth often enroll in school at times outside official registration periods. As a result, they may not be present during standard evaluation periods for services or programs such as special education, before- and after-school care, school meals, vocational and gifted and talented programs and, therefore, may not be receiving services or participating in programs for which they may be eligible.

♦ *Stigma.* Lack of sensitivity by school personnel, administrators, and teachers to the educational needs and life circumstances of homeless children may stigmatize and isolate these children, discouraging their attendance and impeding their success.

THE STEWART B. MCKINNEY HOMELESS ASSISTANCE ACT [3]

The Stewart B. McKinney Homeless Assistance Act, landmark legislation enacted in 1987, provides comprehensive emergency assistance to homeless persons. Title VI-B of the McKinney Act, the Education for Homeless Children and Youth Program, is intended to ensure that homeless children have "equal access to the same free, appropriate public education, including a public preschool education, as provided to other children and youth." The McKinney Act does not create a separate school program for homeless children[4] but rather protects their right to participate in existing public education systems and programs.

The McKinney Act education program authorizes the appropriation of federal funds to carry out this purpose.[5] Under the Act, the U.S. Department of Education distributes the funds to state educational agencies (SEA), which in turn make selected subgrants to local educational agencies (LEA). In addition, the Act imposes specific requirements on all participating state educational agencies and on all local educational agencies, as well as on the U.S. Department of Education.

SEAs' OBLIGATIONS UNDER THE MCKINNEY ACT

States that apply for and receive federal funds under the McKinney Act education program ("participating states") must use these grants to:

♦ Review and revise state laws, regulations, policies or practices that may act as barriers to homeless children's enrollment, attendance, or success in school.[6]

♦ Ensure homeless children have access to the "education and other services" they need to ensure they have an opportunity to meet "the same challenging state student performance standards to which all students are held."[7]

♦ Provide activities for and services to homeless children that enable them to enroll in, attend, and succeed in school or preschool programs.[8]

♦ Develop and implement professional development programs for school personnel to heighten their awareness of and ability to respond to education problems of homeless children.[9]

♦ Establish or designate an Office of Coordinator of Education of Homeless Children and Youth, which must:

  - estimate the numbers of homeless children present in the state;

  - estimate the numbers of children served through grants made under the Education for Homeless Children and Youth program;

  - gather "reliable, valid, and comprehensive information" on the problems they face in accessing public schools, difficulties in identifying special needs, progress made by the SEA or LEAs in addressing such problems, and the success of the state's program;

  - report on this and other information to the Secretary of the U.S. Department of Education;

  - develop and carry out a state plan, as specified in the Act, to provide for the education of homeless children which must address specified issues and problems caused by transportation issues and enrollment delays due to immunization requirements, residency requirements, lack of birth certificates, school records or other documentation, or guardianship issues;

- facilitate coordination between the SEA, state social services, and other relevant agencies providing services to homeless children and youth and their families; and
- develop relationships and coordinate with other providers of services to homeless children and their families to improve the provision of comprehensive services.[10]

LEAs' OBLIGATIONS UNDER THE MCKINNEY ACT

♦ *All LEAs are required to:* continue homeless children's education at either their "school of origin," or the school serving the attendance area in which they are actually residing, based on their "best interest"[11];

♦ Provide homeless children services comparable to those offered other students, including transportation, special education, compensatory education, vocational education, school meals, and programs for talented and gifted students[12];

♦ Maintain school records so that they are available in a timely manner when children enter new school districts.[13]

LEAs receiving subgrants: The McKinney Act also requires participating states receiving grants over a certain amount to make subgrants to LEAs for direct support services to homeless children and youth.[14] LEAs may use the grants for a wide range of activities and services for homeless children; they must also comply with additional requirements under the Act. Information on authorized activities and obligations of LEAs is provided later in this chapter.

THE U.S. DEPARTMENT OF EDUCATION'S OBLIGATIONS UNDER THE MCKINNEY ACT

The McKinney Act places requirements on the U.S. Department of Education (ED) as well, including: reviewing and evaluating state plans, evaluating and disseminating information about programs for the education of homeless children, determining the extent to which SEAs are meeting their responsibilities under the Act, and providing technical assistance to SEAs to help them carry out their statutory responsibilities.[15]

COMPLIANCE

The McKinney Act has resulted in significant changes by states to laws and policies that restricted access. Nevertheless, compliance with the federal statutory requirements has been imperfect, and it is conservatively estimated that 23 percent of homeless school-age children are still not attending school.[16] According to a 1995 ED report, almost all states report success in revising their laws, policies, and regulations to improve educational access[17]; however, compliance problems remained, including:

♦ guardianship and immunization requirements still impede the enrollment of homeless children[18];

♦ homeless students are rarely placed in their school of origin, particularly when it would require transportation across school district lines[19];

♦ homeless youth face major barriers to school access[20]; and

♦ a large proportion of homeless children have difficulty in gaining access to specific educational services such as programs for free school meals, gifted and talented children, vocational education, and preschool.[21]

Further, a 1995 national survey report by the National Law Center on Homelessness & Poverty found:

♦ obtaining birth certificates, transferring school records, and transportation were cited as the most significant barriers still facing homeless children by shelter providers and state coordinators;

♦ approximately 74% of shelter providers surveyed reported that transportation was a barrier for children whose school was in another district and that more than half of the school-age children transferred to a school in the shelter's attendance area.[22]

Finally, in a 1997 national survey report on preschool education, the National Law Center found that lack of transportation, lack of availability of preschool programs, and homeless parents' lack of understanding of their children's educational rights were the major barriers to the participation of homeless children in preschool programs.[23] The National Law Center also found that 70% of State Coordinators were unable to estimate the number of homeless children eligible for public preschool and that 30% of state officials estimated that few or no homeless children were enrolled in preschool.[24]

SEPARATE SCHOOLS FOR HOMELESS CHILDREN

While these access problems continue, a significant new barrier has arisen that challenges the federal policy that "homelessness alone should not be sufficient reason to separate students from the mainstream school environment."[25] Separate schools exclusively for homeless children and youth, sometimes referred to as "transitional schools," have been established in several states nationwide. Often a well-intentioned effort by shelter providers to ensure that homeless students are given some form of schooling, separate schools present concerns to educational access and success for several reasons:

♦ they may conflict with the McKinney Act's policy that "each State educational agency shall ensure that each child of a homeless individual and each homeless youth has equal access to the same free, appropriate public education, including a public preschool education, as provided to other children and youth"[26];

♦ children are isolated from their non-homeless peers;

♦ separate schools may offer a seriously inadequate education (e.g., many programs exist as one-room schoolhouses);

- ◆ separate schools may disrupt the academic coursework of homeless children and youth because such schools often do not follow the curriculum of the mainstream school, causing further gaps in progress;

- ◆ separate schools may be located in inadequate or unsafe physical facilities not designed to be used as schools, such as shelters or converted commercial space;

- ◆ separate schools generally cannot offer the full range of compensatory programs or services such as special education, bilingual education, or programs for gifted and talented children.

Proponents of separate schools argue that these schools help homeless children by ensuring that they are in school somewhere and that they shield children from harassment or ridicule from insensitive classmates or teachers. What both sides of this debate could probably agree upon is that unsupportive or unresponsive public schools are at the root of the establishment of transitional or separate schools and that the remedy lies in addressing this fundamental problem.

LITIGATION TO ENFORCE THE MCKINNEY ACT

To date, two lawsuits have been brought to enforce homeless children's education rights under the McKinney Act. In *Lampkin* v. *District of Columbia*,[27] the U.S. Court of Appeals for the District of Columbia Circuit ruled in a landmark decision that homeless children have enforceable rights under the Act. This case resulted in the first ruling in which a federal court ordered a local government to comply with Title VII-B of the McKinney Act.[28] *Salazar* v. *Edwards*[29] was filed in the Cook County Circuit Court on behalf of homeless children in Chicago in 1992, under both the McKinney Act and a separate Illinois law enacted in 1991 to further protect the rights of homeless children. Following the *Lampkin* decision, the suit was settled in November 1996, with the Chicago Public Schools agreeing to eliminate school enrollment barriers for homeless children and youth and close a "shelter school" where homeless children were segregated.[30]

IMPLEMENTING THE MCKINNEY ACT: COMPLIANCE STRATEGIES

The McKinney Act sets forth detailed directives to state and local educational agencies designed to remove barriers commonly faced by homeless children. In practice, however, questions may arise as to the meaning of the statutory provisions. This section focuses on some specific questions and concerns frequently raised by school systems in the application of the statute to real life situations.

WHAT CHILDREN ARE PROTECTED UNDER THE ACT?

The Education for Homeless Children and Youth provisions of the McKinney Act do not contain a separate definition of "homeless child"; therefore, the Act's general definition applies. That definition is:

"For purposes of this Act, the term 'homeless' or 'homeless individual' includes—

(1) an individual who lacks a fixed, regular, and adequate nighttime residence; and

(2) an individual who has a primary nighttime residence that is—

    (A) a supervised publicly or privately operated shelter designed to provide temporary living accommodations (including welfare hotels[31], congregate shelters, and transitional housing for the mentally ill);

    (B) an institution that provides a temporary residence for individuals intended to be institutionalized; or

    (C) a public or private place not designed for, or ordinarily used as, a regular sleeping accommodation for human beings."[32]

In 1995, ED issued guidance interpreting the McKinney Act's educational provisions. The Department's Preliminary Guidance explains that children and youth living in shelters, transitional housing, the streets, cars, abandoned buildings, and other inadequate accommodations are considered homeless. [33]

In addition, children falling into any of the following categories are considered homeless for purposes of the McKinney Act.

◆ *Children and Youth Living in Trailer Parks and Camping Grounds:* Children living temporarily in trailer parks or camping areas because they lack adequate accommodations should be considered homeless; however, if they are living in such places on a long-term basis in adequate accommodations they should not be deemed homeless.[34]

◆ *Doubled up Children and Youth:* Children living in housing that their family shares with other families or individuals are considered homeless if they are doubled-up due to a loss of housing or "other similar situation;" however, families who are voluntarily doubled-up to save money generally should not be considered homeless.[35]

◆ *Foster Children and Youth:* In general, children in foster homes are not considered homeless; however, children placed in foster homes because of their parents' lack of shelter are deemed homeless.[36] In addition, children living in an emergency shelter or transitional living facility because there is nowhere else to send them and they are awaiting placement in a foster home or home for neglected children are considered homeless—until the placement is made.[37]

◆ *Hospitalized Children and Youth:* Children who are ready for discharge but remain hospitalized because they have been abandoned by their families are considered homeless. Children who were homeless prior to hospitalization are considered homeless while in the hospital unless regular and adequate accommodations will be made available to them upon discharge. [38]

◆ *Incarcerated Children and Youth:* Children who are under the care of the State and are held in an institution because they have no other place to live are considered homeless.[39]

♦ *Migratory Children and Youth:* Children of migrant workers are considered homeless only to the extent they are staying in accommodations not fit for habitation.[40]

♦ *Runaways:* Children who have run away from home and live in runaway shelters, on the streets, in abandoned buildings or other "inadequate accommodations," even if their parents have and are willing to provide a home for them, are considered homeless.[41]

♦ *Throwaways:* Throwaway children—children whose parents or guardians will not permit them to live at home—are considered homeless if they live on the streets, in shelters, or other transitional or inadequate accommodations.[42]

♦ *Unwed Mothers:* School-age children or youth who are living in homes for unwed and expectant mothers and have no other available living accommodations are considered homeless; however, if they are in such homes only to receive specific services and intend to move to other adequate accommodations they should not be considered homeless.[43]

The above categories do not describe all children or youth who could be deemed homeless for the purposes of the McKinney Act. In those cases in which children do not fit neatly into one of these clear categories, state and local educational agencies must make case-by-case determinations. In making such determinations, the ED Guidance advises SEAs and LEAs to consider the relative permanence of the child's living arrangements.[44] In addition, unsheltered homeless children are often overlooked; we recommend that SEAs and LEAs make special efforts to identify and reach out to them to ensure their school needs are addressed.[45]

WHICH SCHOOL SHOULD HOMELESS CHILDREN ATTEND?

The McKinney Act requires LEAs to either continue the child's education in the child's school of origin for the remainder of the academic year or to enroll the child in any school that non-homeless students who live in the attendance area in which the homeless child is actually living are eligible to attend, according to the child's best interest.[46]

Q. How can school districts determine which school it is in a homeless child's best interest to attend?

A. Under the Act, LEAs must comply, "to the extent feasible," with "the request made by the parent or guardian" regarding school selection.[47]

Q. What if a family becomes homeless between academic years?

A. The LEA must continue the child's education in the school of origin for the following academic year, if that is in the child's best interest.[48]

Q. What does "school of origin" mean?

A. The Act defines this term to mean the school the child or youth attended when permanently housed or the school in which the child or youth was last enrolled.[49]

Q. What if a homeless child is not living with his/her parents but has been temporarily placed elsewhere by the parents?

A. The choice regarding school placement must still be made, as above.[50]

Within these requirements, states may develop additional guidelines to assist LEAs in determining homeless children's best interest placement. Relevant factors include:

♦ continuity of instruction
♦ student's need for special instructional programs
♦ quality of instruction in the school of origin
♦ age of the child
♦ school placement of siblings
♦ length of stay in the shelter

♦ likely area of family's future permanent housing

♦ the safety of the child.[51]

WHAT IF THERE IS A DISPUTE REGARDING A CHILD'S EDUCATIONAL PLACEMENT?

The McKinney Act requires states to describe in their plans procedures for the "prompt resolution" of disputes regarding the educational placement of homeless children, [52] but does not otherwise specify what those procedures should be; thus, SEAs must devise appropriate procedures.

In practice, disputes may arise between two schools or between a school and parents, and different resolution mechanisms may be appropriate to each type of dispute. For example, the Oregon State Plan provides that the Homeless Education Program, Office of the State Coordinator will act as a mediator in the event of inter-district or inter-school program disputes.[53] Under this dispute resolution process, the relevant parties to the dispute (e.g., school officials, parents/guardians, the child or youth, and advocate/social worker) meet with a representative of the State Homeless Education Program who hears all sides of the issue.[54] If an agreement between the parties cannot be reached, the Homeless Education Program is authorized to make a decision, based upon the best interest of the child or youth involved.[55]

With regard to disputes between a school and parents, the settlement agreement in the *Salazar* case provides a useful model, including these elements:

♦ designate a school official to receive and process complaints;

♦ establish a short time-frame for resolution of complaints (e.g., within 24 hours after the complaint is made);

♦ require school officials to keep a written record of complaints and their resolution;

♦ if a complaint cannot be resolved through meetings between the designated school official and the parents, develop an appeal process for referring such complaints to the next level of authority (e.g., school superintendent, Coordinator for the State's Education for Homeless Children and Youth program);

♦ develop written and oral information about the school district's dispute resolution policy and procedures, including referral information to local advocacy services, and distribute the policy to all parents at the beginning of each school semester and at the time of enrollment.[56]

SCHOOL ENROLLMENT

Q: What if a homeless child or youth does not have the documents required for school registration, such as a birth certificate or transfer records from a former school?

A: The McKinney Act requires all LEAs in participating states to maintain for each homeless child all records ordinarily kept by a school, including immunization, academic and guardianship records, birth certificates, and evaluations for special services and programs, so that the records are available "in a timely fashion," when the child enters a new school district.[57] Thus, for children who were enrolled elsewhere, the new school in which the child seeks to register should contact the old school for all relevant records.

In cases where the old school cannot or will not transfer the requested records or when children are enrolling in school for the first time, enrollment should not be delayed or denied for lack of records. To the extent that state laws, regulations, or policies governing school enrollment procedures present barriers to enrollment, the state must undertake steps to review and revise these laws to remove such barriers.[58] Further, the McKinney Act requires participating states to address in their state plan enrollment delays caused by immunization requirements, and lack of birth certificates, school records or other documentation, and to demonstrate that the SEA and all LEAs have developed policies to remove barriers to enrollment.[59] In addition, LEAs that receive subgrants are obligated to review and revise policies that present barriers to enrollment, with consideration to issues concerning records requirements.[60]

In compliance with the McKinney Act, some states have reviewed and revised state statutes dealing with school enrollment issues to address the needs of homeless children. A common revision is to establish a statutory grace period for compliance with records requirements. For example, Texas state law allows students up to 30 days following enrollment to submit immunization records.[61]

We recommend that LEAs:

◆ contact the former school and request that the student's records be forwarded immediately (e.g., through the use of facsimile machines or computers);

◆ establish a grace period so that the child may be enrolled pending receipt of any required documentation;

◆ establish procedures for assisting with record transfers or payment of copying fees; establish referrals to nearby health clinics, if any, that perform free immunizations.[62]

WHAT ABOUT TRANSPORTATION TO SCHOOL?

Q: What if it is in a homeless child's best interest to continue in the school of origin, but the child needs transportation to and from that school?

A: Each homeless child must be provided with transportation services "comparable" to those offered to other students in the school selected according to the child's best interest.[63]

Q: What if the child needs transportation that goes beyond what is offered to non-homeless children (for example, if the child is living outside the school district) or if the school does not offer transportation services at all?

A: Under the McKinney Act, the SEA must ensure that transportation issues are addressed so that the lack of transportation is not a barrier to attendance. [64] In addition, the McKinney Act imposes a separate requirement on LEAs that receive assistance under the Act to address any transportation problems homeless children may face in attending schools selected in accordance with their best interests.[65]

There may also be relevant state, city or school district laws that supplement or further clarify the McKinney Act requirements. For example, Illinois state law provides that when a homeless child's education is continued in the school of origin, and that school is located in a school district different from the one in which the family lives, the school district of origin and the school district in which the child is living must meet to determine the apportionment of costs and responsibility for providing transportation services.[66]

Q: If a school district does not receive McKinney funding does that mean it does not have an obligation to assist with transportation needs?

A: No. Each state that participates in the McKinney Program must ensure that all local educational agencies, not just those that receive McKinney subgrants, develop, review and revise policies to eliminate barriers to the enrollment and retention of homeless children and youth in school.[67] LEAs that receive subgrants under the State's McKinney education program have a direct obligation to review and revise policies that act as barriers to enrollment and must take into consideration issues such as transportation.[68] In addition, these LEAs may use their funds to defray the excess cost of transportation, when not otherwise provided for through federal, state or local funds.[69]

Q: How can SEAs and LEAs meet their transportation obligations under the Act?

A: The McKinney Act does not require a specific mode or type of transportation services. Some options include:

Provide passes or tokens for public buses or subways. This was the remedy ordered by the court in *Lampkin v. District of Columbia.*[70] In addition, under the *Salazar v. Edwards* settlement, children who continue in their school of origin are given student-rate tokens and the application fee for a student fare card for the Chicago public transportation system[71]; parents of children in grades six and below are given full-rate tokens so they may accompany them.[72]

Reroute School Buses. School districts can create a procedure for making mid-semester revisions in school bus routes. For example, in Buffalo, New York, the school district has set up a system that enables homeless shelter providers to contact the School District's transportation department directly to arrange for bus service for each new student that moves into a shelter. For students who wish to remain in a school of origin that is outside of the Buffalo School District's geographic boundaries, the School District provides tokens for use on the City's public buses.

HOW CAN SCHOOL DISTRICTS REACH OUT TO HOMELESS CHILDREN AND PARENTS, AND OTHER AGENCIES WORKING WITH THEM?

It is crucial to the implementation of the McKinney Act that schools and school districts take the initiative in reaching out to identify homeless children and their families. Homeless parents often have no idea that their children have rights to equal access and services under the McKinney Act; indeed, because of the crisis nature of homelessness, parents may not be focusing attention on their children's educational needs. Developing contacts with, and becoming part of, an existing network of service providers and advocates is a key part of reaching out.

Q: What does the McKinney Act require regarding identifying homeless children and collaborating with other groups?

A. The McKinney Act requires State Coordinators to collect information about homeless children in their state, including estimating their total numbers and the number served by the state's McKinney education program,[73] difficulties they face in gaining access to school and preschool, and progress made by the SEA and LEAs in overcoming those difficulties.[74] State Coordinators must also develop relationships and coordinate services with the State social services agency and with other agencies providing services to homeless children and families.[75] In carrying out each of these required activities, State Coordinators should develop relationships with service providers and advocates.

Q. What are examples of useful groups to contact?

A. Some relevant organizations to contact include shelter operators, transitional living programs, runaway and homeless youth centers, health clinics such as Health Care for the Homeless Projects, domestic violence programs, Head Start programs, preschool programs for children with disabilities, recreation groups, and local governmental agencies responsible for arranging shelter placements for homeless families.

Q. What information should be provided to homeless parents?

A. To carry out their responsibilities under the Act, we recommend that State Coordinators develop mechanisms for providing information about homeless children's rights under the law to homeless parents as well as to service providers, advocates, and others who work with homeless families and children. Brochures, posters, and other written materials, clearly and simply written, can help; informational presentations or one-on-one discussions can also be useful,

especially for parents with literacy problems. Under
the *Salazar* v. *Edwards* settlement, the Chicago Public
Schools must send a notice, in English and Spanish,
to all students and their parents twice a year, in September and January[76]; and must also post it in a
prominent place in each school.[77]

Q. How else can education be coordinated with other
services?

A. Coordination can occur on many levels; it can help
to eliminate barriers such as transportation problems,
lack of school supplies and clothing, and poor nutrition, and can expand school districts' resources for
assisting homeless children and youth. In addition,
coordination can result in a comprehensive assessment of a homeless child or youth's needs.

State coordinators should become knowledgeable about the
whole spectrum of groups and services working with homeless
families and children in their state. We recommend contacting
the regional U.S. Department of Housing and Urban
Development ("HUD") office to identify local and statewide organizations that are participating in the agency's "Continuum
of Care" approach to the problem of homelessness. The Continuum of Care planning process consists of a coordinated
community-based process through which governmental and
non-profit agencies identify the needs of homeless persons in
their community and the systems or resources needed to
address those needs. The organizations then prepare a community-wide application for housing and supportive services funds
administered by the Office of Community Planning and Development at HUD.

By participating in this process, state and local educational
agencies can play a role in ensuring that educational needs are
linked to the process of planning for shelter or housing resources.
The goal should be to minimize disruption in schooling.[78] Shelter and housing policies and programs can help achieve this goal
by considering the educational needs of homeless children during the shelter or housing placement process, allowing flexibility
in addressing housing needsfor example, providing assistance

with rent arrears to enable a family to stay in its own housing, or eliminating limits on length of shelter stays that are shorter than the academic year.

HOW CAN SCHOOLS PROVIDE A SENSITIVE LEARNING ENVIRONMENT FOR HOMELESS CHILDREN?

Lack of sensitivity by teachers and school administrators to the needs of homeless children and youth can result in lack of success or poor attendance. In particular, the McKinney Act requires the SEA to develop and implement professional development programs for school personnel to heighten their awareness and capacity to respond to specific problems in the education of homeless children and youth.[79] In addition, we recommend that schools consider:

♦ conducting training sessions that focus on homelessness, the challenges it creates for homeless children, and the barriers the children face in their education.[80] Schools also should contact the Coordinator of their State's Education of Homeless Children and Youth program to determine whether the state is sponsoring local, regional or state conferences on this issue.[81]

♦ inviting the staff of local shelters, transitional living facilities, advocacy groups, food banks, or other organizations that work with homeless families to participate in or conduct trainings on the needs of homeless families and children.

♦ including materials about homelessness in the school curriculum.[82]

HOW DOES THE McKINNEY ACT APPLY TO HOMELESS PRESCHOOLERS?

All of the requirements and recommendations regarding school age children and barriers also apply to homeless preschoolers. Each State Coordinator is required to gather information on the needs of homeless preschoolers and the extent of their problems in accessing public preschool programs.[83]

At the local level, school districts with homeless liaisons must identify educational access problems for homeless preschoolers and ensure their participation in programs for which they are eligible.[84] This is where coordinating services with local providers of services to homeless families can be of help as these groups may be able to assist in the identification process.

Schools that offer public preschool should do outreach to homeless parents to encourage enrollment of their children in such programs. Schools without preschool programs should consider how to provide information to homeless parents about other preschool educational programs in the community such as the Head Start program.

Refer to chapter 2, "Meeting the Developmental and Educational Needs of Homeless Infants and Young Children," for more information on homeless preschoolers.

How Do LEAs Receive and Use McKinney Subgrants?

SEAs that receive McKinney Act funding that exceeds the amount received in 1990 must provide grants to LEAs for the purpose of facilitating the enrollment, attendance, and success of homeless children and youth in school.[85] The grants may be used for a wide range of activities including:

◆ tutoring, supplemental instruction, and enriched educational services linked to helping homeless children and youth achieve the same challenging state student content and performance standards established for all students;

◆ expediting evaluations of strengths and needs, including needs and eligibility for programs and services;

◆ professional development and other activities for staff designed to heighten understanding and sensitivity to the needs of homeless children and youth, their rights under the McKinney Act, and the specific educational needs of runaway youth;

◆ referrals for health services;

♦ payment of the excess cost of transportation services not otherwise provided through other federal, state or local funding, where needed to enable homeless students to attend the school that is in their best interest to attend;

♦ provision of early childhood education programs, not otherwise provided through federal, state, or local funding;

♦ provision of before- and after-school programs, mentoring, and summer school programs;

♦ payment of fees and costs associated with tracking, obtaining, or transferring records needed for enrollment;

♦ training for homeless parents regarding their children's rights and resources available for homeless children and youth;

♦ development of coordination activities between schools and organizations providing services to homeless children and youth;

♦ pupil services and referrals for such services;

♦ services to address the needs of children and youth affected by domestic violence;

♦ adaptation of space and services for nonschool facilities used to provide any services through a McKinney subgrant;

♦ provision of school supplies; and

♦ provision of other extraordinary or emergency assistance to enable children and youth to attend school.[86]

LEAs that receive subgrants must also designate a homeless liaison,[87] coordinate with local service providers and social service agencies providing services to homeless families and their children,[88] coordinate with state and local housing agencies responsible for developing comprehensive housing affordability strategies,[89] and review and revise any policies that may act as barriers to homeless children's enrollment in the school that it is in their best interest to attend.[90]

WHAT IS A HOMELESS LIAISON?

A homeless liaison is an individual designated by a LEA to be responsible for ensuring that homeless children and youth are able to enroll in and succeed in school, are able to receive all the services for which they are eligible, and are able to obtain referrals to necessary services such as health care services.[91] While only LEAs that receive McKinney subgrants are required to appoint a homeless liaison, we recommend that all local educational agencies designate a staff member to act as the local liaison because the liaison can become the link between homeless families and schools, facilitating compliance with the McKinney Act education provisions.

For example, we recommend appointing a homeless liaison to:

♦ help a school district develop a process for identifying homeless children and youth in the community;

♦ ensure that parents are informed about their children's educational rights;

♦ assist in the school selection process; and provide referrals to local health, mental health and other services in the community; and

♦ collaborate with shelter providers and other homeless service providers to determine the best method for ensuring that homeless children and youth have equal access to school.

CONCLUSION

Homeless children and youth face multiple barriers to school enrollment, attendance and success. However, federal law—in particular, the McKinney Act education program—offers important tools in overcoming those barriers. To ensure that the Act is implemented to maximum benefit, state and local educational agencies must work together and with parents, service providers, and other government and private entities involved in addressing the needs of homeless parents, children, and youth. Coordination and collaboration, together with careful review and revision of policies, are crucial to the success of these efforts and, ultimately, to the success of homeless children and youth.

ENDNOTES

[1] Bassuk, Ellen L. (1991), *Homeless Families, Sci. Am.* 66, 70-71 (1991); Bassuk, Ellen L., & Gallagher, Ellen M., *The Impact of Homelessness on Children*, 14(1) *Child and Youth Services* 19 (1990).

[2] Yvonne Rafferty, *The Legal Rights and Educational Problems of Homeless Children and Youth*, 17 Educ. Evaluation and Pol'y Analysis 39, 42-45 (1995).

[3] The Stewart B. McKinney Homeless Assistance Act, Pub. L. No. 100-77, Title VII-B, 101 Stat. 482, 525 (1987), amended by, the Stewart B. McKinney Homeless Assistance Amendments Act of 1990, Pub. L. No. 101-645, 104 Stat. 4673, 4735, and the Improving America's Schools Act of 1994, Pub. L. No. 103-382, 108 Stat. 3519, 3957 (codified as amended at 42 U.S.C. §§ 11431-35 (1994)).

[4] 42 U.S.C. §§ 11431(3); 11432(g)((1)(H); 11433(a)(2).

[5] The Act does not contain a specific authorization level for fiscal years 1996 through 1999. 42 U.S.C. § 11435. The actual appropriations for 1998 and 1999 were $28.8 million for each year.

[6] 42 U.S.C. §§ 11431(2); 11432(d)(1); 11432(g)(1) (G) and (8).

[7] *Id.* §§ 11431(4); 11432(d)(1) and (g)(1).

[8] *Id.* § 11432(d)(2).

[9] *Id.* § 11432(d)(5).

[10] *Id.* §§ 11432(d)(3), (f), and (g)(1)-(9). Currently, all states have an Office of Coordinator of the Education for Homeless Children and Youth.

[11] *Id.* § 11432(g)(3)(A).

[12] *Id.* § 11432(g)(4).

[13] *Id.* § 11432(g)(6).

[14] *Id.* §§ 11432(e)(1)(a) and 11433(a)(1). The statute defines the amount as over what the agency received for fiscal year 1990; agencies that receive under that amount may, but are not required to, make subgrants to LEAs.

[15] *Id.* § 11434.

[16] U.S. Dep't of Educ., Preliminary Guidance for the Education for Homeless Children and Youth Program 2 (1995).

[17] Leslie M. Anderson et al., Policy Studies Associates, Inc., An Evaluation of State and Local Efforts to Serve the Educational Needs of Homeless Children and Youth 12 (1995).

[18] *Id.* at 17-21.

[19.] *Id.* at ii.

[20] *Id.*

[21] *Id.*

[22] National Law Center On Homelessness & Poverty, A Foot in the Schoolhouse Door ii-iv (1995).

[23] National Law Center On Homelessness & Poverty, Blocks to Their Future 16-17 (1997).

[24] *Id.* at 18-19.

[25] 42 U.S.C. § 11431(3).

[26] 42 U.S.C. § 11431(1).

[27] *Lampkin* v. *District of Columbia*, Civ. No. 92-0910, slip op. at 14-15, 1992 WL 151813 (D.D.C. June 9, 1992), rev'd., 27 F.3d 605 (D.C. Cir. 1994), cert. denied. U.S. , 115 S.Ct. 578, 130 L.Ed.2d 493 (1994), enforced, 879 F. Supp. 116 (D.D.C. March 7, 1995), dissolved, slip op. (D.D.C. May 4, 1995). This suit was brought by a group of homeless mothers on behalf of their homeless children, and the National Law Center on Homelessness & Poverty.

[28] *Id.* Rather than comply with the Court's order the District of Columbia withdrew its participation in the McKinney Act education program and returned the unspent portion of its 1994 McKinney funds to the U.S. Department of Education. This forced the Court to dissolve its injunction requiring educational services to homeless children.

[29] *Salazar* v. *Edwards*, No. 92-CH-5703 (Ill. Cir. Ct., 1992). Plaintiffs, homeless mothers on behalf of their children, were represented by the Legal Assistance Foundation of Chicago.

[30] Settlement Agreement and Stipulation to Dismiss, *Salazar* v. *Edwards*, 92-CH-5703 (Ill. Cir. Ct., Nov. 21, 1996). The Chicago Coalition for the Homeless, under Laurene Heybach, the original lead attorney for plaintiffs, is monitoring compliance at the time of this printing.

[31] The term "welfare hotels," while not defined in the Act or in regulations generally refers to commercial hotels that are used by government or private agencies to house homeless families temporarily. In some cases, families may themselves select and pay for such accommodations; if their arrangement is inadequate or unstable they may be homeless under the McKinney Act.

[32] 42 U.S.C. § 11302(a). The definition specifically excludes persons who are imprisoned or "otherwise detained" pursuant to federal or state law. Id. at (c).

[33] U.S. Dep't of Educ., *supra* note 16, at 21. Other federal agencies have interpreted the term "homeless individual" for the purposes of other programs under the McKinney Act or other laws. For example, the U.S. Department of Housing and Urban Development's (HUD) Continuum of Care Homeless Assistance Application materials define homeless persons eligible to receive assistance under HUD's homeless programs as including a person who is "being evicted within a week from a private dwelling unit and no subsequent residence has been identified and the person lacks the resources and support networks to obtain housing."

[34] *Id.*

[35] *Id.* at 21.

[36] *Id.* at 21.

[37] *Id.*

[38] *Id.* at 22.

[39] *Id.* at 22. By contrast, children who are incarcerated for violation or alleged violation of a law should not be considered homeless even if they would have been so considered before their incarceration. *Id.*

[40] *Id.*

[41] *Id.* at 22.

[42] *Id.* at 23

[43] *Id.*

[44] *Id.* Within these guidelines, states may set more specific criteria for determining homelessness. For example, Oregon proposes to include as homeless children in "inadequate housing," defined as housing which "lacks electricity, adequate plumbing, or sufficient heating, particularly when such circumstances lead to frequent school absences and/or poor school performance. Children and youth whose living situations involve inadequate or substandard space and sleeping accommodations should be provided enrollment and supplemental services as if they were homeless." Oregon Department of Education, Admission of Students to Oregon Public Schools 7 (1998) (draft policy, on file with the National Law Center on Homelessness & Poverty).

[45] See discussion of recommended practices regarding outreach *infra.*

[46] 42 U.S.C. § 11432(g)(3)(A).

[47] *Id.* § 11432(g)(3)(B). The McKinney Act does not define "feasibility" nor are there regulations that provide any guidance on this issue.

[48] *Id.* § 11432(g)(3)(A)(I)(II).

[49] *Id.* § 11432(g)(3)(C).

[50] *Id.* § 11432(g)(3)(D).

[51] *See, e.g.*, Maryland State Department of Education, Interim Guidelines and Procedures on Education of Homeless Children and Youth 2.

[52] *Id.* § 11432(g)(1)(A).

[53] Oregon Department of Education, State Plan for Education of Homeless Children & Youth 1 (1991).

[54] *Id.*

[55] *Id.*

[56] *See generally*, Settlement Agreement and Stipulation to Dismiss, *Salazar* v. *Edwards*, 92-CH-5703 (Ill. Cir. Ct., Nov. 21, 1996) at par. 15-16.

[57] 42 U.S.C. § 11432 (g)(5).

[58] *Id.* § 11431(2).

[59] *Id.* §§ 11432 (g)(1)(F) and (G).

[60] *Id.* § 11432(g)(8).

[61] Texas Education Code § 25.002(a)(3).

[62] For example, the local health department may sponsor an annual free immunization day or may be part of a community-wide campaign to ensure that all school-age children are immunized schools could join with the local health department in such campaigns to disseminate information to all parents about the need to ensure their children receive immunizations on the proper schedule.

[63] 42 U.S.C. § 11432(g)(4).

[64] Under the Act, SEAs must review and revise any policiesincluding those pertaining to transportationthat may act as barriers to the enrollment of homeless children in the school selected to be in their best interest, 42 U.S.C. § 11432 (g)(8); LEAs that receive assistance under the Act must also remove transportation barriers, id. In addition, SEAs must demonstrate in their plans that they will address problems caused by, among other things, transportation, and demonstrate that the state, as well as the LEAs in the state, will remove barriers to homeless children's enrollment and retention in school, id. at (g)(1)(F) and (G).

[65] *Id.* § 11432(g)(8).

[66] 105 ILCS 45/1-15.

[67] 42 U.S.C. § 11432(g)(1)(G).

[68] *Id.* § 11432(g)(8).

[69] *Id.* § 11433(d)(5).

[70] *Lampkin* v. *District of Columbia*, 879 F. Supp. 116, 126 (D.D.C. 1995) (District ordered to make transportation tokens available to all children and their adult escorts who travel more than 1.5 miles to school).

[71] Settlement Agreement and Stipulation to Dismiss, *Salazar* v. *Edwards*, 92-CH-5703 (Ill. Cir. Ct., Nov. 21, 1996) at par. 13.

[72] *Id.*

[73] 42 U.S.C. § 11432 (f)(1).

[74] *Id.* § 11432 (f)(2).

[75] *Id.* § 11432 (f)(5),(6).

[76] Settlement Agreement and Stipulation to Dismiss, *Salazar* v. *Edwards*, 92-CH-5703 (Ill. Cir. Ct., Nov. 21, 1966) at par. 23. In other communities, other languages may be appropriate.

[77] *Id.*

[78] One way to minimize disruption in schooling would be to consider placing shelter and housing facilities near the schools of origin of children likely to be placed there. Research in some cities indicates that homeless families often come from highly circumscribed neighborhoods; thus, some prediction is possible. *See, e.g.*, Dennis P. Culhane et al., *Where the Homeless Come from: A Study of the Prior Address Distribution of Families Admitted to Public Shelters in New York City and Philadelphia*, 7(2) Housing Policy Debate 340-343 (1996).

[79] 42 U.S.C. §§ 11432(d)(5) and (g)(1)(B).

[80] An example of training materials designed for staff development on the issue of homeless children and youth and the McKinney Act is *Pieces of the Puzzle: Creating Success for Students in Homeless Situations*, published by the Star Center, a collaborative project based in Texas that involved, among others, the office of the State Coordinator for the Education of Homeless Children and Youth.

[81] Local educational agencies that receive subgrants from their State's Education for Homeless Children and Youth Program may also use their funds for professional development and sensitivity training. 42 U.S.C. § 11433(d)(3).

[82] Some model materials as well as course curricula have been developed. *See, e.g.*, The Center on Homelessness at William Penn College, Homeless Resource Guide K-12, available through their Web site: www.wmpenn.edu.

[83] 42 U.S.C. § 11432(f)(2).

[84] *Id.* § 11432(g)(7).

[85] *Id.* §§ 11432(e)(1)(A) and 11433(a)(1).

[86] *Id.* §. 11433(d)(1)-(15).

[87] *Id.* § 11432(g)(7).

[88] *Id.* § 11432(g)(6).

[89] *Id.* § 11432(g)(6),(9).

[90] *Id.* § 11432(g)(8).

[91] *Id.* § 11432(g)(7).

9

BUILDING EFFECTIVE AWARENESS PROGRAMS FOR HOMELESS STUDENTS AMONG STAFF, PEERS, AND COMMUNITY MEMBERS

KEVIN J. SWICK

The substance of what happens in schools is mainly the result of what staff and students accomplish through their social and educational interactions. This reality is very apparent in the school experiences of homeless students. For example, their sense of acceptance or rejection is interrelated with the understanding and treatment they receive from teachers, peers, and other school personnel (Stronge, 1995). Homeless students and their parents develop their "schema" of what schools are through direct experiences, including the messages they receive related to access and participation in social and educational activities.

Staff and students can be a major force in providing empowering learning experiences for homeless students. *Three questions provide the framework for exploring ways to achieve an empowerment approach in staff and students:*

1. How can we build awareness and support for the learning needs of homeless students among teachers and staff?

2. How can we build awareness and support for the learning needs of homeless students among all students?

3. How can we build awareness and support for the learning needs of homeless students among community members?

HOW CAN WE BUILD AWARENESS AND SUPPORT FOR THE LEARNING NEEDS OF HOMELESS STUDENTS AMONG TEACHERS AND STAFF?

Helping staff transform their relationships with homeless students into productive experiences can occur through many strategies.

Use federal, state, and local funding to develop staff teams to study and become insightful into the needs of homeless students. These teams can gain new perspectives as they acquire information and share and learn with others in the school and community. One teacher who participated in such a team effort noted:

> I never thought of the reality that these children do not have a place to study or lack basic resources to work with. Imagine not being able to do your homework when you really want to. (Swick, 1996a, p. 294)

Become a school liaison for homeless students, functioning as an advocate for them and as a leader in educating other teachers in the school. Staff can also function as the linkage to district level resources and activities as well as the contact person to shelters and other service agencies. The *liaison* role can help to accomplish many needed changes:

♦ help other teachers and staff better understand the challenges homeless students experience;

♦ assist shelters in setting up study rooms inclusive of needed materials and resources;

- advocate at the district level for needed adjustments in bus routes and other changes that will increase school attendance of homeless students; and
- serve on community advisory teams to develop improved support services for homeless students and their parents.

Engage in mentoring and tutoring roles with homeless students. In addition to assisting homeless students in strengthening their educational skills, staff can gain valuable insights into the challenges and barriers they experience in trying to achieve educational success. Examples of effective *mentoring* and *tutoring* activities include:

- helping students develop improved study skills in after-school programs;
- becoming a "reading buddy" to a young child on a regular basis; and
- adopting a homeless student and helping him/her develop a positive sense of self and others.

Form a collaborative study and action team with others in the school district and engage university and state education personnel in this process. A course or professional development program on educating homeless students can enlighten faculty and staff about critical issues and strategies. Swick (1996a) used such a model to engage interested teachers in proactive involvement with homeless students and their families, and their helpers. University, community, school leaders, state education personnel, and the participating staff used a collaborative, inquiry approach. Sources of information included:

- Staff from homeless service agencies
- Shelter staff
- District homeless education coordinator and social worker
- State level homeless education director
- Transitional housing coordinator

♦ Cooperative ministry leader

♦ Social service staff

♦ Homeless pre-school child development program director

As Swick (1996a) noted the success of the course was enhanced through the collaborative scheme:

The collaborative effort provided the framework for a successful professional development course that expanded teachers' understanding of and involvement with homeless students and families. Multiple perspectives, participants' involvement in goal setting, use of varied and relevant instructional strategies, and opportunities for applying acquired knowledge in community and school setting were the key means for achieving success. (p. 295)

Service-Learning Enhances Teachers/Staff Understanding of the Needs of Homeless Students

1. Teachers and staff can assess school and community needs of homeless students as a part of professional development or graduate course learning.

2. Identify key needs of homeless students and set goals for:

   a. more supportive teacher/staff-homeless student relationships;

   b. removing barriers that negatively influence student learning;

   c. strengthening homeless students' involvement in educational and social activities;

   d. increasing parent/family involvement in classroom, school, and community; and

   e. improving teacher, staff, and student attitudes toward homelessness.

3. Carry out school and community projects that positively influence the lives of homeless students and families.

   a. Be a liaison for homeless students and advocate and educate others and gain their support and involvement.
   b. Form "leadership teams" that take action to increase the school success of homeless students.
   c. Volunteer at a community shelter for homeless students/families.
   d. Help organize district wide policy changes that improve attendance of homeless students.
   e. Tutor and mentor a homeless student in your school.

4. Reflect on your service involvement.

   a. Develop plans for educating and involving other staff.
   b. Organize more comprehensive school/community strategies to address the problems of homeless students and families.
   c. Initiate staff and faculty professional development workshops on omelessness, especially as related to the needs of students.

Design and carry out a "serve and learn" project that focuses on making the school more responsive and supportive of the needs of homeless students. For example, staff might conduct an assessment that examines barriers to homeless students' full participation in school and related educational pursuits. Similar assessments (Swick, 1996a) have found problem areas such as: enrollment barriers, transportation, lack of basic resources, a need for educational resources, peer rejection, unresponsive teachers, and the need for counseling.

Use home visits with families at local shelters to gain insights into the specific challenges they face in supporting their children educationally and in relation to other needs. As Stronge (1997) noted, homeless students and families are individuals with specific attributes and needs. Home visits also provide educators with information on how they can support students through direct and indirect activities that help the parents and family. One teacher who found success through family visits at a shelter then engaged others in eliminating barriers so these parents could attend parent-teacher conferences and other parenting and school-sponsored activities. She explains:

> During the "family visits" three things were clear: (1) these parents wanted their children to succeed in school, (2) they needed transportation to get to the school, and (3) they needed help in getting their children resources like paper, pens, etc. I met with our principal and we developed a team of faculty who worked on several strategies including: getting a van to transport parents to the school, working with the shelter on setting up a study room, and collaborating with the Cooperative Ministry to provide students with needed study materials. (Reported in this teacher's course journal for the author)

Organize a leadership team of staff who are experienced in educating homeless students and pursue goals such as the following: (1) advocate at the district level for needed changes and resources; (2) sponsor a district professional development program on educating homeless students; (3) develop curriculum materials for classroom use; (4) form a school-community alliance on behalf of homeless students and families; and, (5) create "transition" support resources to assist homeless students in dealing with the many changes they experience. Teaming among staff in efforts like this enhances everyone's learning and effectiveness. It brings staff together to begin to shape a promising vision for their work with homeless students. As Quint (1994) noted:

> When professional isolation of teachers is reduced, the door is opened to the sharing of a common language, successful practices, and a vision of what school life could be like, as well as to joint support, trust, and encouragement. (p. 42)

Form a district-wide faculty team to develop a "resource guide on homelessness" that can be used across different subject areas (Young, 1997). The team might study specific needs in the community, acquire data on homelessness from a national and international perspective, invite input from other staff and students, and organize related curriculum resources. The resource guide should be easily adaptable to different grade levels and to different content areas. Staff development sessions to introduce teachers to the guide are essential. Ideally, this team can continually revise the resource guide to include new materials and ideas gained from their work.

Develop a caring-inquiry relationship with a homeless student, learning all that you can about their specific situation. Involve the student in "co-researching" his/her context, talents, and needs. This can be a valuable learning experience for teacher and student. Some insights might include:

♦ The teacher comes to know the student as a person, not just as a homeless student. At the same time, the teacher can gain a "new perspective" on some of the key issues other homeless students confront. Further, the teacher can begin to see just how much she/he can contribute to the life of even one student.

♦ The student gains a nurturing and trusting relationship with a caring adult. The student also acquires insight into her/his personal strengths, skills for coping with different challenges, and hopefully a vision for achieving educational and life success. (Swick, 1996b)

HOW CAN WE BUILD AWARENESS AND SUPPORT FOR THE LEARNING NEEDS OF HOMELESS STUDENTS AMONG ALL STUDENTS?

The empowerment of students in understanding homeless students and specifically the situation(s) of their homeless peers is critical to developing an effective school and community environment. The following are some examples of ways to increase student awareness of homelessness and the proactive roles they can play in dealing with this community challenge.

Faculty and staff should model sensitive and caring relations with homeless and other at-risk students and families (Schwartz, 1995). Students often follow the lead of teachers and staff in confronting new experiences. Staff who establish positive and supportive interactions with homeless students without stigmatizing or isolating them are providing an exemplary model for all students and parents. Observable indicators of this positive approach might include having needed services on site, using a "buddy system" where students team with a homeless student to help them become familiar with the school, and putting homeless students in leadership roles in the school.

Establish a faculty/staff team that promotes caring activities in the school that enable students to gain positive perspectives and relationships with homeless students (Rafferty, 1997/1998). These activities may range from schoolwide homeless awareness and service projects to individual counseling with students who may hold distorted ideas about their homeless peers. In addition, community service projects should include opportunities where staff and students work together in helping roles that foster a better understanding of the complexities of homelessness. Small group "reflection times" can promote a sharing of insights on being homeless, thus increasing everyone's ability to be more proactive.

Select and train "peer leaders" who serve in leadership roles in the school and community in educating others about the issues involved in being homeless (Swick & Graves, 1993). Mature and sensitive student leaders who are provided with needed training can promote positive and supportive relations with homeless students. In particular, these student leaders can:

♦ provide support to individual students who are homeless;

♦ encourage other students to include homeless students in peer activities;

♦ initiate schoolwide awareness activities on the needs of the homeless;

♦ function as a team in developing a comprehensive program to improve school services for homeless students.

Student leaders gain in the sense of developing leadership skills and by engaging others in the school environment in becoming more supportive of students who have special needs.

Organize a faculty curriculum development team to create units, materials, resources, and service-learning experiences that enhance student understanding of homelessness (Schwartz, 1995). The following possibilities are noted by Young (1997):

- In Art, have the students research the needs of the homeless and create "flyers" that highlight these needs and possible solutions for use in advocacy work in the community.

- In Math, have students try to develop a monthly family budget based on the income of a homeless family in the community. Have them compare this budget to their own family budget.

- In Social Studies, have the students research various aspects of the living conditions of homeless families and possible approaches to resolving these problems. Have them develop a plan of action that might be used in their community.

- In Language Arts, have the students write about "how it would feel to not have a home." Have them study poetry and stories written about homelessness and have them share their findings and their stories on this topic.

Many discussion activities and creative problem-solving opportunities will evolve from the above curriculum experiences. The idea is to engage students in thinking about the issues involved in homelessness so they can develop proactive and supportive approaches to the problems they articulate.

Develop a "Service-Learning Program" that centers on activities that support homeless and other special needs groups in the community (Swick et al., 1998). Students can be engaged in a three-stage process: (1) conducting community needs assessment (particularly for homeless people), (2) designing and implementing service activities based on the assessments, and (3) doing reflective work on their service with an emphasis on how the experiences have increased their understanding of social challenges in the community. To be most effective, these service-learning activities should be long-term, have significant student input, be coordinated with the agencies being served, and be linked to academic and related school objectives. Formally planned service-learning programs communicate the positive value that staff and the total school-community team place on serving and valuing all people in the community. Brophy (as cited in Quint, 1994) notes:

> Consistent projection of positive expectations, attributions, and social labels to the students is important in fostering positive self-concepts and related motives that orient the students toward prosocial behavior. (p. 106)

Develop a counseling intervention plan to address the particular social and emotional needs of homeless students and their non-homeless peers (Vissing, Schroepfer, & Bloise, 1994). Homeless students often feel uncomfortable in the school environment. They need a counselor who can build a trusting relationship with them and support them in negotiating the various social and emotional challenges inherent in their situation. Students who are not homeless often need counseling that empowers them to understand the specific needs and strengths of their homeless peers. Both prevention and intervention activities can focus on developing positive and accurate student understanding of homelessness.

HOW CAN WE BUILD AWARENESS AND SUPPORT FOR THE LEARNING NEEDS OF HOMELESS STUDENTS AMONG COMMUNITY MEMBERS?

The power of staff and student involvement in supporting homeless students is enhanced through collaboration arrangements that "connect" their work with that of the total community (Quint, 1994). Schools must be a significant part of the community and must foster perspectives that encourage everyone to strengthen social and educational opportunities for homeless

Building Community Leadership Skills by Involving Students in Service to the Homeless

1. Organize student leadership teams that are heterogeneous in nature and that focus efforts on community strengthening.

2. Have each team assess critical needs of the homeless in their community such as:
   a. housing   d. food
   b. transportation   e. education
   c. job training   f. other

3. Involve teams in building a "Strengthening Services for the Homeless" plan inclusive of:
   a. goals   d. desired results
   b. organizational plans
   c. specific community
      strategies

4. Students implement plans using strategies such as:
   a. direct service activities such as helping improve shelter facilities,
   b. packaging food and delivering it to shelters,
   c. improving educational access for homeless students,
   d. helping local government develop improved housing plans, and
   e. doing indirect service projects such as fund raising.

5. Student leadership teams evaluate their efforts and refine plans for developing new projects and activities.

students and families. When parents and neighbors are encouraged to participate as partners in building better schools and communities they respond positively if staff are sincere in sharing the power of decision making with them (Quint, 1994).

Thus, the awareness process should involve faculty and students in learning about important community values, needs, and resources, and ways that they can negotiate these issues to advance the education of homeless students.

The move from awareness to action can be further strengthened by forming a systematic means of addressing the needs of homeless students at both the school and district levels (Stronge, 1995). For example, a faculty/student leadership team can become the force for shaping a vision and developing a structure for supporting homeless students, and linking this structure to district-wide efforts. One teacher involved in an awareness course on homeless students provided the leadership in her school to create such a structure and was effective in altering admission policies, transportation schedules, and after-school activity fees, to the advantage of homeless students (Swick, 1996a). Schools can also use the concept of a "Welcome Team" that Woods (1997) describes, where staff and students provide a non-threatening and supportive introduction to the school. The leadership team should be inclusive of the principal, parents, staff, students, and neighborhood/community leaders.

Collaboration of leadership teams from two or three schools can provide the impetus for changing district-wide policies and procedures. Two policy changes that happened in one district as a result of teacher-leadership are noted by Swick (1996a):

♦ provisions for annual awareness workshops on the needs of homeless students within the district's regularly scheduled professional development programs;

♦ adjustments in the placement of homeless students so that they are placed in the school they previously attended or the school most comfortable and convenient for them and their families.

School and district collaboration is a powerful means for transforming the school experience for homeless students. Swick (1996a) noted that:

Collaborative efforts within schools can promote services such as after-school tutoring, easier access to school resources, provisions for needed study materials, increased involvement of homeless students in school activities, and the development of teacher liaisons to local shelters. (p. 295)

Guidelines for Learning about Homelessness in the Community

1. Carry out formal and informal "focus group" and discussion sessions with parents, neighbors, and other professionals and citizens who work with those who are homeless. Swick (1996b) found that as teachers engaged in direct relationships with homeless families and personnel who served the homeless, they enriched their perspectives for strengthening school and community support of homeless students.

2. Conduct assessments that identify needs and strengths of the homeless population in your community, including students. Involve homeless students, social service personnel, and others who have insights into the real situations of those who are homeless or at risk for becoming homeless.

3. Take stock of existing services and resources that can provide assistance to homeless families and students, collating these into a resource guide for use in each school in the district. Carry out staff development and community awareness activities, using the guide as a means of empowering others to support homeless students.

4. Volunteer to serve on community action teams that are designed to help the homeless population. Through this service, staff and students can learn about how the process of support is being achieved, what improvements are needed, and delineate opportunities for strengthening the community support system for homeless students and families.

To optimize the power of faculty/student efforts within schools and districts, efforts must be interrelated with services, advocacy work, and policy planning within the community and in relation to state and national activities.

> ## Collaboration Can Help Us Address Homeless Issues Effectively
>
> ♦ Staff and students can share and learn strategies for being more effective in supporting homeless students (Swick, 1997a).
>
> ♦ Needed support services for homeless students can be better coordinated and accessed more easily (Pawlas, 1994).
>
> ♦ Inter-agency and community policies related to services and supports for homeless students can be more easily changed and adapted (Quint, 1994).
>
> ♦ The particular services each school or community group provides can be more effectively used and directed to best meet the needs of homeless students (Stronge, 1995).
>
> ♦ Long-term educational and support plans to assist homeless students and their families can be more comprehensively designed, pursued, and achieved when all parties are networking and partnering (Stronge, 1997).
>
> ♦ Meeting the individual needs of each student who is homeless is enhanced as a result of collaboration where professionals know and have easy access to services that meet particular needs (Pawlas, 1994).

CONCLUSION: WHERE DO WE GO FROM HERE?

The future of the education of students who are homeless is dependent on having strong school and community collaboration. Three examples of ways to achieve the needed partnerships for homeless students are noted:

1. The "Principal as Leader" scheme described by Quint (1994) offers the benefit of the building leader "taking ownership" of advocating, planning, and guiding

staff and student efforts. At the same time, this approach can only be effective when the power and responsibility for educating homeless students is shared and accepted by everyone in the school culture. In effect, the principal must provide the context for empowering the entire team to engage in creating a supportive and positive climate for homeless students. Staff and students must be engaged as active members of advisory teams, community policy groups, and school-community action efforts.

2. The "Teacher as Leader" scheme discussed by Swick (1996a, 1996b) relies on the power of experienced classroom teachers in developing strategies to reshape school-district-community policies and procedures to better support the education of students who are homeless. An individual teacher, or more likely, a small group of teachers, functions as a team, working closely with the building principal to organize strategies that are responsive to the specific needs of homeless students in the school. This approach is only effective to the degree that teacher leadership parameters are clear, continuous, and interrelated with the work of all staff and students. This scheme is potentially powerful in that teachers have more direct access to students than other personnel and they are more likely to identify key areas that need change.

3. The "Staff/Student Committee" scheme noted by Pawlas (1994) is ideally suited to articulating specific issues in need of urgent attention. It is a very inclusive scheme but is prone to lose power if the membership becomes complacent. Active staff/student teams have proven influential in creating community involvement such as providing for on-site social services, developing special after-school study programs, and encouraging community contributions to fund special-need areas (Quint, 1994).

Regardless of the structure that the collaboration system takes, the following questions provide key insights on areas that staff and students can strengthen through the networking process (Pawlas, 1994):

♦ What are the key needs of homeless students in our school/community, inclusive of needs that reach beyond those observed within the school?

♦ What are key resources in the community that can enhance the educational and social lives of students who are homeless and how can these be most effectively coordinated and accessed?

♦ What school-district-community collaboration scheme seems most effective for our school in achieving optimal networking to empower students who are homeless?

♦ What educational and training resources on homelessness can we access through partnerships with local groups, university faculty, and state education leaders?

♦ How can we engage parents, students, and staff in the total collaboration scheme to assure that our approach of empowering homeless students becomes a shared-ownership process?

Ultimately, moving from awareness to action to empower students who are homeless requires that each of us advocate for more inclusive and compassionate educational conditions in schools and communities. As Swick (1997) noted:

Educators, working in collaboration with many community groups, can create dynamic educational and support services that strengthen homeless students and families. The key is competent and caring staff who use responsive strategies that involve parents and students in using small steps each day to achieve their vision of permanency and care. (p. 34)

REFERENCES

Pawlas, G. (1994). Homeless students at the school door. *Educational Leadership, 51*(8), 79-82.

Quint, S. (1994). *Schooling homeless children: A working model for America's public schools.* New York: Teachers College Press.

Rafferty, Y. (1997/1998). Meeting the educational needs of homeless students. *Educational Leadership, 55*(4), 48-53.

Schwartz, W. (1995). *School programs and practices for homeless students.* New York: ERIC Clearinghouse on Urban Education. (ERIC Document Reproduction No. ED 383 783.)

Stronge, J. (1997). A long road ahead: A progress report on educating homeless children and youth in America. *Journal of Children and Poverty, 3*(2), 13-31.

Stronge, J. (1995). Educating homeless students: How can we help? *Journal for a Just and Caring education, 1*(2), 128-141.

Swick, K. (1997). Strengthening homeless families and their young children. *Dimensions of Early Childhood, 25*(2), 29-34.

Swick, K. (1996a). Teacher strategies for supporting homeless students and families. *The Clearing House, 69*(5), 293-296.

Swick, K. (1996b). Early childhood teachers reconstruct their views about homeless families. *Journal of Early Childhood Teacher Education, 17*(1), 26-36.

Swick, K., Winecoff, L., Rowls, M., Kemper, R., Freeman, N., Somerindyke, J., & Williams, T. (1998). *Service learning and teacher education.* Clemson, SC: National Dropout Prevention Center, Clemson University.

Swick, K., & Graves, S. (1993). *Empowering at-risk families during the early childhood years.* Washington, DC: National Education Association.

Vissing, Y., Schroepfer, D., & Bloise, F. (1994). Homeless students, heroic students. *Phi Delta Kappan, 75*, 535-539.

Woods, C. (1997). Pappas School: A response to homeless students. *The Clearing House, 70*(6), 302-303.

Young, N. (1997). *Teaching our students about homelessness.* Unpublished document available from the author. Chapel Hill, NC: University of North Carolina.

ADDITIONAL RESOURCES

Hightower, A., Nathanson, S., & Wimberly, G. (1997). *Meeting the educational needs of homeless children and youth: A resource for schools and communities*. Washington, DC: U.S. Department of Education. Available from the U.S. Government Printing Office.

Hoffbauer, D., & Prenn, M. (1966). A place to call one's own: Choosing books about homelessness. *Social Education, 60*(3), 167-169.

Pawlas, G., West, G., Brookes, C., & Russell, T. (1994). A safety net for homeless students. *Educational Leadership, 51*(8), 82-83.

Uline, C. (1998). *Homeless curricula: Five exemplary approaches*. Harrisburg, PA: Pennsylvania Department of Education, Education of Homeless Children and Youth Program. Available from the Office of Educating Homeless Children and Youth of the Pennsylvania Department of Education in Harrisburg, PA.

10

DESIGNING EFFECTIVE SCHOOL PROGRAMS FOR HOMELESS STUDENTS

BRENDA TOLER WILLIAMS AND LORI KORINEK

> Write all the books you want. Give all the speeches you
> want. Run all the meetings you want. Bleat out your
> longing for how the world (education) should work,
> and you will get only one question back . . . "How?"
>
> (Block, 1993, p. 233)

The statement above implies that there are no easy answers to the complexity of creating effective educational programs. This is especially true when attempting to design programs for students who are homeless and other students who are at-risk for school failure because of poverty, disabilities, or cultural and linguistic differences. Society is becoming more diverse—racially, linguistically, and culturally. The social fabric is unraveling for many families with children who comprise more than one-third of all homeless people (Vissing, 1996). Poverty is increasing and the indices of physical, mental, and moral well-being are declining (Children's Defense Fund, 1998). Students with disabilities represent approximately 12% of the school-age population (U.S. Department of Education, 1998).

The response to this diversity has been the promulgation of "special" programs and services which target each category of student need. This has resulted in duplication of services and fragmented delivery systems. In addition, many students experience the cumulative, adverse effects of poverty, homelessness, disabilities, and cultural differences (Williams & DeSander, 1999). There is a need to unify and coordinate educational programs and services to transform schools into diverse, problem-solving organizations that share responsibility and emphasize learning for all students. (Working Forum on Inclusive Schools, 1994).

This chapter identifies primary characteristics of effective school programs which are responsive to varying educational needs of students and families. A framework is provided for designing programs which facilitate educational achievement for all students but which are essential to removing the barriers to educational opportunity for students who are homeless. Additionally, resources are described to assist educators in comprehensive program planning.

COMPONENTS OF EFFECTIVE SCHOOL PROGRAMS FOR HOMELESS STUDENTS

HOW ARE EFFECTIVE SCHOOL PROGRAMS DEFINED?

Effective school programs for students who are homeless are those that successfully address the complexity and diversity of homeless students' needs—educational, emotional, behavioral, and physical—to produce positive outcomes for these students. Effective programs employ creative strategies for overcoming barriers to school attendance such as transportation, residency, health, and records requirements. Moreover, effective programs will provide an array of services that can be combined, adjusted, or reconfigured to provide the support needed for school success (Edmonds, 1982; Lezotte & Jacoby, 1990).

WHAT ARE THE CHARACTERISTICS OF EFFECTIVE SCHOOL PROGRAMS?

Effective school programs for students who are homeless are characterized by:

- ◆ multilevel collaboration;
- ◆ authentic family involvement;
- ◆ strong leadership;
- ◆ comprehensive planning;
- ◆ adequate resources; and
- ◆ ongoing staff development.

These characteristics are very similar to those identified by Walther-Thomas, Korinek, McLaughlin, and Williams (2000) as essential features of inclusive programs to support students with disabilities and others with special needs due to a variety of risk factors. In concert, these characteristics allow school programs to be responsive to diverse and changing needs. They also allow programs to be proactive in preventing school difficulties that might compound the hardships already encountered by students who are homeless. Each program characteristic is described below.

Multilevel Collaboration. Because of the complexity of needs presented by students who are homeless, teamwork is crucial among school personnel, other service providers, and families for successful planning, problem solving, and program implementation. Collaboration begins with a common commitment of participants to supporting all students in their learning and development regardless of student labels or circumstances. Teamwork brings together diverse perspectives and expertise, allowing for more comprehensive and creative solutions to complex problems. At its best, collaboration involves voluntary participation, mutual goals, parity among participants, and shared decision making, resources, responsibility, and accountability (Friend & Bursuck, 1999). In the most successful school programs, collaboration is evident at and across multiple levels—the classroom, school, district, and community.

In the classroom, teachers, specialists, and para-educators model collaboration, acceptance, and belonging. They make students feel that they are an integral part of the learning community, both giving and receiving support. Students are afforded learning experiences that foster peer interaction, teamwork, and group decision making through support structures such as buddy systems, cooperative learning groups, and peer tutoring.

At the school level, administrative, instructional (e.g., teachers, specialists), and support staff work together to serve students with special needs. Korinek, Williams, McLaughlin, & Walther-Thomas (2000) noted that a variety of teaming approaches developed in schools to encourage collaborative planning and problem solving can also be used to provide support to students without homes. These structures include departmental or grade-level teams, assistance teams, consultation, and cooperative or co-teaching. In different ways these approaches provide a forum for discussing unique needs, identifying problems and resources, brainstorming, problem solving, and implementing accommodations and interventions. If students are identified as having disabilities, even more extensive supports and program modifications can be accessed through the special education process.

Because the needs of homeless students extend beyond any one school, collaboration is critical among school leaders *within a district,* among district-level personnel in localities where homeless students may hold temporary residence, and among staff at schools and shelters housing school-aged children and youth. Schools and shelters tend to be central agencies among those providing assistance to families who are homeless. Designated liaisons between shelters and schools can facilitate communication, prompt enrollment or transfer of records, and effective use of available resources. Leaders or their designees from community agencies such as Social Services, Mental Health, the Red Cross, and Salvation Army also serve as valuable collaborative partners in meeting the needs of students and families who are homeless. In addition, churches, civic organizations, university programs, volunteer groups, and others in the community can play important roles as part of the larger system mobilized to provide a network of support to homeless individuals. Close collaboration ensures that needs are met, gaps and overlaps in services are avoided, and resources are used most efficiently and effectively.

Authentic Family Involvement. Effective school programs have found meaningful ways to involve parents and family members in the educational process despite many obstacles and challenges they face because of homelessness. Professionals recognize these challenges and try to work with family members in ways that convey respect and facilitate participation. Such strategies include:

♦ conveying genuine commitment to serving children;

♦ scheduling meetings at convenient times and places;

♦ providing assistance to attend educational meetings and complete forms;

♦ encouraging participation in creative ways such as supplying food or essential items at school meetings.

Staff recognize family members as valuable sources of information about their child's functioning and educational experiences. They may have records, names of contact persons from previous settings, and unique insights into students' situations outside of school. Parents and family members are viewed as educational partners with unique strengths and coping mechanisms—essential collaborators in achieving positive outcomes for students who are homeless.

Strong Leadership. Strong leadership is another hallmark of effective school programs for students who are homeless. The role of principals at the school level is pivotal in articulating school missions, managing curriculum and instruction, supervising teachers, promoting positive climate, and fostering collaborative interactions (Krug, 1992; Tindall, 1996). But principals are not the only leaders in successful school programs for homeless students; leadership and advocacy must be shared and employed at every level of involvement with students and their families (classroom, school, district, and community). State and local school boards can enact policies that increase access to and the quality of educational opportunities. Teachers, specialists, and agency personnel can highlight needs, help align key players, motivate and inspire others, maintain critical directions and initiatives, and work together to implement the comprehensive effort needed to meet needs of homeless students and their families.

Comprehensive Planning. Comprehensive planning that characterizes effective school programs for homeless students is coherent, coordinated, and long-range. Comprehensive plans serve as tools for articulating and communicating the program vision and for demonstrating commitment to sustained support for initiatives. They guide immediate and long-term decision making about resource allocation, staff development, personnel assignments, student programming, and evaluation (Walther-Thomas et al., 2000).

Adequate Resources. Appropriate educational programs for students who are homeless require adequate resources including personnel, funding, facilities, collaboration time, and materials. But few programs have all the resources considered desirable by implementers. Most successful programs have creatively allocated or reallocated resources to make most efficient use of available resources and tapped into additional assets by combining funding streams and services for at-risk populations, applying for grants, and leveraging existing funds and personnel across schools within a district. Again, support from and collaboration among leaders at the state, division, school, and community levels are essential to providing the required resources for successful implementation of school programs for homeless students over time.

Ongoing Staff Development. A well-developed, ongoing, multidimensional program of staff development experiences to facilitate within-school and within-district awareness, understanding, and capability to respond to identified needs of homeless students also characterizes effective school programs serving these students (Walther-Thomas et al., 1996). All administrative, instructional, and support staff who need to be aware of their respective roles in assisting students and families receive preparation regarding topics such as legal and procedural issues, warning signs of homelessness and needs for extra support, communication skills with families and community agencies, and strategies for supporting students academically and socially. Formal staff development sessions are often supplemented with video- and audiotaped materials, computer software and Internet information, resource manuals, case studies, articles, and newsletters which can reach a wider audience with diverse needs and schedules. Opportunities to visit shelters, dialogue with community staff and families, and network with other service providers are also used to increase awareness and skills.

In summary, this section has identified several critical characteristics of effective school programs serving students who are homeless. Suggestions for accomplishing quality programs are offered in the next sections.

PLANNING EFFECTIVE SCHOOL PROGRAMS FOR HOMELESS STUDENTS

WHAT IS PROGRAM PLANNING?

Planning for program improvement is a systematic process for developing a new or refined vision, setting priorities, and defining a more effective school organization and governing structure. It is a mechanism for building a constituency to support school change (U. S. Department of Education, 1998). In most school districts, planning should be implemented at three levels: in policy, in program development, and in program delivery (McCune, 1986). Each planning level provides a different element for the success of schools. Strategic planning involves the analysis of current policy and addresses the relevancy of the total educational program. It begins with the question, "What knowledge, skills, and capabilities will youth and adults need in the future?" Relevant programs meet the needs of the community and the students and families served while maintaining a perspective on national trends and issues that impact education (Rothwell & Cookson, 1997). Strategic planning requires the development of a vision or an approximation of the future that provides the assumptions for developing the district's or school's mission and strategic goals.

Program planning activities address the issue of effectiveness. "Are we doing the things that will help us achieve our mission and goals?" This question may easily relate to curriculum and instructional systems, but is equally important to review the budget, physical facilities, staff development, technology, personnel systems, and other factors to ensure that they support the attainment of the mission and goals.

The third level of planning is for program delivery, which asks, "How well are we doing things? Does the day-to-day delivery of services support the attainment of our mission and goals?" Program delivery planning addresses efficiency issues.

WHO SHOULD BE INVOLVED IN THE PLANNING PROCESS?

While federal initiatives, state legislation, and school district restructuring may be strong forces for change, it will be the efforts of teachers, specialists, principals, and families working together persistently over time on goals that are important to them that will improve the quality of education for all students (Hirsh & Murphy, 1991; Quint, 1994; Walther-Thomas, et al, 2000). Planning efforts should include a broad array of people who are involved in deliberating on behalf of children and youth. Such people, who have a vested interest in the use of resources and in the skills and knowledge that students will possess when they exit the system, are referred to as "stakeholders" (Holcomb, 1996). Both internal (i.e., administrators, teachers, specialists, psychologists, social workers, clerical, school health personnel) and external (i.e., parents, agencies, business community, shelter staff) stakeholders should be represented in the planning process. Team building activities and professional development on group process skills will enhance program planning initiatives.

WHAT ARE THE STEPS FOR DESIGNING RESPONSIVE SCHOOL PROGRAMS?

Literature on organizational development, school change, and effective inclusive schools (Fullan, 1993; Holcomb, 1996; Korinek, McLaughlin, & Gable, 1994; Lezotte & Jacoby, 1990; Wood, 1989) suggests that program planning that considers all segments of the student population should respond to the following questions:

- Where are we now?
- Where do we want to go?
- How will we get there?
- How will we know we are (getting) there?
- How can we keep it going?

The planning process essentially becomes a matter of working through these basic questions. Each of the questions corresponds to planning steps which can assist school districts in building school capacity to respond to the needs of students who are homeless and other at-risk populations.

Step 1: Develop Division-Wide Commitment to All Students. Question: Where Are We Now? At this stage an environmental scan or internal audit is conducted to determine the current "state of the school(s)" in responding to student, family, and staff needs. Figure 1 summarizes some of the data that can be collected to support activities at this step. Specific activities include:

- Identify current rates of student success; analyze these data for specific student groups (e.g., homeless students, students from low socioeconomic backgrounds, students of color).
- Review existing philosophy, mission, and belief statements in light of student success data. Is there an expressed commitment to helping *all* students succeed?
- Identify strengths and weaknesses of current programs to raise awareness of the need for change (e.g., strength: existence of pamphlets and posters describing available services for students who are homeless; weakness: absence of school-community liaison or single point of contact for families and shelter personnel).

- ◆ Identify barriers to achieving success for all students including those obstacles which might exist in current governance, policies, and procedures (e.g., policy requiring receipt of transfer records before enrollment; lack of transportation to support continuation at former school in the district; lack of communication mechanisms between school and shelter).

- ◆ Identify current "bridges" which facilitate student success. What is working (e.g., school-shelter liaison position, donations of school supplies and clothing from community agencies; office procedures that permit flexibility in enrolling homeless students)?

- ◆ Identify indicators of readiness for change in the district's or school's culture and climate (e.g., presence of support programs for other students with special needs, existence of School Improvement Teams which support problem solving at the school level).

- ◆ Communicate roles and responsibilities. *Who* will do *what* by *when* on behalf of homeless students and their families?

- ◆ Diagnose stakeholder perceptions and expectations (e.g., interviews, surveys, or focus groups of family members, teachers, administrators, shelter personnel, community agencies).

The environmental scan represents the context, or needs assessment stage, of program planning. At this stage planners should review the current status of programs in operation, staffing patterns, technology, curriculum, instructional strategies, and existing evaluations (Hoyle, English, & Steffy, 1998). The results of this audit can be compared with vision and mission statements which reflect where the district or school wishes to be in the next five or ten years. One way to organize the environmental scan is to conduct a SWOT analysis, identifying the perceived **S**trengths, **W**eaknesses, **O**pportunities and **T**hreats in the internal and external environments.

FIGURE 1. POSSIBLE SOURCES OF INFORMATION FOR THE
ENVIRONMENTAL SCAN

♦ A demographic profile of students served by the school
  (gender, race/ethnicity, language differences, family
  income, indicators of special needs, etc.)

♦ Evidence of levels of parent participation/involve-
  ment

♦ Summary of existing assessment data
  - aptitude test scores
  - achievement test scores
  - state and city-wide test assessment results

♦ Discipline records

♦ Attendance records for students and staff

♦ Tardiness records

♦ Dropout records

♦ History of interagency contacts and collaboration

♦ Transfer and mobility records

♦ Descriptions of current programs

*Step 2: Identify Goals That Are Central to the School
District's Mission. Question: Where Do We Want to Go?*
Holcomb (1996) offered specific activities for this planning step:

♦ Revise or affirm the district's mission statement (i.e.,
  ensure wording is inclusive of special groups such as
  homeless students).

♦ Engage stakeholders in visioning or a description of
  the desired future for the district or school as it relates
  to students who are homeless.

♦ Prioritize concerns. What needs to be addressed immediately? What are long-range issues?

♦ List unmet student, family, and staff needs (e.g., information, transportation, expedited enrollment and
expedited evaluation when a disability is suspected).

♦ Develop goals and objectives that focus on students
(e.g., academic success, social skill mastery, self-advo-
cacy skill development).

♦ Identify practices that have promise for success with
homeless students (e.g., curriculum-based assessment,
cooperative learning, in-school homework groups).

Defining clear goals and objectives based on the identified
needs of students and staff facilitates program improvement.
Brainstorming is one technique that facilitates generation of as
many ideas as possible related to a particular problem, issue, or
goal. Because the brainstorming process is not tied to current
realities it aids in the shaping of new visions for educational
programs. Posing a question such as "What are *all* the things
that anyone might say could be improved about our educational
services for homeless students and their families?" is a good
way to generate a list of issues. Brainstorming is most effective
when participants share ideas freely but briefly, everyone contributes, quantity of ideas is stressed, and explanations and
evaluation of suggestions occur *after* brainstorming.

Having individual group members rank order the five items
they are most concerned about facilitates prioritizing of concerns.
This technique, known as Nominal Group Process, gives planning team members the opportunity to participate in selecting
which areas to work on first (Holcomb, 1996).

***Step 3: Develop Multiple Strategies to Ensure Goal Achieve-
ment for Students With Diverse Educational Needs. Question:
How Will We Get There?*** After a school plan which includes
beliefs, mission, priorities, objectives, and strategies has been
completed, action plans should be developed. Action plans are
detailed descriptions of the specific tasks required to implement
the strategies of the plan and achieve its objectives. This step
involves the following:

- Identify and prioritize strategies to accomplish goals.

- Develop responses to barriers.

- Identify success indicators and data sources to monitor progress.

- Affirm mission and beliefs.

Figure 2 provides an example of an action plan format which can be used to ensure implementation of strategies. This format facilitates sequencing tasks, establishing timelines, and identifying key persons to carry out specific tasks.

Step 4: Plan for Continuous Evaluation and Improvement. Question: How Will We Know We Are (Getting) There? Program evaluation addresses the design of the program and committed resources, program implementation, and results or outcomes (McLaughlin & McLaughlin, 1993). Planners should not try to evaluate everything at once, but focus on established priorities within the context of program development. For example, if the program is in the beginning stages, it may be appropriate to collect information on stakeholder perceptions of services and resource commitments; once the program is implemented, student outcome data should become the focus. Guidelines for evaluation include:

- Focus on established priorities.

- Monitor progress data on identified indicators.

- Identify and respond to individual concerns.

- Affirm mission and beliefs.

- Adjust program as needed.

Continuous evaluation yields information to support decision making. Planners should formulate evaluation questions that shape the processes for collection, analysis, and reporting of information about the school program to various audiences (e.g., families, school board members, the media, citizen groups). Evaluation also provides evidence to continue, adjust, or refine

FIGURE 2. SAMPLE ACTION PLAN FORMAT

Action Plan Title: *Improvement of Educational Services for Homeless Students*

Clarifying Statement: In order to facilitate enrollment and attendance of students who are homeless, plans will be designed and implemented to overcome barriers currently confronting these students.

Task #	Tasks to be completed	Timelines Begin Date	End Date	Person(s) Responsible	Resources Required/Costs (measurable outcomes)	Progress Indicators
1.0	Review school intake policies and procedures	Sept.	Nov.	Team A	None	Elimination of cases of delayed enrollment of students who are homeless
1.1	Revise procedures to expedite access of records	Nov.	Jan.	Team B	None	
1.2	Provide in-service to office personnel on revisions	Nov.	Jan.	Sarah Jones School-Shelter Liaison	Stationery, postage	
1.3	Inform shelter staff of revisions					

what is being done. It shows if resources are being used efficiently and effectively or if changes are needed.

Step 5: Employ Techniques to Maintain Momentum and Sustain Implementation. Question: How Will We Keep It Going? Lambert (1998) stated that a commitment to a culture of inquiry provides a forum in which educators can continue to identify and respond to the most compelling questions which frame their work. Such a culture develops the knowledge base of professionals and staff to ensure that planning efforts address research-based as well as "cutting edge" issues and practices. Maintaining momentum and sustaining implementation involves the following:

♦ Monitor progress and adjust strategies.
♦ Build a culture of inquiry. Consider strategies such as:
  - convening faculty study groups on issues related to education of homeless students;
  - inviting shelter personnel to speak to school faculty and staff; and
  - visiting successful programs.
♦ Design a process for problem solving as conflict arises (i.e., identify the problem, brainstorm solutions with stakeholders, weigh advantages and disadvantages of alternatives, select and implement a solution).
♦ Affirm mission and beliefs.

Strategies for orienting new staff members and planning team members about the planning process are suggested in some of the resources listed at the end of this chapter (see, for example, Arcaro, 1995; Hirsh & Murphy, 1991). In addition, second or third year plan updates provide the opportunity to assess progress, analyze new information, and adjust the plan accordingly. Such updates also provide the opportunity to celebrate tasks that have been completed and communicate new activities that have been added.

CONCLUSION

Rothwell and Cookson (1997) discussed program planning as a comprehensive process in which planners, exercising a sense of professional responsibility, designate specific strategies to engage relevant contexts, design specific sets of learning outcomes, and plan relevant administrative aspects. More simply stated, such planning affords participants the opportunity to describe the desired future of the organization and identify what action and resources are necessary to achieve that future.

This chapter has described the components of effective programs for students who are homeless and others who are at-risk for school failure. Steps for design and implementation planning have been delineated. The suggestions that have been offered represent a "menu" of planning options rather than a prescription that should be followed in a linear fashion. Planning teams will need to develop site-specific "plans to plan" based on the unique features and characteristics of their respective schools or districts. The resulting planning road map must allow flexibility to respond to changing needs of students, families, and staff. The end result can be the development of a school climate where meaningful learning takes place and in which everyone feels safe and cared for.

REFERENCES

Arcaro, J.S. (1995). *Teams in education: Creating an integrated approach.* Delray Beach, FL: St. Lucie.

Block, P. (1993). *Stewardship.* San Francisco: Berrett Koehler.

Children's Defense Fund (1998). *The state of America's children: Yearbook 1998.* Washington, DC: Author.

Edmonds, R. (1982, December). Programs of school improvement: An overview. *Educational Leadership, 40* (3), 4-11.

Friend, M., & Bursuck, W. (1999). *Including students with special needs: A practical guide for classroom teachers* (2nd ed.). Boston: Allyn and Bacon.

Fullan, M. (1993). *Change forces: Probing the depths of educational reform.* New York: Falmer.

Hirsh, S., & Murphy, M. (1991). *School improvement planning manual.* Oxford, OH: National Staff Development Council.

Holcomb, E. (1996). *Asking the right questions: Tools and techniques for teamwork.* Thousand Oaks, CA: Corwin.

Hoyle, J.R., English, F.W., & Steffy, B. (1998). *Skills for successful 21st century school leaders: Standards for peak performance.* Arlington, VA: American Association of School Administrators.

Korinek, L., McLaughlin, V. L., & Gable, R. A. (1994). A planning guide for collaborative service delivery. *Preventing School Failure, 38*(4), 37-40.

Korinek, L., Williams, B., McLaughlin,V., & Walther-Thomas, C. (2000). Improving educational opportunities for students with disabilities who are homeless. In R.A. Mickelson (Ed.), *Children on the streets of the Americas: Globalization, homelessness and education in the United States, Brazil and Cuba.* New York: Routledge.

Krug, S. E. (1992). Instructional leadership: A constructivist perspective. *Educational Administration Quarterly, 28*(3), 430-433.

Lambert, L. (1998). *Building leadership capacity in schools.* Alexandria, VA: Association for Supervision and Curriculum Development.

Lezotte, L., & Jacoby, B. (1990) *A guide to the school improvement process based on effective schools research.* Okemos, MI: Effective Schools Products.

McLaughlin, J. A., & McLaughlin, V. L. (1993). Program evaluation. In B. Billingsley (Ed.), *Program leadership for serving students with disabilities* (pp. 343-370). Richmond: Virginia Department of Education.

McCune, S.D. (1986). *Guide to strategic planning for educators.* Alexandria, VA: Association for Supervision and Curriculum Development.

Quint, S. (1994). *Schooling homeless children: A working model for America's public schools.* New York: Teachers College.

Rothwell, W.J., & Cookson, P.S. (1997). *Beyond instruction: Comprehensive program planning for business and education.* San Francisco: Jossey-Bass.

Tindall, E. (1996). *Principal's role in fostering teacher collaboration for students with special needs.* Unpublished dissertation. Williamsburg, VA: College of William and Mary.

U.S. Department of Education. (1998). *To assure the free appropriate public education of all children with disabilities: Twentieth annual report to Congress on the implementation of the Individuals with Disabilities Education Act.* Washington, DC: U.S. Government Printing Office.

Vissing, Y. (1996). *Out of sight, out of mind: Homeless children and families in small-town America.* Lexington: University of Kentucky Press.

Walther-Thomas, C., Korinek, L., McLaughlin, V. L., & Williams, B. T. (1996). Improving educational opportunities for students with disabilities who are homeless. *Journal of Children and Poverty, 2*(2), 57-74.

Walther-Thomas, C., Korinek, L., McLaughlin, V., & Williams, B. (2000). *Collaboration for inclusive education: Developing successful programs.* Boston: Allyn & Bacon.

Williams, B. T., & DeSander, M.K. (1999, January). Dueling legislation: The impact of incongruent federal statutes on homeless and other special-needs students. *Journal for a Just and Caring Education, 5* (1), 34-50.

Wood, F.H. (1989). Organizing and managing school-based staff development. In S.D. Caldwell (Ed.), *Staff development: A handbook of effective practices* (pp. 26-43). Oxford, OH: National Staff Development Council.

Working Forum on Inclusive Schools (1994). *Creating schools for all our students: What 12 schools have to say.* Reston, VA: The Council for Exceptional Children.

ADDITIONAL RESOURCES

The following resources are available to assist planning teams to design responsive programs:

Arcaro, J.S. (1995). *Teams in education: Creating an integrated approach.* This book describes a structured process for creating and managing teams in education and provides information on selecting team members, developing the team, organizing and measuring team activities, and documenting results. Publisher: St. Lucie Press, Inc., 100 E. Linton Blvd., Suite 403B, Delray Beach, FL 33483, telephone: (407) 274-9906; fax: (407) 274-9927.

Heflin, L.J., & Rudy, K. (1991). *Homeless and in need of special education.* This monograph provides useful information on strategies for overcoming barriers to appropriate education for homeless students. Publisher: Council for Exceptional Children (CEC), 1920 Association Drive, Reston, VA 22091-1589, telephone: (703) 620-3660.

Hirsh, S., & Murphy, M. (1991). *School improvement planning manual.* This manual provides lesson plans, resource materials, and transparency masters to facilitate strategic planning at the school level. Publisher:

National Staff Development Council, P.O. Box 240, Oxford, OH 45056, telephone: (513) 523-6029.

Holcomb, E.L. (1996). *Asking the right questions: Tools and techniques for teamwork*. This practical book is organized around five questions that represent stages of the school improvement process. Tools that are most relevant to each phase are identified. Publisher: Corwin Press, Inc., A Sage Publications Company, 2455 Teller Road, Thousand Oaks, CA 91320, e-mail: order@corwin.sagepub.com

Maddux, R.B. (1992). *Team building: An exercise in leadership*. This self-paced resource helps readers recognize the differences between groups and teams and can be used for individual study, workshops and seminars, remote location training, or informal study groups. Publisher: Crisp Publications, 1200 Hamilton Court, Menlo Park, CA 94025, telephone: (800) 442-7477.

Walther-Thomas, C., Korinek, L., McLaughlin, V., & Williams, B. (1996). Improving educational opportunities for students with disabilities who are homeless. *Journal of Children and Poverty, 2* (2), 57-74. This article provides useful strategies for program development for homeless students. Publisher: Institute for Children and Poverty, 36 Cooper Square, New York, New York 10003, telephone: (212) 529-5252, Fax: (212) 529-7698.

11

ADVOCATING FOR HOMELESS STUDENTS

BARBARA J. DUFFIELD

In the United States today, children are more likely than any other age group to experience poverty. Despite a "booming" economy and a decline in the overall child poverty rate, the number of children living in extreme poverty—below half the poverty line—is increasing (Children's Defense Fund and National Coalition for the Homeless, 1998). It is not surprising, therefore, that the number of children without homes is also growing. In some states, children under the age of 18 now represent the majority of persons who are homeless: for example, 50% of all sheltered homeless persons in Minnesota, 64% of those seeking shelter in Oregon, and 55% of homeless people in Iowa.[1]

Poverty and homelessness hurt children. Poor children are twice as likely as non-poor children to be born at low birth weight; they also suffer more mental and physical disabilities (Children's Defense Fund, 1997). Homelessness during childhood is associated with higher infant mortality, developmental delays, asthma, chronic diarrhea, delayed immunizations, ear infections, elevated lead levels, dental problems, and family separation (Mihaly, 1991; Sherman, 1998).

Deep poverty and housing instability—especially during the earliest years of childhood—also have clear, long-lasting effects on children's academic learning and school completion (Duncan & Brooks-Gunn, 1997). Poor children are more than twice as likely as non-poor children to repeat a grade in school (Children's Defense Fund, 1997). In addition, frequent changes of residence and schools are associated with educational and behavior problems. A child who never moves is one-half as likely to drop out of high school as a child who moves four times, other factors being equal (Haveman & Wolfe, 1994). And children who have to change schools frequently because they move tend to score lower on math and reading tests (U.S. General Accounting Office, 1994).

School should be an oasis for homeless children and youth—a stable place where they receive sustenance, guidance, and support in learning the skills they will need to escape poverty as adults. Efforts to help homeless children and youth enroll, attend, and succeed in school are critical to their health and well-being.

Title VII B of the McKinney Homeless Assistance Act (PL100-77) provides the legal framework for homeless children and youth's right to an education. However, without the active participation of teachers, administrators, parents, policymakers, and advocates, the rights conferred by the McKinney Act are merely theoretical. Creative, effective, and persistent advocacy is the key to making educational rights real for homeless children and youth—and ultimately to ending the conditions of homelessness and poverty from which they suffer. This chapter outlines basic principles of advocacy on behalf of homeless students, provides examples of effective advocacy practices, and offers resources for budding and veteran advocates alike.

ADVOCACY 101: THE BASICS

WHAT IS ADVOCACY?

The word "advocacy" has a number of different meanings. Often, and particularly within the context of educational or social service programming, advocacy involves pleading the cause of another person—helping a child get a referral to needed medical care, obtain school records, or enroll in school. This kind of "one-on-one" advocacy is the backbone of most homeless education programs. Advocacy of this nature is accomplished family by family, child by child.

Advocacy also can focus on arguing in favor of a cause, idea, or policy. This kind of advocacy affects more than one person at a time, and is undertaken frequently on behalf of a whole group of people. Although "advocacy" in this latter sense is often used in reference to legislation, advocacy need not be restricted to legislative policy issues. Encouraging a school district to help provide transportation, to revise immunization requirements, or to drop school fees for lab classes or extracurricular activities so that homeless children may participate are all examples of essential community and school-based advocacy on behalf of homeless students. While this chapter focuses on issue-oriented advocacy rather than "one-on-one" advocacy, the strategies recommended in the chapter may be useful for both kinds of advocacy.

WHAT ARE THE GREATEST BARRIERS TO ADVOCACY?

Despite the importance of advocacy in ensuring homeless children and youth's enrollment, attendance, and success in school, many people who work directly with homeless children and youth are reluctant to get involved in advocacy efforts. While the reasons for this reluctance vary, they often fall into the following categories.

Fear of the Unknown. Many people who work with homeless children do not take part in advocacy efforts because they have never done so before and they believe that they do not know how to go about it. Advocacy may appear to be the preserve of activists, local "politicos," or influential community members, and not the realm of teachers, service providers, and administrators. The process for getting involved—whether attending a school board meeting, visiting a local elected official, or writing a letter to Congress—may appear too foreign and cumbersome.

There are plenty of "how to" resources that teach the basics of getting involved (see *Additional* Resources at the end of this chapter). In addition, there may be other groups in the community that can provide a vehicle for advocacy activities and help interested persons get their feet wet. But most importantly, the research, writing, and organizing skills that are used in everyday work activities by teachers and service providers are the same skills that are used in advocacy.

Power Differentials. Homeless children are among the least powerful people in our society. People who work with them may also feel as though they have little power in their communities. Advocacy may seem intimidating because of the apparent disparity in power between decision makers and affected parties.

Yet, most policymakers—local, state, and national—are dependent upon their constituents to elect them and to help them govern. Elected officials fully expect that their constituents will call them, write them, and ask them to do things. Similarly, school boards and other education bureaucracies must contend with various interest groups by virtue of their position in the community. Keeping this in mind may help reduce anxiety about power differentials: decision makers need and expect input from all sectors of the community.

There is another kind of power that can help assuage fears: the power of numbers. Convening a group of people with similar concerns—other teachers, volunteers, coalition members—may help overcome feelings of intimidation.

Knowledge Base. People who work with homeless children may feel that they lack sufficient substantive knowledge to be able to get involved in advocacy efforts. They may feel that because they are unfamiliar with some aspects of homelessness or education in their community, they don't "know enough" to speak to policymakers or other stakeholders. Or, perhaps most commonly, lack of familiarity with the content of legislation or the legislative process prevents people from getting involved in advocacy.

It is of utmost importance to remember who the experts on child homelessness are: homeless families and children. However, after homeless families, people working directly with homeless families and children are the foremost experts on homelessness in their communities. The particulars of legislation and the legislative process matter far less than the day-to-day activities and knowledge of practitioners and affected people.

Anti-lobbying Regulations. In recent years, a wave of "anti-lobbying" legislative initiatives have caused many people who work with homeless children and youth to question their ability to get involved in advocacy activities. This is particularly true of persons whose positions are paid for, in part or in full, by federal grants, such as the McKinney Education for Homeless Children and Youth program.

There is a great deal of confusion and misunderstanding surrounding "lobbying" and "advocacy." Advocacy should not be confused with lobbying. Lobbying, as defined by the IRS, involves attempts to influence legislation at the local, state, or federal level. To constitute lobbying, a group or individual must either support or oppose legislation. Using federal funds to lobby is prohibited. However, making a general argument—for example, that homelessness is increasing, or that homeless children need support in order to enroll, attend, and succeed in school— is not considered lobbying, but advocacy.

Thus, advocacy encompasses a broad range of activities not included in lobbying. For example, educating elected officials by informing them of the needs of homeless students is advocacy, and therefore not prohibited—even for people in federally funded positions. Moreover, staffing a federally funded position does not mean giving up the privileges of citizenship. Many child advocates engage in advocacy and lobbying activities in "after-hours" or other non-official capacities.

Another area of confusion is the ability of non-profits to engage in advocacy. Nonprofit (501c3) organizations that receive government funding can engage in direct lobbying activities, provided that their activities are documented and that those activities account for no more than a specified percentage of their overall budget (Alliance for Justice, 1996).

It is important not to let fear of anti-lobbying regulations prevent active participation in advocacy efforts. As noted earlier, advocacy takes many different forms, and there are ways that persons in all positions can take action on behalf of homeless children and youth in their communities.

Lack of Time. Working with homeless children is exhausting, consuming work. It may seem as though there is no time left at the end of the day to write a letter, attend a meeting, or make a phone call.

Fortunately, there are a number of ways to incorporate advocacy activities into daily work and to plan for them well in advance (these methods will be covered in more detail later in this chapter). However, it is also worth pointing out that advocacy can also make day-to-day work easier—it can result in changes in policies and programs that ultimately reduce time, effort, and stress. Furthermore, advocacy offers opportunities for creative, inspiring work that can improve services and lessen suffering.

Thus, there are many compelling reasons to incorporate advocacy into programmatic work for homeless children and youth. The following section describes effective practices for doing so.

EFFECTIVE PRACTICES IN ADVOCATING FOR HOMELESS STUDENTS

The struggle for homeless children and youth's right to an education has provided numerous examples of effective advocacy. Some of those examples, the effective practices they exemplify, and strategies to incorporate these practices into a total school/community program are described below.

MAXIMIZING THE IMPACT OF ADVOCACY: PRIORITIZING ISSUES

Picture this: confusion over the definition of homelessness is preventing children who are living in doubled-up situations from enrolling in school; the City Council is considering limiting the length of time families can stay in shelter; Congress is preparing to vote on next year's funding for the Education for Homeless Children and Youth program; and lack of awareness about homelessness appears to be at an all-time high. Which issue deserves immediate attention and action?

On any given day, there are numerous issues that cry out for concerted advocacy on behalf of homeless children and youth. Advocacy efforts will be maximized if participants carefully choose which issues to work on and when to work on them.

Strategies. The following questions may help guide efforts to prioritize advocacy:

Who else is working on this issue? Depending upon the size of the community, there may be several organizations that are active in children's advocacy. Are any of these groups taking the lead on the issue in question? If so, it may be more useful to support their efforts by signing letters, endorsing positions, etc., rather than spend a lot of time on activities that may be duplicative.

What will have the greatest impact on homeless children and youth? The causes and consequences of homelessness are complex; a policy change in one area can have ramifications in other areas. It is important to try to weigh the direct impact of the issue in question on homeless children and youth. What will have the greatest impact on their education, health, and well-being? For example, the restriction on the length of time families can stay in shelter, might have the greatest negative impact, as it would increase mobility and instability for the community's homeless children.

How much time is available? People who work with homeless children and youth respond to an ever-changing series of crises and demands upon their time.

Balancing competing demands is a necessary struggle in advocacy, and one that pre-planning may help ease. There are some national, state, and local advocacy events that happen on a regular basis each year, such as National Hunger and Homelessness Awareness Week and annual funding decisions for the Education of Homeless Children and Youth program. Other times of the year may be appropriate for more local advocacy events: for example, the "back to school" season in September, and the holiday season in late November and December. Pre-planning to include such events in annual work agendas helps to improve their effectiveness and reduce last-minute stresses associated with participating in them.

Often, however, issues come up unexpectedly or with little warning. In these instances, it is important to consider what can be done in the available time. If a vote is pending in Congress in a matter of hours, for example, it may be more effective to initiate a call-in campaign rather than writing letters; if there are

---

Kids in Advocacy

Homeless children in Minneapolis have had a big impact on city policy decisions that directly impact them. In November 1997, the Hennepin County Board debated a proposal to limit the shelter stay of families new to the county to 10 days. If adopted, the proposal would have forced homeless families to look for alternative emergency accommodations in the midst of a freezing Minnesota winter. With help from the Minnesota Coalition for the Homeless, two dozen homeless children attended the County board meeting and presented commissioners with a book about homelessness. The children held signs reading "Reduce Shelter Use—Build Affordable Housing" and told the commissioners what homelessness was like. The *Minneapolis Star Tribune* featured pictures of the children and details of the meeting. The result: the County retreated from its plan.

---

several days or weeks before a vote, a letter-writing campaign might be more appropriate because letters can convey more information and, therefore, have a greater impact.

Finally, there are some advocacy issues that will demand a carefully thought-out strategy that requires more time in order to be successful. Matters relating to multiple agencies and involving complex policymaking fall into this category. A less rushed, more deliberative advocacy campaign might yield better results in these instances.

What are your strengths? Another important consideration in prioritizing advocacy issues is determining an agency's or individual's strengths. For example, an agency may have developed excellent relationships with local news reporters. It may be that such an agency could most effectively contribute to an advocacy issue by contacting reporters to give them the "inside scoop." Other agencies may have extensive phone and fax networks. These agencies may be most effective in sending out alerts or letters requesting support. Yet other agencies or individuals may have key contacts in places of power. In this instance, arranging a private meeting to discuss issues out of the glare of the spotlight might be the best approach.

Ideally, advocacy can be pursued along all of these lines by working with a diverse coalition of partners (see *Community-Wide Collaboration* below). When time is short, however, it is necessary to evaluate your strengths and weaknesses before proceeding with an advocacy initiative.

COMMUNITY-WIDE COLLABORATION: CREATING PARTNERS IN ADVOCACY

An essential ingredient in effective advocacy is broad, diverse, community-wide collaboration. Collaboration is important in advocacy for homeless children and youth for a number of reasons. Some reasons are more obvious than others: there is strength in numbers, and resources can be quickly deployed by working with other groups. Other reasons are less obvious but equally compelling. For example, it is important that homeless children and youth not be perceived as a "special interest" population that only a small segment of the community cares about. For this same reason, it is important to try to involve as many "mainstream" groups as possible in advocacy activities—groups that might not be expected to take a strong interest in homeless children, but that have high visibility and legitimacy in the community. Such groups include faith-based organizations, parent associations such as the PTA, and businesses.

Another important reason to emphasize collaboration in advocacy efforts is to increase the visibility of homelessness in the community. Building a broad coalition of groups that are interested in helping homeless children—by lending their name to a letter, speaking up at an important community meeting, etc.—not only helps legitimize advocacy efforts but also helps educate more people about the problem of homelessness.

Collaboration is of particular importance to those who are limited in their advocacy efforts by the nature of their employment. Many people who work for government agencies, for example, are not free to engage in certain kinds of advocacy activities. By working in coalition, such individuals can share information with people who are free to advocate in the manner that best suits the issue at hand.

Finally, collaboration in advocacy is essential because of the kinds of connections to key players or "insiders" that other groups may have. The power of personal relationships in advocacy at all levels should never be underestimated; these relationships can often be discovered and employed by pulling together as diverse a community-wide coalition as possible.

Strategies.
♦ In thinking about how to build a diverse coalition around advocacy for homeless children and youth, start by examining all existing organizational relationships, including those based on services, funding, or staffing. Which of these relationships might be broadened to include advocacy?

♦ In most homeless education programs, there are likely to be two major groups: the education system and the homeless services system. Is there a key contact in each group who might be interested in helping to identify advocacy partners?

♦ Other important constituencies to approach include homeless parents, volunteers, civil rights groups, homeless/housing coalitions, child advocates, anti-poverty advocates, student groups, parent associations, faith groups, businesses (for example, those who donate to programs), law firms (for example, those who do *pro bono* work), and other education advocates (special education, etc.).

♦ Once potential partners have been identified, there are a number of ways to engage them in advocacy efforts. Holding an "open house" or "town hall meeting" in an available shelter, school, or church building might be one way to bring people together to discuss advocacy for homeless children. Inviting them to participate in other regular community meetings is an additional possibility.

♦ Campaigns are another good way to build partnerships—for example, identified partners can be approached to participate in a winter clothing drive or to sign on to a letter. Sign-on letters can range from asking the Mayor to issue a proclamation on Homeless Persons' Memorial Day (December 21) to a letter to the editor of the local newspaper on homelessness.

♦ Finally, newsletters are a great vehicle for community outreach. They can be used to educate about homelessness and to make appeals for support of advocacy initiatives. Identified partners might be added to the mailing list with a special cover letter for their first issue.

ESTABLISHING AND MAINTAINING RELATIONSHIPS WITH KEY PLAYERS

In addition to building community-wide collaboration in advocacy, it is important to develop relationships with "key players": people in positions of power in the community who have the ability to make decisions impacting homeless children and youth's lives. Key players can be highly visible figures or people who work predominantly "behind the scenes." They include, but are not limited to, elected officials (local, state, and national), superintendents, school board members, and reporters.

It is not uncommon for advocates to contact key players only after an emergency has arisen and immediate action must be taken. In these instances, advocates are likely to be in the position of needing something (a vote, decision, money, etc.) and/ or of reacting to a decision that already has been made. While these situations are unavoidable, advocates can be more effective if they have established a relationship with the key player *prior to* the emergency, when there is less political pressure and more time to develop an understanding of the issues and to build a solid relationship.

Strategies. There is no substitute for face-to-face meetings with key players. Opportunities for meetings include meeting people who are new to their position; discussing the content of a new report or of new data[2]; inviting input into important decisions that an agency is making; discussing outstanding problems or issues that homeless children and youth face in the commu-

---

A Meeting that Made a Difference

In July 1997, two Pennsylvania educators of homeless children took a road trip to Washington, D.C. to meet with the staff of their Senator, who also happened to be the chair of the appropriations subcommittee with jurisdiction over the McKinney Education for Homeless Children and Youth program. The educators brought letters, poetry, and art from the homeless children they served; they described their programs' activities and their struggles to meet the needs of increasing numbers of children. Staff from the National Coalition for the Homeless accompanied the educators to argue for an increased appropriation. The Senate committee staff person listened to the educators, asked them questions, and, while they were seated in front of her, crossed out the proposed funding level (which had been the same as the previous year) and increased it by $2 million. In the end, the Senate-proposed level was adopted and homeless education programs across the country received more funding to help homeless children and youth enroll, attend, and succeed in school.

---

nity; and reviewing proposed legislation or desired changes to legislation. Scheduling meetings with key players during "off-season," less busy times of the year (summer, Congressional recess) is an excellent way to begin building relationships.

Here are some considerations for planning face-to-face meetings with key players:

♦ If possible, arrange for a small group of people who share your concerns to participate in the meeting. It is important to include homeless parents, and children, when feasible, so that key players can put faces on the issue of homelessness and hear from those who have direct experience.

♦ Decide ahead of time what issues the group will discuss and who will cover each issue.

- Limit discussion in your visit to one, or at most two, topics.

- If homeless parents or children cannot attend the meeting, give specific examples of the situations they are facing—a series of case studies. Bring art work, poetry, or other materials that homeless children and youth have produced to help humanize the issue and make it more compelling.

- Sometimes it is not possible to meet with the key player and a meeting with staff will have to suffice. Even if a meeting with a key player is obtained, it is important to understand the role of staff in a particular office and to build good working relationships with them.

- Prior to the meeting, let the key player or staff member in charge of setting up the meeting know who will attend and what you will discuss. The key player can then prepare for the meeting, which will make it more productive. Present the case at hand, and if you are asking for something, explain what you want the key player to do and why.

- If you don't know the answer to a question, don't make it up. Offer to find out and send information back to the key player later.

- Try to keep control of the visit. Don't be put off by smokescreens or long-winded answers. Tactfully ask for specific answers if you don't feel you are getting them.

- Don't make promises you can't deliver.

- If you are coming to discuss a contentious community issue, try to find out if the key player has heard opposing views. If so, ask what the arguments were and what groups were involved. Also, try to find out whether the key player has made public statements on the issue.

- Spend time with the key player even if his or her position is different than yours. Sometimes it is possible to lessen the intensity of the opposition.

- Don't confront, threaten, pressure, or beg.
- Follow up the visit with a thank you note.

In addition to arranging meetings at a key player's office, it is important to invite him or her to participate in a program or organization's activities. For example, a key player might be asked to address the organization, or the organization might present him or her with an award. These events leave a lasting positive impression about the organization and build a relationship with the key player that can be useful.

While face-to-face meetings are the best way to establish relationships with key players, letters are also important tools. Letter writing can be the first step in building an ongoing relationship with a key player—a way of introducing yourself and the issue of homeless children and youth. It is also a critical means of staying in touch and maintaining relationships.

Considerations for letter writing include:

- Stay on one topic. If you want to write about other issues, send another letter later on.

- Give reasons for your letter and/or your position. As appropriate, use personal experience or a concrete example to make your case.

- Raise questions. A question can get a personal response.

- Keep it short. One page is best. Use two pages only if necessary for clarity and completeness.

- Be polite, positive, and constructive. Don't plead, and never threaten.

- If you are writing to impact a decision, be timely. Write before decisions are made and action is taken. But don't write too long before—a letter six months before a vote will probably be forgotten.

- Use your name and address on both the envelope and the letter. This helps staff in replying and identifies you as a constituent if you are writing an elected official.

♦ Keep writing! It is important to keep your agency's name and the issues facing homeless children and youth in front of key players. Add their names to your agency's or program's mailing list.

STAYING IN THE LOOP: INFORMATION IS POWER

In order to be successful, advocates need accurate, timely information about issues that impact homeless children and youth. Information is needed to help prioritize efforts, identify partners, determine strategies, and plan advocacy campaigns.

Strategies. Given the busy schedules of people who work with homeless children and youth, the complexity of the issues, and the enormous amount of information available, staying informed can present a challenge. It is best to find ways to incorporate the flow of information into daily routines. There are a number of ways that this can be achieved.

First, become a member of local, state, and national homeless coalitions. Homeless coalitions are often the best sources of information about new data, reports, programs, and impending policy decisions. Many coalitions publish newsletters, hold annual conferences and regular meetings, and administer fax or e-mail alert lists. By joining homeless coalitions, child advocates can receive regular information to help keep them in the loop.

Another way to build information gathering into daily routines is to appoint someone (a volunteer or staff person) to the role of "advocacy liaison." This person might attend community and coalition meetings, subscribe to newsletters and e-mail listservs, and distribute advocacy materials to the rest of the program staff. Having one person who agrees to take on this function creates a regular vehicle for dissemination of information to the entire program.

There are two other organizations that serve as important information clearinghouses on the education of homeless children and youth: the National Association for the Education of Homeless Children and Youth (NAEHCY) and the National Center for Homeless Education (NCHE). NAEHCY produces a newsletter, *The Beam,* which contains valuable information on programs, policies, and legislation. NAEHCY also holds the largest national conference on homeless education each fall. NCHE is a new clearinghouse and technical assistance resource. Both organizations offer information and networks that can be utilized in advocacy efforts (see *Additional Resources*).

Finally, the Internet is the largest and fastest growing source of information on homelessness. The Web sites of the National Coalition for the Homeless (NCH) and NCHE are vital sources of information on homeless children and youth. The NCH web site includes regular legislative updates, fact sheets, comprehensive directories of state and local advocacy coalitions, and numerous other resources (see *Resources* for Web site addresses).

CREATIVE PUBLIC EDUCATION: CHANGING HEARTS AND MINDS

Homeless families with children are invisible to the public; they do not readily identify themselves as homeless out of fear of losing custody of their children and because of the enormous stigma associated with poverty in this country. This makes the task of raising awareness extraordinarily difficult.

And, yet, it is imperative that the general public be better educated if we are to change hearts and minds. Communities and schools that do not acknowledge the existence of homeless children cannot act to meet their needs. Similarly, communities that are uninformed about impending public policy or program decisions cannot weigh in on behalf of homeless children and youth.

Strategies. Public education is both a general strategy to lift barriers to education and pave the way to positive community action, and an advocacy tool to help push through specific program or policy objectives. Strategies to help accomplish both functions are described below; however, it is useful to begin with a few general guidelines concerning public education.

First, it is important to combine "hard" data about homelessness, such as statistics, with "soft" data, such as anecdotes and stories. Numbers explain the dimensions of homelessness, and they also add credibility. If possible, it is best to combine local and national statistics, so that readers/viewers

---

Photography and Advocacy

Illinois photographer Pat Van Doren has teamed up with Illinois Coalition to End Homelessness President Diane Nilan to grab attention with moving photography of homeless children. One of Van Doren's most chilling photos, a close-up of an infant's toes with "These Little Piggies Are Homeless" written below them, has been used across the country by child advocates and educators to help raise awareness in their communities. In 1994, Nilan and Van Doren worked together on a state homeless education law. A photograph of "Charlie," a homeless child who had been denied enrollment at his school, was affixed to flyers, talking points, and other advocacy materials. The photo of Charlie—an impish 6-year old holding a cat at least half his size—helped remind lawmakers and the public who the law was intended to help. The bill became known as "Charlie's Bill." It was passed and signed into law, making Illinois the state with the strongest legal protections for homeless children and youth's education.

---

understand that homelessness is a problem in their own communities and that it is a national problem.

But numbers are not enough. The realities of homelessness and its impact on children must also be conveyed through stories and the voices of people who have direct experience with homelessness. Interviews, personal narratives, art, and poetry are just a few of the ways that the "human dimension" can accompany statistics to create powerful public education materials.

Recent media studies have suggested that public education materials about poverty are best accompanied by descriptions of concrete solutions to the problem—examples of successful programs or policies (National Low Income Housing Coalition, 1998). The message is that homelessness is not an unsolvable problem and that there are positive initiatives that can be replicated and expanded. If there are no specific examples to draw from locally, it may be helpful to draw from the practices of other communities or school districts that have adopted desirable policies or programs. At a minimum, it is critical to present specific solutions to the problems that are described in awareness-raising campaigns.

Finally, the saying, "a picture is worth a thousand words" is certainly true when it comes to homelessness. Homelessness, especially when described in numerical terms, is all too often thought of as an abstract social problem and not an immediate human crisis. Photographs help put faces on the issue of homelessness and remind the reader that human lives are at stake. The use of photographs of homeless children and families, however, raises difficult issues of confidentiality and exploitation. Some agencies circumvent these problems by using non-identifying pictures such as shadows, profiles, heads turned, or backs of children at play or in school. At a minimum, parental and child consent must be obtained before a photograph is taken, and its usage should be explained to parents.

General Awareness-Raising Strategies. As mentioned earlier, annual campaigns are an excellent way to plan ahead for awareness-raising advocacy events. National Hunger and Homelessness Awareness Week, held each year the week before Thanksgiving, is an opportunity to create a week's worth of awareness-raising events before the Holiday season. An organizing manual for National Hunger and Homelessness Awareness Week is available on the NCH Web site.

As practical and important as annual events are, awareness-raising and public education are a continuous effort, one that should not be confined to one a year. The high amount of turnover in school personnel alone necessitates regular vehicles for public education about homelessness—its impact on children, the role of schools, and the educational rights of homeless children and youth. Staff development in-service days, pamphlets and flyers, and official postings of notices are all ways that schools and communities can be regularly informed about homelessness and homeless children's and youth's educational rights (see *Additional Resources* below).

Finally, a critical but often overlooked population for public education campaigns are children themselves. As future voters and citizens, children's attitudes about poverty and homelessness will shape the public policy of tomorrow; as neigh-

---

Homeless Children in the Headlines

In the Spring of 1995, the Budget Committee of the U.S. House of Representatives debated a proposal that would eliminate all funding for the McKinney Education for Homeless Children and Youth program. In the course of the debate, one Arizona representative challenged another representative to "show him one child who had ever been helped" by the program. What the Arizona representative did not know is that there were two homeless education programs in his district. One program contacted the *Arizona Daily Star* and told them about the Representative's comments. Not only did the newspaper print a cover story on the program profiling its successes, it also produced an editorial chastising the Representative for his remarks. While the Representative ultimately did not change his vote, he has ceased his attacks on the homeless education program. Moreover, the community responded to the article with increased support (donations, volunteers, etc.) for the program's efforts.

---

bors and classmates, their attitudes about homelessness impact the self-esteem and mental health of the homeless children in their schools now. Educating housed children about poverty and homelessness is an awareness-raising and advocacy activity with current and long-lasting benefits. Several curricula have been developed for teaching about homelessness. One of the best comes from the Minnesota Coalition for the Homeless; this K-6 guide provides information and activities for teachers and students to explore as they learn about the causes, consequences, and solutions to homelessness (see *Additional Resources* below).

Using Public Education as Part of Targeted Advocacy Initiatives. Public education can be an invaluable tool in targeted advocacy initiatives. For example, sometimes it is necessary to influence key players by appealing to the community directly. One of the best ways to do this is by working with the local media. While media work may seem daunting at first, it is well worth the effort—the media can help carry a specific message far and wide and, at the same time, educate large numbers of people. Some general guidelines include the following:

♦ Keep the message very simple.

♦ Provide accurate information.

♦ Do not exaggerate claims.

♦ Be specific about the solution proposed and the desired outcome.

♦ Be creative.

♦ Be persistent.

A few informative, easy-to-use media guides that have been developed for people who work in human services are highly recommended (see *Additional Resources* below).

CONCLUSION

As a new century dawns, we—in the richest country in the world—face the prospect of increasing child homelessness. There is nothing inevitable about homelessness, however, nor about how the poorest and most vulnerable children in the nation will fare in school. Advocacy is one key to making rights real and to ending homelessness. No special training or expertise is needed to become an effective advocate—merely practice and commitment.

People who work with homeless children and youth are uniquely positioned to work for lasting change—to alter the conditions that create homelessness and its many barriers to education. The wealth of knowledge and insight gained in everyday work with homeless children can and should be marshaled toward creating the day when every child has access to the education to which he or she is entitled, and when every child has a place to call home.

REFERENCES

Alliance for Justice (1996). *Regulation of advocacy activities of nonprofits that receive federal grants*. Washington, DC: Author.

Children's Defense Fund and the National Coalition for the Homeless (1998). *Welfare to what: early findings on family hardship and well-being*. Washington, DC: Author.

Children's Defense Fund (1997). *Poverty matters: The costs of child poverty in America*. Washington, DC: Author.

Duncan, G., & Brooks-Gunn, J. (Eds.) (1997). *Consequences of growing up poor*. New York: Russell Sage.

Haveman, R., & Wolfe, B. (1994). *Succeeding generations*. New York: Russell Sage.

Mihlay, L. (1991). Homeless families: Failed policies and young victims. Washington, DC: Children's Defense Fund.

National Low Income Housing Coalition (1998). *Media advocacy project*. Washington, DC: Author.

Sherman, P. (1998). Health care for homeless children: A clinician's perspective. *Healing Hands, 2*(6), 1-2.

U.S. General Accounting Office (1994). Elementary school children: Many change schools frequently, harming their education. Washington, DC: U.S. Government Printing Office.

ADDITIONAL RESOURCES

Publications:

How to tell and sell your story: A guide to media for community groups and other nonprofits. How to plan a media campaign, bring attention to your group's work or issue, stage a press conference, write a press release, write and place "op-eds," influence editorials, and more. 1997, Center for Community Change. Cost: $7.00. Address: 1000 Wisconsin Avenue, NW, Washington, DC 20007. Phone: 202.342.0567.

How to tell and sell your story—Part 2: A guide to developing effective messages and good stories about your work. How to find and tell good stories about your work; frame an issue or an organization's work; do your own focus group. 1998, Center for Community Change. Cost: $7.00. Address: 1000 Wisconsin Avenue, NW, Washington, DC 20007. Phone: 202.342.0567.

How—and why—to Influence Public Policy: An Action Guide For Community Organizations. How to do effective advocacy, select issues, decide how much and what kind of lobbying and voter work your group can do, etc. 1996, Center for Community Change. Cost: $5.00. Address:

1000 Wisconsin Avenue, NW, Washington, DC 20007. Phone: 202.342.0567. Web: http://www.communitychange.org/advocacy.htm

On the street where you live: Lesson plans on homelessness for k-6th grade students and middle school students. 1998, Minnesota Coalition for the Homeless. Cost: $25.00. Address: 122 West Franklin, Suite 5, Minnesota, MN 55404. Phone: 612.870.7073.

Pieces of the puzzle: Creating success for students in homeless situations. A training kit for educational programs; includes sections on awareness, identifying barriers, creating opportunities for success, resources, and an appendix of useful documents such as the McKinney Act. 1997, University of Texas at Austin. Phone: 512.475.9702. Web: http://www.tenet.edu/OEHCY/publications_Pieces.html

Stand for children: A parent's guide to child advocacy. This guide tells how to advocate for your own children and for all children. 1996, Children's Defense Fund. Cost: $4.95. Address: 25 E Street, NW, Washington, DC 20001. Phone: 202.628.8787.

Organizations:

Chicago Coalition for the Homeless. 1325 S. Wabash Ave., #205, Chicago, IL 60605. Phone: 312.435.4548. Web: http://www.cchomeless.org/~cch.

National Center on Homeless Education at SERVE. 1100 West Market Street, Suite 300, Greensboro, NC 27403. Phone: 1.800.755-3277. Web: http://www.serve.org/nche

National Coalition for the Homeless. 1012 14th Street, NW, Suite 600, Washington, DC 20005. Phone: 202.737.6444. Web: *http://nch.ari.net*

National Law Center on Homelessness and Poverty. 918 F Street, NW, Suite 412, Washington, DC 20037. Phone: 202.635.2535. Web: *http://www.nlchp.org*

ENDNOTES

[1] Minnesota Department of Children, Families, and Learning, 1998; Oregon Housing and Community Services Department, 1997; Iowa Coalition on Housing and Homelessness, 1997.

[2.] The release of national, state, and local reports presents excellent opportunities for meetings, as do new annual program statistics or survey results. Even if national or state reports do not directly address the education of homeless children and youth, they can be used to call attention to the overall conditions facing poor and homeless children—including educational issues.

12

ENHANCING COLLABORATION ON BEHALF OF HOMELESS STUDENTS: STRATEGIES FOR LOCAL AND STATE EDUCATIONAL AGENCIES

PAMELA D. TUCKER

As educators become more sensitive to the unique circumstances and needs of individual children, they are beginning to recognize homelessness as a significant risk factor which can have debilitating effects on the educational attainment of children and adolescents. These students are present in most schools and many classrooms; approximately one out of every 100 school-age children is homeless.[1] Food, clothing, shelter, and security are daily struggles for these students and their families. What is the role of schools in their lives? What is our role as educators to help homeless students? How can we possibly meet the myriad needs they present? One of the more compelling responses was made by Alker (1992, p. 192): "For many homeless children, school may be the only stable setting in their daily lives.

Few would deny that any group of children is more in need of education than those without a place to call home."

Historically, education in America has had the role of assimilating new immigrants, blurring class distinctions, and more recently, serving all children regardless of race or disability (Tyack, 1992). Extension of this basic educational opportunity to homeless students is both a caring response and legally mandated by relatively unknown federal legislation, found in the Stewart B. McKinney Homeless Assistance Act (P.L. 100-77). To meet the pervasive problems homeless students present, something more than the traditional, school-centered delivery model is required. A broad-based and comprehensive approach resulting from collaborative efforts of various agencies working together at the local and state levels offers the greatest hope to educators of having a meaningful and lasting influence on our neediest clients.

WHY IS COLLABORATION IMPORTANT?

WHY IS COLLABORATION NEEDED?

While homeless children and youth are a relatively small percentage of the student population, they arguably are one of its most vulnerable (Stronge, 1997). Children and youth are estimated to constitute 26 percent to 33 percent of the total homeless population (Nunez, 1995). As a consequence of their circumstances, many children and youth experience extreme poverty with attending health, nutrition, and safety problems (Nunez, 1995). The impact of homelessness on children manifests itself in their psychosocial development and academic achievement. Homeless preschoolers are much more likely to be developmentally delayed in areas such as language, attention span, sleep patterns, social interaction, and aggressiveness (Reed-Victor & Stronge, 1997). School-aged homeless children score lower on standardized tests, are referred more often for special education, and repeat a grade more frequently (Rafferty, 1997; Stronge, 1995).

Despite the fundamental commonality of no home, homeless children and youth are a heterogeneous group. They find themselves homeless due to a widely varying combination of factors which have differential effects on their educational needs (Stronge, 1995). Precipitating factors may include those related to the economy, government policies and legislation, the community, individual problems, and even the ravages of nature. See Table 1 below for specific examples. As Stronge (1997) noted, "the problems associated with homelessness are multidimensional and rooted in the broader community; so too, must the solutions to homelessness be multidimensional and based squarely in the broader community" (p. 25).

The broader nature of issues that contribute to homelessness force a shift in focus from the child to the whole family, which is a difficult challenge for schools in working with homeless students. Even if school enrollment is achieved, which historically has been a major barrier to education for homeless students (Stronge, 1995), it is unlikely that the child will be able to attend class regularly and focus on learning. There are many associated issues such as proper immunizations, clothing, school supplies, transportation, and academic support to offset gaps in previous school attendance which impede academic success (Virginia Commission on Youth, 1998). When parents are "ex-

TABLE 1. FACTORS PRECIPITATING HOMELESSNESS

Economy	unemployment, underemployment, labor pool
Government policies	social welfare policy, low cost housing, childcare, social security, educational/training opportunities
Community	housing market, healthcare, job market, available services
Individual problems	domestic violence, mental illness, substance abuse, lack of job skills/education, disabilities, chronic health problems
Nature	tornadoes, hurricanes, landslides, fires

hausted from trying to supply the daily necessities of food, clothing, and shelter" (Mickelson, Yon, & Carlton-LaNey, 1995, p. 357),
these routine school requirements take on formidable propor-
tions. Without a broader, more coordinated effort to assist with
the provision of these materials and services, the provision of "a
free, appropriate public education" (P.L. 101-645, Title VII, Subtitle B, Sec.721(1)) to homeless students as mandated by the
Stewart B. McKinney Homeless Assistance Act is meaningless.

WHY HAS COLLABORATION BEEN NEGLECTED?

The physical and psychological needs of homeless children
and adolescents are immediate and pressing. Educators and social service agents who work with this population are often
responding to a steady stream of crises, making the time and
effort required for collaboration difficult to find. It is often easier
to respond with resources at hand, however limited, than to work
with another agency or bureaucracy.

A second major issue is the categorical funding mechanisms
for children's services which are restricted to specific programs
and population groups (Verstegen, 1996).

> In an effort to simplify compliance with fiscal require-
> ments, many states and localities have segregated
> children's services according to funding channels and
> have been hesitant to collaborate with outside agencies
> due to perceived increased administrative burdens and
> turf questions. (p. 285)

While the McKinney Act calls for states to enhance interagency cooperation, First (1992) found in a national study that it
was one of the responsibilities which was most poorly implemented. She concluded that "the advocacy and coordinating role
that some dream of is not there for [homeless] children, and the
school may be the only agency positioned to fill that societal
need" (p. 91). Many authors (Quint, 1994; Rafferty, 1997; Stronge,
1995; Sullivan & Sugarman, 1996) argue that collaboration holds
great promise for leveraging resources and linking services, and
yet few organizations have demonstrated the capacity to do so.

WHAT IS THE ROLE OF COLLABORATION IN SERVING HOMELESS STUDENTS?

WHAT ARE THE BENEFITS OF COLLABORATION?

The actual benefits of collaboration go far beyond serving the specific needs of children and youth, homeless and those more fortunate. Working together with other agencies is a means of:

♦ building bridges of understanding;

♦ developing new perspectives;

♦ illuminating new options;

♦ providing new resources;

♦ stretching existing resources; and

♦ creating a sense of community.

When educators become members of groups with common concerns and goals, such as the education of homeless students, they are able to exert more influence on policymaking across agencies based on trust and an enhanced appreciation for the interdependent roles of each organization and agency. For example, coordination between housing officials and educators can help school systems anticipate higher enrollments and the need for additional services.

WHAT IS THE LEGISLATIVE BASIS FOR COLLABORATION?

The specific legislation that addresses education of homeless students originated in 1987 as Title VII, Subtitle B of the Stewart B. McKinney Homeless Assistance Act (P.L. 100-77). The program was amended by the McKinney Homeless Assistance Act Amendments of 1990 (P.L. 101-645), and more recently under the Improving America's Schools Act of 1994 (P. L. 103-382), which reauthorized the education portion of the McKinney Act. Two important roles of both state and local educational agencies under this Act are:

1. facilitating coordination among educational and social agencies, and

2. developing relationships and coordinating among
   homeless service providers to "improve the provision of comprehensive services to homeless children
   and youth and their families" (P.L. 103-382, Title VII,
   Subtitle B, Sec.722(f)(6)).

In addition, multiple pieces of recent federal legislation have
recognized the "importance of health, nutrition, and social services to student achievement" (Sullivan & Sugarman, 1996, p.
287) and as a result, have supported school-linked integrated
services. Examples of such legislation include the Improving
America's Schools Act (P.L. 103-382), Goals 2000: Educate
America Act (P. L. 103-227), and the reauthorized Elementary
and Secondary Education Act (P. L. 104-208). Title I of the Elementary and Secondary Education Act (ESEA) specifically
addressed children in high poverty schools and the need for
coordinated services to meet their many needs. This policy focus of coordinating services is being adopted at the local level
and Title I programs across the country provide much of the
additional support available for homeless students in school
systems that do not have McKinney homeless education programs. For example, Title I Coordinators often take the lead in
finding school supplies, arranging testing, and obtaining support services for homeless students.

WHAT IS THE NATURE OF COLLABORATION?

WHAT DOES COLLABORATION INVOLVE?

For the purposes of this article, collaboration is used to refer
to all the formal and informal efforts by individuals across agencies and institutions to work together on behalf of homeless
children. They include "integration of education and human
services, school-linked services, services integration,
interprofessional collaboration, coordinated services for children,
and family support" (Knapp, 1995, p. 5). While most schools

have not conceptualized themselves as social agencies, it is an inevitable paradigm shift if the needs of the whole child are to be recognized and addressed (Pawlas, 1996; Yon, Mickelson, & Carlton-LaNey, 1993). The recent focus on the integration of education and human services (Dryfoos, 1998) is an acknowledgment that not all children come to school "ready to learn" and it is unrealistic to push for higher academic standards when these basic needs are not being met. For homeless students in particular, "the nature of services is likely to be more social support oriented and less academically oriented than traditional education services" (Stronge, 1993, p. 355).

WHO SHOULD BE INVOLVED IN COLLABORATIVE EFFORTS?

Potential collaborative partners for meeting the needs of homeless children and youth are multiple, especially in urban areas. The following list in Table 2 provides broad categories of potential team members.

By working together, resources can be pooled and leveraged to achieve a more extensive response to the various problems of

TABLE 2. POTENTIAL COLLABORATIVE PARTNERS

Categories	Examples
Service providers	Social Services, Domestic violence shelters, Health department, Community services board, Emergency food networks, Mental health clinics, Employment services, Job training programs, Housing programs
Faith community	Churches, Synagogues
Business community	Department stores, Grocery stores, Local industry
Civic and social organizations	Salvation Army, Rescue Missions, YMCA, YWCA, Volunteers of America, United Way

the child and family. Working with others as a team to achieve a common goal is the simple essence of collaboration. The ultimate goal is to connect homeless children and their families with services and programs more quickly so that they are responsive and amenable to efforts to enroll their children in school and help them succeed in that environment.

HOW CAN COLLABORATION SERVE THE MULTI-FACETED NEEDS OF HOMELESS STUDENTS?

Collaboration among community groups can link resources and services making broad-based services possible. By meeting basic needs that threaten family survival, attention can be focused on other concerns such as school attendance. Model programs create "communities of learning" which include "specialized education for homeless children, contextualized education for parents, and linkages to needed services" (Nunez & Collignon, 1997, p. 57). Model programs reflect the diversity of resources available within the communities where they exist. Some, such as the Oak Street School[3] in San Juan County, California, provide for the basic needs of students by offering breakfast, lunch, transportation, and clothing (Newman & Beck, 1996). Oak Street School is a collaborative venture by the San Juan County Department of Education, the Neighborhood Club, and a church. Other programs, such as the Brownstone School[4] in the Bronx, exist in a context that provides extended family-oriented services that include adult education programs, job training, and housing referral services (Nunez & Collignon).

For collaborative teams to work at the state or local level, it is important for them to focus their energies by:

1. defining a common goal;
2. collecting information on needs and resources;
3. identifying priorities based on needs; and
4. developing a mutually agreed upon strategic plan.

Because each participant in a collaborative effort has differing mandates, funding procedures, and administrative policies, organizing group efforts around a process like this encourages cooperation instead of competition among participating agencies. In addition, it is important to clarify roles and responsibilities of each collaborative team member, clearly delineate resource allocations, and specify procedures for coordinating the delivery of services and resources (Olsen, 1983).

WHAT ARE SUGGESTED STRATEGIES FOR COLLABORATING AT THE STATE LEVEL?

Each state differs in the mechanisms for coordination of educational and social services, and their level of success, but most are making an effort to integrate available resources and services for needy students (First, 1992). The office of the State Coordinator for the Education of Homeless Children and Youth should take a lead role in fostering collaboration at the state level. Recommended strategies to achieve this goal include the following.

Strategy 1.1: Develop a working relationship with other programs in the state department of education. The department of education within each state can serve an important coordination role through internal associations or councils of various federal program administrators, such as Title I and Headstart Coordinators. The federal government has encouraged this process with an explicit policy shift to "cross-program coordination" which is clearly evident in the consolidated planning process to procure federal grant funding. According to the U.S. Department of Education (1995), consolidation is:

> . . . intended to improve teaching and learning by encouraging greater cross-program coordination, planning, and service delivery; enhance integration of programs with educational activities carried out with State and local funds; and promote the State's educational goals for all students while effectively meeting the needs of the programs' intended beneficiaries. (pp. 4–5)

It is especially important to build trusting relationships with specialists from Title I, special education, Headstart, and Even

Start. These program areas provide essential services for homeless students, and yet, homeless students often are not served either because of waiting lists or delays in necessary evaluations. By alerting these specialists to the unique challenges of homeless students in accessing services, strategies can be developed to overcome existing obstacles, such as reserved slots for homeless preschoolers or expedited evaluations for possible special education students.

Strategy 1.2: Search for and take advantage of opportunities to work with interagency associations. In many states, there are organizations such as the Virginia Interagency Action Council for the Homeless[5] which assist in the coordination of agencies that serve the homeless. They use strategies such as conferences, newsletters, and Web pages to disseminate useful information and extend the network of individuals and agencies that can interact and learn about available programs and services. These groups typically are composed of members from state and federal agencies representing health care, employment, mental health, education, social services, housing, and social security. In addition, there can be representatives of advocacy groups, food banks, the faith community, and charities such as Salvation Army and United Way. The members reflect varied backgrounds and disparate funding streams but similar goals of assisting the homeless in numerous domains. Interdisciplinary organizations such as these provide valuable forums to share information, build working relationships, leverage resources, and develop action agendas.

Strategy 1.3: Participate in the National Association for the Education of Homeless Children and Youth (NAEHCY). This professional organization sponsors annual conferences that afford educators and service providers at both the state and local levels an opportunity to develop relationships with professionals serving children and youth across the state and country. State programs can be enhanced through collaboration with others who have more experience and, in some cases, more resources due to the size of their state grants. The exchange of ideas and promising practices serve an important professional development function for participants and enhances the collective capacity of coordinators to resolve the difficult problems and dilemmas that arise on a daily basis in working with homeless students and their families.

Strategy 1.4: Work with state legislators to introduce legislation for homeless students. One of the mandates of the original McKinney legislation was to identify state policies that create barriers for educating homeless children and youth, such as immunization requirements, proof of residency, proof of guardianship, and prior school records. Today, more than a decade later, these barriers have not been totally eliminated and they often require further legislative action to fully implement (Stronge, 1997).

WHAT ARE SUGGESTED STRATEGIES FOR COLLABORATION AT THE LOCAL LEVEL?

Collaboration at the local level is more varied and reflective of the capacities of community resources such as charitable organizations, social services, health care, and the faith community. Even more important the "quality of leadership of the people who are part of the interagency partnerships is critical" (Stronge, 1997, p. 25).

Strategy 2.1: Develop working relationships with social services serving homeless students. Networking with potential collaborative partners is an important first step in learning about available community resources. As Holtzman (1995) noted, "the most creative initiatives for the near future will be those that grow out of local partnerships rather than federal mandates" (p. 60). Through the resulting information exchange and interaction, the level of collaboration is elevated from one of parallel or overlapping services for similar populations to one of awareness and the possibility of future cooperation around commonly agreed upon problems and goals. No matter how well-intentioned federal and state policy may be regarding coordination, it takes people developing trusting relationships with one another to foster meaningful collaboration (Olsen, 1983). It is through the understanding of respective capacities and the development of mutual goals that agencies can work together on behalf of children. Ultimately, over time, working relationships and voluntary cooperation among agencies can evolve into institutional changes and better ways of doing business together.

Strategy 2.2: Involve the whole community in building support for special programs. Community involvement through civic organizations and the faith community, offer a wealth of resources to programs for homeless students. To truly be successful, "jointly funded projects require that there be extensive local involvement [and] high visibility increases the likelihood of local individual involvement in the program" (Olsen, 1983, p. 25). By creating a "community" program versus a school or shelter program, there is a greater sense of ownership and commitment from a wide range of organizations that can offer broader and more comprehensive support as well as long-term viability.

Strategy 2.3: Make connections with other school systems serving homeless students. The state office for the Education of Homeless Children and Youth can play an important role in building a sense of community and collaboration among school systems that are facing similar issues, regardless of whether or not they receive grants. This leadership role also can be filled by other federal program coordinators who address a wide range of risk factors, including homelessness, or by highly committed individuals, such as school counselors, who step forward to focus attention on the homeless issue. What is crucial is the development of informal relationships with individuals in other school systems because similarly situated schools often have much to offer each other in terms of basic information, support, and guidance.

Strategy 2.4: Modify administrative roles and practices. One of the major barriers to establishing effectively integrated services for children identified by Sullivan and Sugarman (1996) was administrative practices that preserve the status quo and don't adjust to changing circumstances. Key recommendations made by Sullivan and Sugarman for modernizing the administration of services included:

- ♦ unified systems for planning;
- ♦ client-friendly transitions from program to program;
- ♦ joint program-supportive activities with cost sharing; and
- ♦ a shift from a top-down, compliance approach to a flexible, community-responsive orientation.

Model programs, such as Oak Street School in San Juan County, are employing strategies such as these to the benefit of children (Newman & Beck, 1996). They provide almost seamless service delivery by building on the strengths of each participating partner to provide resources such as transportation by the Neighborhood Club, clothes and class space by the church, and certified teachers from the school system.

Strategy 2.5: Obtain support for cooperative efforts from the state level. In recent years, the federal government has devolved authority to the states for program design and permitted more flexibility in the use of funding streams with block grants. A likely outcome of this shift predicted by Sullivan and Sugarman (1996) will be that states "devolve much of their authority to counties or other regional or local jurisdictions" (p. 292). Successful interagency efforts in the area of special education have found that it is important to gain support for cooperative efforts from state level agencies to ensure the ongoing viability of their programs and to encourage their replication (Olsen, 1983).

Strategy 2.6: Recognize the importance of small victories. Homeless children and youth present a complex set of problems requiring multifaceted responses. Successes tend to be small and tenuous but must be savored and built upon incrementally. It is not sweeping federal programs that will help homeless children, but the fundamental ethic of caring by individuals that collectively can change lives. Stronge (1993) captured this spirit with the following: "We can help, first, by caring individually and, second, by joining our efforts collectively in providing an appropriate educational opportunity for homeless students" (p. 137).

How Can the Effectiveness of Collaboration Be Assessed?

Why Is Program Evaluation Important?

Program evaluation is important for many reasons, most broadly, for program accountability and program development. More specifically, reasons include the need to:

♦ assess effectiveness of local programs;

◆ document progress for state Departments of Education;

◆ advocate for needs with state and federal legislatures;

◆ request funding from local school systems, charitable organizations, or foundations;

◆ develop public awareness of the problems and the successes in working with homeless students; and

◆ comply with federal requests for information as required by the Stewart B. McKinney Act.

WHAT HAVE BEEN IMPEDIMENTS TO EVALUATION?

Educators serving homeless children and youth face numerous challenges in evaluating programs. Reservations about program evaluation can be related to the time and money required by them, which diminish efforts in other critical areas such as direct service with students. The benefits of program evaluation tend to be less tangible and immediate but offer long-term program viability both in terms of funding and effectiveness. A secondary issue is the complexity of coordinating and standardizing data collection, analysis, and interpretations, especially when collaborative partners are involved. Lastly, given the transient nature of homeless families, it is difficult to determine *even* short-term effects of service delivery, such as the number of homeless students served within a locality, students' school attendance, and students' adjustment to school. Long-term effects of service delivery are seldom assessed. A national evaluation of state and local efforts to serve homeless students (Anderson, Janger, & Panton, 1995) found that few local school districts measure program impact on any outcome measure.

WHAT SHOULD BE THE BASIS FOR ASSESSING THE EFFECTIVENESS OF COLLABORATION?

Current program evaluation efforts typically address input and process measures, such as students served, school supplies distributed, and hours of tutoring provided. However, the greatest concern among many educators is the lack of data on the *impact of services* on the academic success of children and youth (Stronge, 1997). At present, longitudinal studies of services provided to students and their ultimate effect on "academic achievement, attitude, self-esteem, and school access and attendance" (Anderson et al., 1995, p. xv) are nonexistent and beyond the grasp of current data-gathering strategies. Without this kind of information on program efficacy, it may become increasingly difficult to maintain public support for educational services for homeless students.

WHAT ARE STRATEGIES TO EVALUATE THE EFFECTIVENESS OF COLLABORATION?

Knapp (1995) offered an in-depth discussion of the challenges confronting evaluators and researchers in the area of collaborative services for children and families and suggested a number of methodological approaches to address the identified problems. He recommended that "studies need to be strongly conceptualized, descriptive, comparative, constructively skeptical, positioned from the bottom up, and collaborative" (p. 10). In practical terms, he advised that the participants in program evaluation:

♦ define goals to determine valid measures of achievement;

♦ use extensive description to capture the impact of programs on the recipients;

♦ use evidence of contrasting cases to highlight effects;

♦ remain skeptical about the reliability and validity of information collected;

♦ anchor the study in the client's needs and perceptions; and

♦ involve all collaborative partners in designing and implementing the study, if feasible.

A mixed design study of this nature has methodological integrity and merit but may be beyond the expertise and financial resources of many programs for homeless students.

CONCLUSIONS

Schools may be "the only source of stability in the life of a homeless child" (Rafferty, 1997, p. 50). As educators, we have the power to mitigate the effects of homelessness with our understanding and compassion. We can provide a successful educational experience and a chance to break the cycle of poverty, but schools cannot do it alone. It requires supportive communities with a range of necessary services and concerned individuals to negotiate the boundaries of educational, medical, housing, and social service agencies on behalf of homeless children and their families. With the trends toward non-categorical funding of programs and an emphasis on coordination, schools have a better opportunity than ever before to make a difference for our most vulnerable students.

Successful school programs for homeless children are characterized by communication and collaboration and "yet this critical step . . . is the piece most often missing" (Nunez & Collignon, 1997, p. 59) from most school efforts. Communication and collaboration take time and effort, but the more we promote them and support educators who are willing to take the challenge of meeting the physical, emotional, and educational needs of children through collaboration with other professionals, the more humane and responsive schools will be for all children, including those who are homeless.

WHAT ELECTRONIC RESOURCES ARE AVAILABLE FOR EDUCATORS?[6]

A review of the Internet resources on collaboration and homeless students yielded relatively few with broad utility, indicating the pressing need for further efforts in these areas. Table 3 presents the Web sites that address homelessness and the needs of children and adolescents living in poverty. Table 4 includes Web sites that address collaboration with parents or across agencies at the community level.

TABLE 3. ELECTRONIC RESOURCES ON HOMELESSNESS AND THE NEEDS OF CHILDREN

Web site	Sponsor	Focus
www.opendoor.com/hfh/icp.html	Institute for Children & Poverty (sponsor: Homes for the Homeless)	Community building, dissemination of research, development of public policy to combat homelessness and its effects on children and their families
nch.ari.net	The National Coalition for the Homeless	Public education and advocacy with the purpose of ending homelessness
www.nlchp.org	National Law Center on Homelessness & Poverty	Protection of the rights of homeless people, special section: Education of Homeless Students
www.childrensdefense.org	Children's Defense Fund	Advocacy for the needs of all children
www.alliance1.org	Alliance for Children & Families	Public policy and advocacy for children and their families
www.hud.gov/homeless.html	U.S. Department of Housing and Urban Development	Information and resources for the homeless, special section: Kids

TABLE 4. ELECTRONIC RESOURCES ON COLLABORATION

Web site	Sponsor	Focus
proto.wce.wwu.edu/Depts/HS/community/index.html	Western Washington University, Woodring College of Education	Community collaboration and interprofessional education
www.ed.gov/pubs/AchGoal8/about.html	Federal Interagency Committee Parental	National Education Goal 8: Involvement & Participation
www.ccnet.com/~educoal/	The Education Coalition	Creation of "new educational systems, models and partnerships"
www.ncrel.org	North Central Regional Laboratory (sponsor: U.S. Department of Education)	Research-based information on a wide range of educational issues
www.nn4youth.org	National Network for Youth	Community-based services for youth through partnerships
www.ed.gov/databases/ERIC_Digests/ed371108.html	ERIC Digest	article: "Urban teachers and collaborative school-linked services"
www.ed.gov/databases/ERIC_Digests/ed377414.html	ERIC Digest	article: "School counselors collaborating for student services"

REFERENCES

Alker, J. (1992). Ensuring access to education: The role of advocates for homeless children and youth. *Educating homeless children and adolescents: Evaluating policy and practice*. Newbury Park, CA: Sage.

Anderson, L., Janger, M., & Panton, K. (1995). *An evaluation of state and local efforts to serve the educational needs of homeless children and youth*. Washington, D.C.: Department of Education.

Dryfoos, J. G. (1998). *A look at community schools in 1998*. Occasional Paper #2. New York: National Center for Schools and Communities.

First, P. F. (1992). The reality: The status of education for homeless children and youth. *Educating homeless children and adolescents: Evaluating policy and practice*. Newbury Park, CA: Sage.

Holtzman, W. H. (1995). Commentary: Local partnerships as the source of innovative policy. In L. C. Rigsby, M. C. Reynolds, & M. C. Wang (Eds.), *School-community connections: Exploring issues for research and practice* (pp. 59-67). San Francisco: Jossey-Bass.

Knapp, M. S. (1995). How shall we study comprehensive, collaborative services for children and families? *Educational Researcher, 24*(4), 5-16.

Mickelson, R. A., Yon, M. G., & Carlton-LaNey, I. (1995). Slipping through the cracks: The education of homeless children. In L. C. Rigsby, M. C. Reynolds, & M. C. Wang (Eds.), *School-community connections: Exploring issues for research and practice* (pp. 283-309). San Francisco: Jossey-Bass.

Newman, R. L., & Beck, L. B. (1996). Educating homeless children: One experiment in collaboration. In J. G Cibulka, & W. J. Kriteck (Eds.), *Coordination among schools, families*, (pp. 95-133). Newbury: State University of New York Press.

Nunez, R. D. (1995). The new poverty in urban America: Family homelessness. *Journal of Children and Poverty, 1*(1), 7-28.

Nunez, R. D., & Collignon, K. (1997). Creating a community of learning for homeless children. *Educational Leadership, 55*(2), 56-60.

Olsen, K. R. (1983). Obtaining related services through local interagency collaboration. ERIC Document No. ED 239439.

Pawlas, G. E. (1996). Homeless children: Are they being prepared for the future? *Educational Forum, 61*(1), 18-23.

P.L. 100-77, Stewart B. McKinney Homeless Assistance Act of 1987. Codified at 42 U.S.C. 11301. (1987, July 22).

P.L. 101-645, Stewart B. McKinney Homeless Assistance Amendment Act of 1990. (1990, November 29).

P.L. 103-382, Improving America's Schools Act of 1994. (1994, September 28).

P.L. 103-227, Goals 2000: Educate America Act of 1994. Codified at 20 U.S.C. 5801. (1996, April 26).

P.L. 104-208, Elementary and Secondary Education Act. Codified at 20 U.S.C. 6301. (1996, September 30).

Quint, S. (1994). *Schooling homeless children: A working model for America's public schools.* New York: Teachers College Press.

Rafferty, Y. (1997). Meeting the educational needs of homeless children. *Educational Leadership, 55*(4) , 48-52.

Reed-Victor, E., & Stronge, J. H. (1997). Building resiliency: Constructive directions for homeless education. *Journal of Children and Poverty, 3*(1), 67-91.

Stronge, J. H. (1993). From access to success: Public policy for educating urban homeless students. *Education and Urban Society, 25,* 340-360.

Stronge, J. H. (1995). Educating homeless students: How can we help? *Journal for Just and Caring Education, 1*(2), 128-141.

Stronge, J. H. (1997). A long road ahead: A progress report on educating homeless children and youth in America. *Journal of Children and Poverty, 3*(2), 13-31.

Sullivan, C. J., & Sugarman, J. M. (1996). State policies affecting school-linked integrated services. *Remedial and Special Education, 17*(5), 284-292.

Tyack, D. (1992). Health and social services in public schools: Historical perspectives. *The Future of Children, 2*(1), 19-31.

U.S. Department of Education. (1995). *Preliminary guidance for the Education for Homeless Children and Youth Program, Title VII, Subtitle B.* Washington, D.C.: Author.

Verstegen, D. (1996). Reforming American education policy for the twenty-first century. In J. G Cibulka & W. J. Kriteck (Eds.), *Coordination among schools, families, and communities: Prospects for educational reform* (pp. 269-296). Albany: State University of New York Press.

Virginia Commission on Youth. (1998). *Study of the educational needs of homeless children* (House document no. 52). Richmond: Commonwealth of Virginia.

Yon, M. G., Mickelson, R. A., & Carlton-LaNey, I. (1993). A child's place: Developing interagency collaboration on behalf of homeless children. *Education and Urban Society, 25,* 410-423.

ENDNOTES

[1]This statistic is based on the estimate made by the U.S. Department of Education (1995) of 750,000 homeless school-age children and 50 million total school-age children in 1995.

[2] Joyce Askew of the Virginia Beach City Public Schools in Virginia Beach, Virginia coordinated this effort.

[3] Oak Street School is staffed by a public school teacher and instructional aide from San Juan County Department of Education. Students come from slum motels in the area, attend classes in a church, and are fed by volunteers from the Neighborhood Club.

[4] The Brownstone School is operated by Homes for the Homeless at the Prospect Family Inn in the Bronx, New York.

[5] Visit their webpage at http://www.state.va.us/VIACH

[6] Appreciation is expressed to Tiffany Barber for her assistance in searching for relevant resources.

13

EDUCATING HOMELESS STUDENTS: LINKING WITH COLLEGES AND UNIVERSITIES

PATRICIA A. POPP

A growing proportion of America's children needs easy access to a broad array of high quality services and supports that seek to prevent, as well as to treat, their problems and that recognize the interrelationship among their education, social service, health, child welfare, and employment and training needs. (Melaville & Blank, 1991, p. 6)

INTRODUCTION

Among students with the most complex needs are those experiencing homelessness. Maslow, in his hierarchy, recognized that basic survival needs must be addressed for academics to progress. Masten and her colleagues (1997) reiterated the importance of meeting basic needs to address education, based on their research looking at the educational risks homeless students face. "Programs to unobtrusively boost the nutrition, hygiene, and appearance of these children at school may need to be considered along with programs to boost school stability, attendance, reading skills, perceived belonging, and home-school connections" (Masten et al., 1997, p. 43). This complexity requires shared efforts of many players, including higher education.

There are numerous avenues to meet the varied needs of students in homeless situations by linking with colleges and universities. Linkages between schools and other service providers and communities at-large can occur in professional development schools for educators and among other disciplines in the university. Such opportunities are timely as the relevancy of American colleges and universities is questioned and these institutions engage in reexamination of their missions. Across higher education programs, there are calls to reconnect with the community (Corrigan, 1997). By helping meet the needs of homeless students, colleges and universities may reconnect with their communities and possibly rediscover a part of their mission for service.

This chapter will explore a variety of linkages with colleges and universities that hold promise in meeting the educational needs of homeless students, the processes for creating such links, and the benefits and challenges that are likely to emerge. The following questions provide a framework for the chapter:

♦ Why are college and university linkages important?
♦ What do college and university linkages look like?
  - Where can linkages originate?
  - What existing structures can provide linkages?
♦ What are the essential elements of successful linkages?
♦ What conditions should be met?
♦ What qualities should participants possess?
♦ What stages can be anticipated?

WHY ARE COLLEGE AND UNIVERSITY LINKAGES IMPORTANT?

The importance of school-university linkages in education has been recognized for more than a century. School-university partnerships are an example of cyclical reform that emerges over and over. In the late nineteenth century, the Committee of Ten called for dialogue between universities and schoolteachers to discuss methods for improving education (Clark, 1988). During the same period, John Dewey advocated for the development of laboratory schools jointly run by school systems and universities as sites to train future teachers, for research, and to develop more effective teaching methods. Possible causes for the failure of early efforts include the lack of systematic evaluation, overly top-down structures, and narrowly defined goals that sought to change practice in classrooms but ignored the need for systems-level reform. More recent efforts acknowledge the importance of addressing multiple fronts from university teacher and administrator preparation through school system and individual school structures to nurture and support classroom changes (Winitzky, Stoddart, & O'Keefe, 1992).

In the 1980s, the Holmes Report and the Carnegie Forum again suggested the need for schools and universities to join forces, providing "sites of research, development, and practice where state-of-the-art knowledge could be tested, refined, and transformed into practice" (Winitzky, Stoddart, & O'Keefe, 1992, p. 5). With attention to lessons learned, today's efforts hold promise to shape partnerships that acknowledge and respect the wisdom of practitioners and attempt to build bridges between theory and practice, frameworks for development and research, and policies that reflect this merger of perspectives and experiences (Hargreaves, 1996).

Criticism of the chasm between university programs and community life is not unique to education. "Universities seem to be disconnected from the neighborhoods as well as the society that surround them" (Corrigan, 1997, p.14) and are asking what it means to educate people for citizenship in today's world and how "people form and sustain commitment to a common good that includes the whole earth community" (Parks Daloz, Keen, Keen, & Parks, 1996). The complexity of needs that must be considered to support the learning of students in homeless situations invites the inclusion of other disciplines from the university and creates a kaleidoscope of options for linkages. One response has been the adoption of service learning opportunities. Service learning can be found in K–12 education, but is often associated with undergraduate education.

Higher education is being urged "not only to prepare the undergraduates for careers, but to enable them to live lives of dignity and purpose; not only to give knowledge to the student, but to channel knowledge to humane ends" (Boyer, 1987, p. 219). Service learning offers opportunities for involvement not obtainable through traditional coursework and establishes connections between academic life and the larger society (Boyer, 1987). Critical experiences possible through service learning in college have been identified among the significant factors that lead to a life of commitment to the larger world (Parks Daloz et al., 1996).

Linking with colleges and universities, whether schools of education, undergraduate programs, or other disciplines within the university, can fulfill a number of goals. Linkages can meet the immediate needs of students experiencing homelessness, reshape the systems which impact these students, and nurture the development of young adults with a sensitivity to, understanding of, and ability to better meet the needs of individuals, especially children, living in poverty and homelessness.

WHAT DO COLLEGE AND UNIVERSITY LINKAGES LOOK LIKE?

The types of linkages with colleges and universities can vary widely. The appearance of such linkages depends on a number of factors, including:

♦ Where the impetus for change originated; and

♦ What existing structures in the higher education site can be accessed and how they can be modified.

This section will describe possible options for each of these factors and highlight several programs that illustrate the diversity of arrangements.

WHERE CAN LINKAGES ORIGINATE?

One consideration that may shape the appearance of college and university linkages is the level at which the relationship originates. Local, state, and national initiatives can be catalysts for creating linkages or enhancing existing ones.

At the *service delivery level*, linkages focus on meeting the needs of individuals. Examples include:

♦ using pre-service teachers as tutors in after-school programs at local schools or homeless shelters;

♦ recruiting school psychology students to assist with developmental screenings provided through collaboration among the local shelters, school division, and university;

♦ placing social work interns with case managers in shelters or assigning them to multidisciplinary teams working to coordinate services for homeless families; and

♦ enlisting sociology students to participate in ethnographic studies to gain insights into the perceptions of clients toward the services provided and identify possible means of improvement.

The Big Buddy program provides an example of a service delivery level link.

At the *systems level*, linkages can be initiated to create new policies and practices while building community-wide networks of comprehensive service delivery (Melaville & Blank, 1991). Creating professional development schools and research consortiums are two examples of linkages focusing on system-level improvements.

Local, state, or national level initiatives can be catalysts for university involvement. *Local* needs in the community may lead service providers to approach neighboring colleges and universities for volunteers or support in specific areas of expertise, such as education, mental health, nutrition, medicine, law, or social work. The service mission of universities may provide the impetus for outreach. This may result from administrative networks, the commitment of a single faculty member, or the resourcefulness of a small group of concerned students. Cornell University's School of Hotel Administration illustrates the influence of university administration and one professor who saw connections where none had existed.

States can promote the development of linkages through the provision of special funding and technical assistance in the creation of projects seen as priorities (Teitel, 1993). State departments of education have called upon the research expertise of universities in meeting the requirements of the McKinney Act, such as conducting the child estimate (Dail, Fitzgerald, & Shelley, 1998) and program evaluations (Williams, Korinek, & Popp, 1996). Several State Coordinators for Homeless Children and Youth are located within universities (e.g., Florida, Texas, and Virginia). This creates linkages between state administration and university resources to support research and evaluation efforts, publications, material development, and the creation of new initiatives, as illustrated in the Texas SHELTRS Project.

National programs, such as America Reads and AmeriCorp, promote relationships between colleges and universities and

---

The Queens College Big Buddy Program

The Big Buddy Program at Queens College, New York, began in 1987 with the commitment of three faculty members, representatives from the local school district, a homeless mother, and consultation with the New York City Human Resources Administration. College students, acting as mentors, are paired with homeless children living in hotels. The partners spend one day each weekend together. Mentors serve as friends, confidants, role models, and educational and cultural guides during outings around the city. Mentors keep journals and attend special seminars that target working with children and dealing with problems that arise. There is no remuneration, but mentors receive two credits per semester. Impact on feelings and attitudes across racial and ethnic lines have been noted. Benefits for homeless children have included a secure environment, the building of positive relationships, an expanded view of the world, and improved attitudes toward school. (Salz & Trubowitz, 1992, 1997)

Linking with Schools of Business: Cornell's Initiative

Since 1987, the School of Hotel Administration at Cornell University has incorporated meeting the needs of the homeless into its program, following the lead of a professor of financial management who saw the connection between the hotel industry and crises of homelessness and hunger. Students with expertise in food preparation and short-term hotel stays can share these skills in developing and improving programs to feed and house those in need. The program developed as a response to the university president's call for proposals for Educational Initiatives that would include community outreach and offer students interdisciplinary learning experiences. Components include a credit-bearing course, an Industry Linkage Program which builds awareness within the business and hospitality communities of their potential roles in serving individuals experiencing poverty and homelessness, and a Research, Resources, and Advocacy Center including local service providers. (Hales, 1996)

agencies providing services to homeless children and youth. Federal grants can provide incentives for developing linkages. During the writing of this chapter, the U. S. Education Department issued an alert for Teacher Quality Enhancement Programs requiring at least one college or university with a teacher preparation program to partner with a school of arts and sciences and a high-need local school division. The $33.3 million in funding for these grants could be an incentive for partners to address the needs of homeless students as one of their targeted objectives. Presidential proposals also have the potential for nurturing relationships among service providers, local schools, and higher education.

Impetus for initiating a relationship is recognition of a need and a potential source for fulfilling it. Recognition can begin with K–12 schools, homeless service providers, or colleges and universities, resulting from organizational missions or a vision that begins with a single individual.

Creating New Initiatives: The SHELTRS Project

The Office for the Education of Homeless Children and Youth at the Charles A. Dana Center of the University of Texas at Austin was awarded a $272,000 grant from the Department of Commerce. The SHELTRS Project (Support for Homeless Education: Linking Technology Resources to Shelters) will develop computer networks at shelters to provide nearly 1,000 students access to individualized tutoring tailored to the state-mandated curriculum. Partners in this endeavor include LifeWorks, Inc. (an organization providing support and shelter for youth in crisis), Safe Place (a domestic violence shelter), Community Advocates for Teens and Parents, the Austin Children's Shelters, the Austin Independent School District, Microsoft, Boundless Technologies, Southwestern Bell Telephone Company, and Education Service Center (ESC) Region 8. (B. E. James, personal communication, November 4, 1998)

WHAT EXISTING STRUCTURES CAN PROVIDE LINKAGES?

When considering how a college or university can support the needs of homeless students, a number of existing higher education structures can become starting points. Structures that provide direct and indirect experiences that build awareness, meet immediate needs, and offer suggestions for long-term systems change include:

♦ coursework;

♦ service learning;

♦ professional development schools, and

♦ research consortiums.

Traditional coursework is one structure to link to the educational needs of homeless students with the resources of higher education. Pre-service and in-service education courses focusing on students in poverty can be shaped to ensure that issues of homelessness are covered. Separate courses and seminars may be developed as the sampler below illustrates. Linkages need not be limited to education courses. Psychology, sociology, economics, government, law, nursing, and medicine are some of the disciplines to consider when comprehensively addressing the needs of homeless students. Faculty may invite the involvement of homeless service providers as guest lecturers and as consultants in shaping courses, or service providers may contact the college to offer their support.

Service learning projects, when carefully planned, structured with opportunities for serious reflection, and evaluated for impact, can help college students become community-minded adults and enrich the teaching of faculty who participate (Boyer, 1987). Projects may be connected with coursework or exist independently and should emphasize the empowerment of individuals to gain independence. These projects should build

---

Courses on Homeless Issues: A Sampler

- The University of Illinois at Urbana-Champaign's non-credit course, "Homelessness: A Comprehensive Approach" was designed for teachers, social workers, and medical personnel. Board Credit or CEU's may be earned (Meyer, 1998).
- "Homelessness and Public Policy" is an example of an on-line course developed by San Francisco State University (Wagner, 1998).
- Social work undergraduates have access to "Homelessness: A Service Learning Course," that combine traditional course work and field work (Wasow, 1999).
- The University of Oregon has offered a sociology course entitled "Homelessness in Contemporary Society" (Southard, 1996).
- "Housing and Feeding the Homeless" developed at Cornell University has had three and four credit options incorporating field-based practicums locally and in Washington, DC (O'Connor, 1999).

in dialogue with and among college students to shape understanding, increase interpersonal perspective-taking by imagining how the world might look to another, and nurture critical systemic thought to identify connections and patterns and evaluate their meanings (Forte, 1993; Parks Daloz et al., 1996). Drake University and William Penn College offer two examples of service learning in action.

Service Learning in Action

Drake University in Des Moines has developed a variety of service learning activities in the form of internships, research, and volunteer projects to assist homeless individuals. Experiences may be tied to homelessness, throwaway children, or poverty courses. Whether assisting with the child estimate, re-vamping a van to serve breakfast, or researching who is using a particular food pantry, students have opportunities for one-to-one interactions that not only provide service and help students develop academic and leaderships skills, but build relationships that can break down stereotypes. (Wright & Noah, 1998)

◆ ◆ ◆

In 1991, William Penn College offered tutoring to residents of a homeless shelter and, with seven volunteers from the college, began the Literacy Tutoring Project. Within a month, 30 children were being tutored. The program has expanded to additional shelters in the region, a complementary course has been added for college students, and a summer camp for homeless students has been created. By 1998, over 5000 tutoring contacts had been recorded and The Center for Homeless Education and Information at William Penn College maintains a Web site, bringing together general information on homelessness, educational materials, including lessons plans about homelessness for grades K–12, and highlighting the work of student volunteers. (Noah, 1999; Wright & Noah, 1998)

Another vehicle for supporting homeless students by linking with colleges and universities involves general improvements in the educational system that have the potential to benefit all students. *School-university partnerships,* such as professional development schools and research consortiums, are examples of such system-level reform. These partnerships are aimed at improving education through changes at all levels by involving college faculty, K-12 administrators, and teachers. The goals include improved teacher preparation, facilitated translation of research and theory into meaningful practice, and shaping research efforts to meet the needs of practitioners (Goodlad, 1993).

Professional development schools attempt to expand our knowledge of school practices, improve initial teacher and administrator preparation, and increase the use of research findings. Activities may include involving university faculty in school-based ongoing professional development activities—such as seminars, classroom observations, demonstration lessons, and collaborative teaching—while master teachers share their expertise in university courses and mentoring practicum students, student teachers, and novice teachers (Zetlin, Harris, MacLeod, & Watkins, 1992). *Research consortiums* call upon schools and universities to identify needs for original research, translate research in practical knowledge, and develop means for implementing new knowledge by synthesizing and disseminating findings at the school level.

A literature review describing this level of systems change did not reveal any examples focused specifically on homeless issues. However, the needs of students in extreme poverty, including those experiencing homelessness, can be woven into such structures through the active voices of individual participants who wish to make this population visible and audible. Evaluative questions such as, "How are these new relationships impacting the delivery of instruction to our students facing the challenges of poverty and homelessness?" and process questions such as, "Have we included the necessary participating agencies to ensure the voices of homeless students are heard?" can be reminders to consider the impact on all students in major reforms.

Partnerships in Action: A University Example

The Georgetown University Child Development Center has implemented a University Affiliated Program focusing on the developmental needs of children from birth through age five who are homeless as well as their families in the District of Columbia. As an example of community collaboration, the project provides service, community outreach, training, technical assistance, and policy development. Interdisciplinary teams comprised of faculty, staff, and trainees from the Center are involved in the identification and referral of children with developmental delays and disabilities. Other goals include supporting families in culturally respectful ways and facilitating the inclusion of these children in childcare programs and transitioning into kindergarten programs. Collaborators include Shelter providers, the D.C. Public School System and Commission on Social Services, Child Care and HeadStart centers, health care and mental health care providers, and legal advocates. (Taylor & Brown, 1996)

WHAT ARE THE ELEMENTS OF SUCCESSFUL LINKAGES?

As suggested above, linkages should be sought to meet a need or solve a perceived problem. It may seem advantageous to begin linkages between universities and school/service providers with clear expectations, goals, and operating procedures; however, such neatly structured elements may be closer to wishful thinking than reality. Those considering the creation of new connections must recognize the fact that such endeavors can be messy business. The process is rarely linear and logical, yet those willing to broach their separate organizations and cultures must find a way to move from problem to vision, from fuzzy roles and responsibilities to a well-defined relationship, and from activity to a focus on meaningful outcomes (Melaville & Blank, 1991). For this to occur, a number of conditions should be met.

CONDITIONS

Goodlad (1993) proposed that school-university partnerships should be symbiotic in nature and suggested that three conditions must be met:

- ◆ There must be dissimilarity between or among partners. Each partner should bring something unique to the relationship.
- ◆ The relationship must allow for mutual satisfaction of self-interests.
- ◆ Participants must be selfless enough to assure that the interests of other participants are fulfilled.

QUALITIES OF PARTICIPANTS

In addition to the conditions listed above, researchers and theorists who study interorganizational collaboration suggest that participants interested in initiating linkages should possess the following characteristics (Zetlin, Harris, MacLeod, & Watkins, 1992):

- ◆ a commitment to working together with mutual trust and respect;
- ◆ flexibility as goals are clarified and strategies to reach them are developed; and
- ◆ a willingness to take risks, be comfortable with ambiguity, and learn from mistakes.

Starting with a limited number of highly committed individuals and experimenting with small beginning activities can nurture respect and trust. Throughout the process, open communication is critical and key to developing more collaborative relationships over time. Individuals in leadership positions should be included. Direct dialogue among the leaders can facilitate or jump-start linkages that are feeling "bogged down" and demonstrate to all parties the level of support needed to further the initiative.

As schools, universities, or service providers consider initiating new linkages, the following questions and steps may provide direction and assist in decision making (Melaville & Blank, 1991; Whetten, 1981):

♦ Ask the following questions.
  - How are we doing? Do we need to change? Why is this linking needed?
  - Are we ready to pursue new linkages? What is our organization's level of commitment to and comfort with linkages?
  - Can we justify the resources required for success against the needs identified?

♦ Identify potential partners.
  - Evaluate these partners in terms of their commitment to linking, common goals, and compatibility with your organization.
  - Determine partners' ability to maintain the relationship and manage ongoing coordination.

WHAT STAGES CAN BE ANTICIPATED?

The time commitment for linking will influence the stages that occur. Some projects may be intentionally short-term, especially during early efforts at linkages. The five-stage approach (Karge & Robb, 1996) in Figure 1 may prove helpful for more contained endeavors. Recognizing these stages and helping the group identify the level on which they are working can facilitate smooth transitions to completion.

If a potential goal of linking with higher education is to create a long-term relationship, the need for extended time in building the relationship should be recognized. Initial planning and implementation are likely to be time-intensive and progress slowly at the start. Trubowitz (1986), in describing school-university unions, suggested that eight stages occur before the union has high likelihood of being sustained. In addition to the stages similar to those listed above, *regression* may occur with blurring of the original vision. Regression due to the loss of original core participants may result from promotion, relocation, or changes

FIGURE 1. STAGES FOR LIMITED-TERM COMMITMENTS

Stage	Label	Description
I	*Forming*	Orientation activities, introductions, and defining purpose occur.
II	*Norming*	Establishing norms for group responsibility, decision making, and confronting problems begin.
III	*Storming*	Coping with conflict is more likely to emerge as communication becomes more open. Turf issues, reconciling different organizational cultures, and resource allocation and distribution may need to be addressed. The group should recognize that confronting differences can be a positive force and reduce the potential for later conflicts.
IV	*Performing*	With purpose and responsibilities understood, the group becomes productive and works toward its goal. Recognize that some regression is possible.
V	*Adjourning*	Termination may not have impact if the group has never connected. A group that has passed through the stages will need opportunities to reflect on changing impressions and celebrate growth and accomplishments.

in funding. *Renewal* occurs as new members are included who can infuse new energy and ideas. *Continuing progress* is possible when structures are in place to ensure communication and strategies to meet future challenges.

CONCLUSION

What roles can colleges and universities fill in meeting the educational needs of homeless students? Many possibilities can be pursued. The three-part mission in higher education includes teaching, research, and service. Colleges and universities can assume roles that include all three of these components. Roles for faculty, students, and staff can include *teaching* to build an information base for understanding the complex issues of homelessness; *research* across disciplines to understand issues more fully and evaluate interventions that are implemented; and *service* through volunteer work, provision of resources, and sharing expertise while connecting with the community.

Opportunities for specific higher education links for supporting homeless students do exist. Some initiatives may not relate directly to education at first glance, but the complex needs of these children and youth justify a broad approach to tapping college and university resources to meet their needs. Physical and mental health, nutrition, recreation, and legal rights are just a few of the avenues that can be explored that ultimately impact students' ability and desire to learn.

Structures for improving the educational system for all students through the linking of schools and universities, especially those facing the challenges of poverty, also can be found. Homeless students most certainly should benefit from these ventures. However, to ensure that they are seen and heard, advocates must continue to build awareness through shared vignettes of successes and failures for these students and through challenging questions, such as: How do we ensure that our homeless students have access to these opportunities? How can we determine if our new approaches are beneficial for our homeless students? What else can we attempt and who else can we include to strengthen the comprehensiveness of our efforts?

As the needs of homeless students are met through links with colleges and universities, college students and faculty have opportunities for integrating learning across fields and disciplines. Higher education benefits from a richer understanding and ability to connect with the larger community. Future citizens are nurtured who share a commitment to that community. These linkages and shared commitments are summed up in a quote by Woodrow Wilson, "'It is not learning, but the spirit of service that will give a college place in the public annals of the nation'" (cited in Boyer, 1987, p. 219).

REFERENCES

Boyer, E. L. (1987). Service: Getting involved. In The Carnegie Foundation for the Advancement of Teaching (Ed.), *College: The undergraduate experience in America*. New York: Harper & Row.

Clark, R. W. (1988). School-university relationships: In interpretive review. In K. A. Sirotnik & J. I. Goodlad (Eds.), *School-university partnerships in action* (pp. 32-65). New York: Teachers College Press.

Corrigan, D. (1997). The role of the university in community building. *The Educational Forum, 62*, 14-24.

Dail, P., Fitzgerald, S., & Shelley, M. (1998). *Homeless in Iowa: Findings from the 1997 Statewide Study*. A paper presented at the Tenth Annual National Association of State Coordinators for Educating Homeless Children and Youth Conference, Des Moines, IA.

Forte, J. A. (1997). Calling students to serve the homeless: A project to promote altruism and community service. *Journal of Social Work Education, 33*, 151-166.

Goodlad, J. I. (1993). School-university partnerships and partner schools. *Educational Policy, 7*, 24-39.

Hales, A. (1996). Cornell University's Homeless Program: The "give and take" process of service. *The Journal of General Education, 45*, 306-318.

Hargreaves, A. (1996). Transforming knowledge: Blurring the boundaries between research, policy, and practice. *Educational Evaluation and Policy Analysis, 18*, 105-122.

Karge, B. D., & Robb, S. M. (1996, October). *Simulations for training future leaders*. A paper presented at the Council for Learning Disabilities International Conference, Nashville, TN.

Masten, A. S., Sesma, A., Jr., Si-Asar, R., Lawrence, C., Miliotis, D., & Dionne, J. A. (1997). Educational risks for children experiencing homelessness. *Journal of School Psychology, 35*, 27-46.

Melaville, A. I., & Blank, M. J. (1991). *What it takes: Structuring interagency partnerships to connect children and families with comprehensive services*. Washington, DC: Education and Human Services Consortium.

Meyer, J. D. (1998). *Homelessness: A comprehensive approach*. [On-line]. Available: *http://pweb.netcom.com/~jdmeyer/series.index.htm*.

Noah, R. (1999). *Center for Homeless Education and Information, William Penn College.* [On-line]. Available: http://www.wmpenn.edu/Pennweb/LTP/ltp2.html.

O'Connor, T. (1999). *Housing and feeding the homeless.* [On-line]. Available: http://courses.sha.cornell.edu/courses/ha490/courseinfo.html.

Parks Daloz, L. A., Keen, C. H., Keen, J. P., & Daloz Parks, S. (1996). Lives of commitment: Higher education in the life of the new commons. *Change,* , 11-15.

Salz, A., & Trubowitz, J. (1992). You can see the sky from here: The Queens College Big Buddy Program. *Phi Delta Kappan, 73,* 551-556.

Salz, A., & Trubowitz, J. (1997). It was all of us working together: Resolving racial and ethnic tension on college campuses. *The Educational Forum, 62,* 82-90.

Southard, P. A. (1996). *Sociology of homelessness.* [On-line]. Available: http://csf.colorado.edu/homeless/hmout.html.

Taylor, T. D., & Brown, M.C. (1996). *Young children and their families who are homeless: A university affiliated program's response.* Washington, DC: The Georgetown University Child Development Center. (ERIC Document Reproduction Service No. ED 406 500.)

Teitel, L. (1993). The state role in jump-starting school/university collaboration: A case study. *Educational Policy, 7,* 74-95.

Trubowitz, S. (1986). Stages in the development of school-college collaboration. *Educational Leadership, 43,* 18-21.

Wagner, J. (1998). *HED/URBS 582 Homelessness and Public Policy, Fall 1998.* [On-line]. Available: http://thecity.sfsu.edu/~bahp/hed_urbsf98.htm.

Wasow, M. (1999). *University of Wisconsin - Madison: Social Work 664, Homelessness: A service learning course.* [On-line]. Available: http://thecity.sfsu.edu/~bahp/education.htm.

Whetten, D. (1981). Inter-organizational relations: A review of the field. *Journal of Higher Education, 52*(1), 1-28.

Williams, B. T., Korinek, L., & Popp, P. A. (1996). *Virginia Homeless Education Project: External Evaluation Report, 1995-96.* Williamsburg, VA: The College of William and Mary.

Winitzky, N., Stoddart, T., & O'Keefe, P. (1992). Great expectations: Emergent professional development schools. *Journal of Teacher Education, 43,* 3-18.

Wright, R. D., & Noah, R. (1998, November). *Teaching about homeless through service learning*. A paper presented at the Tenth Annual National Association of State Coordinators for Educating Homeless Children and Youth Conference, Des Moines, IA.

Zetlin, A. G., Harris, K., MacLeod, E., & Watkins, A. (1992). The evolution of a university/inner-city school partnership: A case study account. *Urban Education, 27*, 80-90.

ADDITIONAL RESOURCES

Melaville, A. I., & Blank, M. J. (1991). *What it takes: Structuring interagency partnerships to connect children and families with comprehensive services*. Washington, DC: Education and Human Services Consortium. Available from the Education and Human Services Consortium c/o IEL, 1001 Connecticut Avenue, N. W., Suite 310, Washington, D.C. 20036-5541. Telephone: 202-822-8405. Information in this report can be freely reproduced and duplicated without prior permission provided the citation is included.

The National Network for Collaboration. (1996). *Collaboration Framework . . . Addressing Community Capacity*. Fargo, ND: The National Network for Collaboration. Available from: The National Network for Collaboration, 219 FLC, Box 5016, Fargo, ND 58105-5016. Telephone: 701-231-7259.

International Homeless Discussion List and Archives HOMEPAGE. Available on-line: *http://csf.colorado.edu/homeless/index.html* This Web site provides over 450 links to sites with information on homelessness, including academic courses, education, articles, and fact sheets.

MEET THE AUTHORS

Linda J. Anooshian (Ph.D. University of California at Riverside, 1974) is currently Professor in the Department of Psychology at Boise State University. Her research includes publications in *Child Development*, *Developmental Psychology*, *Cognitive Development*, *Memory & Cognition*, and *Journal of Personality and Social Psychology*.

Tina D. Butcher is an Assistant Professor of Education and Director of Field Experiences and Undergraduate Student Services at Columbus State University in Columbus, Georgia. In October 1998, she was selected as Outstanding Early Childhood Educator by the Georgia Association on Young Children.

Kate Collignon is currently pursuing a Master's Degree in Public Policy at Harvard University's Kennedy School of Government. Prior to returning to school she served as Research Coordinator with the Institute for Children & Poverty in New York City, where she directed research on family homelessness and provided technical assistance to homeless service providers across the country.

Tim L. Davey received his MSW and Ph.D. degrees from Florida State University and is currently an Assistant Professor at the University of Tennessee College of Social Work, Nashville. He is currently the program evaluator for the McKinney supported HERO Program for Nashville Public Schools.

Barbara Duffield is Director of Education for the National Coalition for the Homeless. She was recognized by the National Association of State Coordinators for the Education for Homeless Children and Youth for outstanding leadership on behalf of homeless children (1995 and 1996) and received the Association's Presidential Award in 1998.

E. Anne Eddowes has recently retired as an Associate Professor in the Department of Curriculum and Instruction at the University of Alabama at Birmingham, where she taught courses in early childhood education. Currently, she works with early childhood programs in the areas of accreditation and personnel evaluation. Several of her articles on the problems of educating homeless children have appeared in *Childhood Education* and *Education and Urban Society*.

Maria Foscarinis, a 1981 graduate of Columbia Law School, is the founder and director of the National Law Center on Homelessness & Poverty, a not-for-profit organization dedicated to legal advocacy for solutions to homelessness. She is a primary architect of the Stewart B. McKinney Homeless Assistance Act, the first major federal legislation addressing homelessness. Her writing has appeared in scholarly journals, general audience publications, and books.

Lori Korinek, Ph.D., is Professor of Curriculum and Instruction with an emphasis in special education, School of Education, College of William and Mary, Williamsburg, VA. She teaches courses and conducts professional development in the areas of learning disabilities, behavior disorders, curriculum development, and instructional strategies.

Sarah McCarthy is a staff attorney at the National Law Center on Homelessness & Poverty in Washington, D.C. She is engaged in legal and policy work that seeks to enforce the educational provisions of the Stewart B. McKinney Homeless Assistance Act and other relevant federal educational laws. She received her B.A. from Bowdin College and J.D. from Northeastern University School of Law.

Ralph da Costa Nunez is President and CEO of the Institute for Children & Poverty and Homes for the Homeless in New York City, and a Professor at Columbia University's School of International and Public Affairs. He also has served as Deputy Director for the New York City Mayor's Office of Homeless and SRO Housing Services. Recent publications include *The New Poverty: Homeless Families in America; Hopes, Dreams and Promise: The Future of Homeless Children in America;* and a children's book *Our Wish*.

Bill Penuel is a research social scientist at the Center for Technology in Learning at SRI International. Currently, he is working as an evaluator on the Joint Venture: Silicon Valley Challenge 2000 project, the GLOBE project, and the Joyce Foundation funded study of technical supports for urban high school reform.

Patricia A. Popp is currently a doctoral candidate in Educational Policy, Planning, and Leadership with an emphasis in special education at The College of William and Mary. She also currently serves as Program Administrator for the Virginia Homeless Education Program.

Evelyn Reed-Victor is Assistant Professor in Early Childhood Special Education and Co-Director of New Connections, an Interdisciplinary Early Intervention Graduate Training Program at Virginia Commonwealth University, in Richmond, Virginia. She also co-directs the Training and Technical Assistance Center for Personnel Serving Infants, Children, and Youth with Disabilities at VCU. She has also co-authored publications about educational practices that support the resilience of homeless children and youth.

James H. Stronge is Heritage Professor of Educational Policy, Planning, and Leadership at The College of William and Mary in Williamsburg, Virginia. He served as editor and contributing author for the Sage Publications book, *Educating Homeless Children and Adolescents: Evaluating Policy and Practice*, which received a 1994 American Library Association Book of the Year Award. He has written on homeless education issues for the *Journal of Law and Education, Journal of Children and Poverty, Journal for a Just and Caring Education, Educational Policy*, and *Education and Urban Society*. Additionally, he serves as State Coordinator for the Stewart B. McKinney Homeless Education Program in Virginia.

Kevin J. Swick is Professor of Education and Director of the Service-Learning and Teacher Education Project in the College of Education at the University of South Carolina – Columbia. He has published recent work on homeless students and families in *The Clearing House, Dimensions of Early Childhood, Journal of Early Childhood Teacher Education*, and *Early Childhood Education Journal*. He was recently recognized for his work with teachers on better supporting homeless students and received the South Carolina Department of Education's "Education of Homeless Students" Award.

Pamela D. Tucker is Assistant Professor of Education at the University of Virginia in Charlottesville, Virginia and Director of the Principal Preparation Internship Program in the Curry School of Education. For two and a half years, she was Program Administrator of Project HOPE, which coordinates educational programs for homeless children in the Commonwealth of Virginia.

Yvonne Vissing, Ph.D., is Professor of Sociology at Salem State College. She is the author of *Out of Sight, Out of Mind: Homeless Children and Families in Small Town America*, and has authored articles on homelessness for publications that *include Phi Delta Kappan*, the McCormick Institute for Public Policy, Sage Publications, Social Work, and the *Journal of Housing Distress and Homelessness*.

Brenda Toler Williams, Ed.D., is Associate Professor in the Educational Policy, Planning and Leadership area, School of Education, College of William and Mary, Williamsburg, VA. She has an extensive background in special education administration and university teaching.